Simon Sandall

Custom and Popular Memory in the Forest of Dean, c.1550-1832

tial Re
019f

≡
2

D1355214

Simon Sandall

Custom and Popular Memory in the Forest of Dean, c.1550-1832

Scholar's Press

Impressum / Imprint
Bibliografische Information der Deutschen Nationalbibliothek: Die Deutsche
Nationalbibliothek verzeichnet diese Publikation in der Deutschen Nationalbibliografie;
detaillierte bibliografische Daten sind im Internet über http://dnb.d-nb.de abrufbar.
Alle in diesem Buch genannten Marken und Produktnamen unterliegen warenzeichen-,
marken- oder patentrechtlichem Schutz bzw. sind Warenzeichen oder eingetragene
Warenzeichen der jeweiligen Inhaber. Die Wiedergabe von Marken, Produktnamen,
Gebrauchsnamen, Handelsnamen, Warenbezeichnungen u.s.w. in diesem Werk berechtigt
auch ohne besondere Kennzeichnung nicht zu der Annahme, dass solche Namen im Sinne
der Warenzeichen- und Markenschutzgesetzgebung als frei zu betrachten wären und
daher von jedermann benutzt werden dürften.

Bibliographic information published by the Deutsche Nationalbibliothek: The Deutsche
Nationalbibliothek lists this publication in the Deutsche Nationalbibliografie; detailed
bibliographic data are available in the Internet at http://dnb.d-nb.de.
Any brand names and product names mentioned in this book are subject to trademark,
brand or patent protection and are trademarks or registered trademarks of their respective
holders. The use of brand names, product names, common names, trade names, product
descriptions etc. even without a particular marking in this works is in no way to be
construed to mean that such names may be regarded as unrestricted in respect of
trademark and brand protection legislation and could thus be used by anyone.

Coverbild / Cover image: www.ingimage.com

Verlag / Publisher:
Scholar's Press
ist ein Imprint der / is a trademark of
AV Akademikerverlag GmbH & Co. KG
Heinrich-Böcking-Str. 6-8, 66121 Saarbrücken, Deutschland / Germany
Email: info@scholars-press.com

Herstellung: siehe letzte Seite /
Printed at: see last page
ISBN: 978-3-639-51455-1

Copyright © 2013 AV Akademikerverlag GmbH & Co. KG
Alle Rechte vorbehalten. / All rights reserved. Saarbrücken 2013

To my parents and my wife

i

ACKNOWLEDGEMENTS

In 2006, I accepted an exciting offer to work on a project at the University of East Anglia, exploring the way that ordinary people thought about the past in early modern England. Within one or two meetings with my doctoral supervisor, Andy Wood, it was clear that my research would focus on the Forest of Dean in Gloucestershire. The foresters enjoy a particularly keen engagement with their history which builds on strong traditions that have long underpinned collective identities in this area. Memories of local events are kept alive in schools, while recent plans to privatise the Forest evoked a fierce reaction. Protest leaders such as Warren James are a source of pride, symbolising this type of resistance in earlier centuries. This book aims to continue this tradition, examining the deeper histories of protest in the region and the ways that local people deployed the past in defence of a way of life increasingly under threat from the late sixteenth century onwards. These histories not only tell us about the experience of being a forester during the sixteenth, seventeenth, and eighteenth centuries, but also lend new perspectives to the way we understand many aspects of the national past. The events explored in this book explain, in part, why the memories of these people and their lives are still so persistent in the modern Forest of Dean.

During the eight years that I have worked on this project I have incurred many debts of gratitude and it is a huge pleasure to be able to acknowledge the support and friendship which has helped me along the way. Research grants from the AHRC and the Economic History Society allowed me to undertake this study in the first place. I am enormously grateful for the encouragement, patience and friendship of Andy Wood and David Rollison who guided me so expertly through my initial research and who are a constant source of support to the present day. While studying at the UEA I was very fortunate to be part of a group of historians who added so much to the way that I think about the past but, more importantly, made my postgraduate research an enjoyable and inspiring experience. For this, I would like to thank Janka Rodziewicz, Gesine Oppitz-Trotman, George Oppitz-Trotman, Karl Bell, Fiona Williamson and Joy Hawkins. Since completing my doctoral research and venturing into the world of work I have enjoyed the support of so many generous people. I am especially grateful for the friendship and encouragement shown to me by Miri Rubin,

Keith Snell, Malcolm Gaskill, Jess Sharkey, Peter King, Steven King and Andy Hopper.
Historical archives can reveal much about a region but, at the risk of resorting to cliché, the Forest of Dean is best understood from a local perspective. I am very grateful for the support of many forest history societies as well as the insights of experts such as Gordon Glissold, Robin Morgan, Ian Wright and others who embody the local knowledge that lies at the heart of this study. I am also indebted to many colleagues, both past and present, at the University of Winchester and the University of Leicester. I have always been fortunate enough to have the support of close friends and family, and I would particularly like to thank my brother, Stuart Sandall, my sister, Sally Sandall, and my grandmother, Dorothy Willsea. In this regard, I owe a huge debt of gratitude to my parents, Barbara and Roger Sandall, for their constant and unswerving emotional and material support. Finally, while this has been such a rewarding period of my life in so many ways, this project will always be associated with meeting and falling in love with my wife, Bronach Kane, a constant source of love, humour, insight, and friendship. I am immensely grateful for her patience in reading and commenting on endless drafts of this book. It is to my parents and my wife that I dedicate this work.

Custom and popular memory in the Forest of Dean, c.1550-1832

TABLE OF CONTENT

Introduction

Well to be a free miner, this only come into being about seven hundred years ago, King Edward the first ... actually gave us, officially he gave us the rights but miners in the Forest of Dean long before King Edward was born, right back before the Romans got here, were still mining coal. But seven hundred years ago, Edward the first came here and at that time he was fighting with the Welsh and the Scotch and he used to take ... he used to come here and take so many miners with him and march them all the way to Scotland and he used to get them to dig under the castle walls, see the siege of Berwick castle, well they were involved in that and that's when that stone of destiny was taken, that's the stone that Kings and Queens of Scotland were crowned on and he took that back to Westminster and it's not all that many years ago that they've had it back ... and what he used to get the miners to do was, of course some of those walls might have been about eight or ten foot thick, you know, and he used to get them to dig under the wall, they didn't go right under the wall and come up the other side cause the Scotch would've had them straight away, like, they used to go under the wall and turn round and follow the wall from underneath putting up timbers and they'd move across for about twenty or thirty metres and then, when they'd got the tunnel dug, they would come back out and tell the soldiers to get ready and in one would go, knocking the timbers out as he was coming back. And because those castles were only built with lime, and mortar, they'd come tumbling down. And for doing that he, then he made it official then, he granted us a royal charter and ... to be a free miner, you've got to be born ... what they say in the hundred of St Briavels, which is basically in the Forest of Dean. If you were

1

born in the Forest of Dean, could prove you'd worked a year and a day in a coal mine, so which means you've got to get someone who owns a coal mine and he's got to write a letter for you saying you've actually worked in his mine for a year and a day, reached the age of twenty one and your name is put in a book in the crown offices incorporate and you can take a mine out. [1]

72 year-old free miner of the Forest of Dean. Interviewed in September, 2007.

I A miner's recollections

Describing the origins of free mining custom in the Forest of Dean, the interviewee whose words introduce this book recalled several aspects of the culture in which he worked and was raised. His history of the Forest reflects many characteristics of what has been termed popular, local, or peasant memory. National events are remembered but recalled in reference to local events, people and places rather than being structured by dominant chronologies.[2] His account evokes differing, yet coexistent, collective memory patterns which have underpinned local occupational identities and

---

[1] 72 year-old free miner of the Forest of Dean. Interviewed in September, 2007.

[2] James Fentress and Chris Wickham outline a tentative and potentially overlapping distinction between the less diachronically ordered historical senses of a local community (particularly within the classical 'peasant' community of the late medieval period) and the linear recollections which constitute national and more abstracted forms of collective consciousness. J. Fentress and C. Wickham, *Social Memory* (Oxford, 1992), Ch. 3.

industrial rights for centuries. He foregrounds Edward I's bestowal of these rights in recognition of service provided to the realm, but there is a clear sense that this historical event was merely the 'official' sanctification of a local system that had been operative since antiquity, irrespective of royal approval. Recalling the moment at which Dean's customary free-mining rights were confirmed by the Crown, he is evidently confident of their legitimacy from 'timeless' practice.

Despite a lack of formal education in this area, the miner's account suggests a working knowledge of England's constitutional history, at least those aspects which directly bore on the legitimacy of his occupational rights. Referring to the linear narrative of the English monarchy as it strove to impose a sense of common identity and allegiance within the British Isles, his local and more immediate historical sense is more malleable and contingent. His discussion of ancient and current mining practice constantly works to collapse the temporal separation between himself and his occupational antecedents. His account moves directly from the moment - *only* seven hundred years ago' - at which the royal charter was granted, through a barely perceptible tense change, to assert that 'if *you were* born in the Forest of Dean' and 'could prove that you'd worked a year and a day in a coal mine', *'your name is* put in a book' and *'you can* take a mine out'. At the point of interview in 2007 this miner was working a seam that had last been used during the 1830s, referring to these tunnels as the 'Old men's works' and describing various pieces of 'ancient' equipment that could be found during the course of his working day. He quite clearly recalls beginning his working life in the larger early twentieth-century mining operations alongside men that had been mining coal in the Forest since the 1870s and thus feels a connection with nineteenth-century free miners. The

3

somewhat exceptional nature of his occupation and Dean's idiosyncratic environment seems to have left him less inclined than many in the twenty-first century to regard his ancestors as 'other' to modern culture.[3]

The free miner's account demonstrates the remarkable transmission of 'unofficial' popular histories of the region through the survival of local mentalities. In contrast to diachronic constitutional histories, he describes the past in a more synchronic sense, resisting sharp, teleological, distinctions between his industrial activity and that of his ancestors.[4] The reasons for these regionally idiosyncratic collective mnemonic strategies are explored below. Here, it suffices to say that this miner's version of the origins of free-mining custom remains similar to claims that were being made four hundred years earlier. Extant seventeenth-century court records suggest that national events, significant regnal years and statutes were regularly called upon, not chronologically, but in accordance with their pertinence to present and local necessity. In this earlier context, however, the contrast between this type of historical memory and the diachronically ordered written record was more explicitly tied to aggressive conflict

---

[3] D. Lowenthal, *The Past is Another Country* (Cambridge, 1985); regarding Lowenthal's work, Elizabeth Tonkin explains that 'Some think that ordinary Europeans and Americans only began to think of the past as qualitatively different from the present in the late eighteenth century'. E. Tonkin, *Narrating our pasts: The social construction of oral history* (Cambridge, 1992), 10. Tonkin's central hypothesis suggests a distinction between 'history' and 'tradition' in that the former implies the objectifying stance of 'official' records and interpretations of the past, whilst the latter refers to a living connection with, and a more subjective embroilment within, those elements of the past that are recalled in the context of present action.

[4] Fentress and Wickham, *Social Memory*, Ch. 3.

between those protecting common rights and those who sought to profit from enclosure and disafforestation.

Claims to timeless and collective uses were ubiquitous in conflicts over attempts to improve the Forest during the early seventeenth century.[5] Moreover, frequent attempts to settle or pacify the region during the following two centuries were unable to quell the overwhelming and popular force of local custom in 1831. On 3 June that year, Warren James, son of a free miner, circulated posters at various points in the Forest. These posters declared that:

> the FREE MINERS of the said Forest, intend to MEET on Wednesday next the 7th instant for the purpose of OPENING the FOREST, and their RIGHT of COMMON to the same, so long deprived of and All those Persons who may chance to have Stock thereon contrary to the Rights and Privileges of the Miners; are required hereby to remove the same forthwith otherwise they will have their Stock impounded without Further Notice.[6]

James' call to action met with huge support. During a four day period, up to three thousand inhabitants of the forest mustered at various strategic

---

[5] A heated and long-running debate in the Forest relates to whether there were ever rights to common rather than tolerated privileges. This has recently been resolved in favour of their definition as privileges. During the seventeenth century, however, this was demonstrably a matter of legal debate with many records claiming commoning and mining rights against those who contended that these were only allowed by grace. As this monograph is a study of popular mentalities in this region, these uses will be referred to as rights because this properly reflects the language of the groups that form the core focus of this research.

[6] TNA, (CL) Assizes 6/2 pt. 29.

locations to begin the arduous task of breaking up the enclosures which had become the focus of much local antagonism.[7] The claims of the Forest commoners in 1831 bore a remarkable resemblance to those of their seventeenth-century predecessors. The strongest line of continuity was the role of miners in organising resistance to encroachments, not only on their mining rights, but on common grazing and fuel rights which had been exercised by the wider forest commonalty since a 'time out of mind of man'.[8] Later chapters explore the interconnection of these customary practices and uses that constituted Dean's popular *habitus*. Resisting these encroachments, the mining community not only defended their own occupation but also the rights of the poor and propertyless in the Forest community. This study seeks to identify and examine the cultural position of Dean's free-mining community. Why did this group provide such an effective organisational focus for the vigorous expression of local popular communalism during the seventeenth century? Judging by the evidence of the 1831 protests, this was still true in the nineteenth century.

The 1831 protest receives a more nuanced analysis towards the end of this study but it is instructive, briefly, to consider the efficacy of James'

---

[7] Estimated numbers are taken from a letter from *Magistrates to Home Office*, 11 June 1831, TNA, HO 52/12.

[8] The claim that rights or uses had been enjoyed since 'a time out of mind of man' was ubiquitous in litigation and other disputes over customary practice in the Forest of Dean and, indeed, England more generally. Signifying the supposed timeless nature of local custom, there were many variations on this theme such as 'since before the memory of man runneth not to the contrary' or, simply, 'time out of mind'. When these phrases are used from here onwards, it is to refer to this general idealised claim to the antiquity of custom.

strategy, certainly by contrast to Edward Machen's riposte. As Deputy Surveyor of the Forest, Machen spread his own posters throughout the area, warning of the consequences for those who answered James' call. Together, these two posters neatly condense the central concerns of this work. The proposal to restore the landscape to its earlier condition evidently drew upon a particularly strong and broad sense of collective identity among Dean's residents. Machen's warning was grounded in those acts of Parliament that were seen to be responsible for the offending enclosures. In popular perceptions, Machen had allied himself with those forces that had reshaped the physical environment, and so had fundamentally subverted local senses of the past which are explored in Chapter One. James foregrounded connections between the destruction of this landscape and the loss of customary rights. By opening the forest, the gathered crowd sought to recover 'their right of common to the same'.[9] James' poster proposed to assert the legitimacy of these customary uses by restoring the landscape through which they had traditionally been transmitted through popular memory, while Machen appealed to the abstracted written memory of statute law. His attempt at persuasion simply did not have the same impact as the free miner's call to defend an environment which could secure the future of subsistence rights. Contrasting with the broad consensus for action achieved by James and the Committee of Free Miners, Machen's power to reassert control within the Forest ultimately rested with the coercive powers of the army.

---

[9] TNA, HO 52/12.

II The Forest of Dean in Gloucestershire

The Forest of Dean is situated towards the west of Gloucestershire in the south-west of England, designating the triangular area between the Rivers Severn and Wye as they flow south towards the Bristol Channel. In legal terms, the name has often been taken to refer, more specifically, to the boundaries of St. Briavels Hundred, corresponding closely with the outline of the mineral basin which has been integral to this region's economy for many centuries.[10] The boundaries of the Forest, as an area governed by forest law and defining customary rights attached to residential status, have been subject to change several times since the twelfth and thirteenth centuries.[11] In its broadest interpretation, the Forest has been understood as all of the land between the two rivers and northwards into Herefordshire, thus including thirty-three parishes from both counties. These bounds were revised during the early fourteenth century, reducing the area to fourteen Gloucestershire parishes and the extraparochial, central crown demesne lands which together constituted St. Briavels Hundred.[12] N. M. Herbert explains that, following the Dean Reafforestation Act of 1668, the region was reduced to the royal demesne lands which were roughly coterminous

---

[10] Herbert, N.M. (ed.), *A History of the County of Gloucester: Volume V. Bledisloe Hundred, St Briavels Hundred, The Forest of Dean* (Oxford, 1996), 285-9.

[11] Ibid., 285.

[12] Ibid., 285.

with the area of approximately 23,000 acres (9,308 hectares) that are currently understood to represent the

Parishes in the Forest of Dean, c. 1538-1838

Royal Forest of Dean.[13] The 1840s finally witnessed attempts to impose a formalised parochial structure upon Dean's central demesne lands. To the west, the River Wye separates Dean from the Welsh county of Monmouthshire while, to the east, the Severn divides this area from the rest of Gloucestershire, a boundary which, during the sixteenth and seventeenth centuries, was as much cultural and economic as geographical.

E. Muriel Poggi explains the geological history of the region, noting that:

> It was the accepted opinion for many years that the South Wales and Forest of Dean coalfields were originally united. Folding from the north and south took place in late Carboniferous times and gave the basin-like form to the two coalfields, and at a later period denudation along the Usk anticline separated the two fields. The area is formed almost entirely of Carboniferous rocks enclosing the Coal measures of the Forest ... the Forest is practically enclosed by a rim of higher land except on the south, from which direction routes penetrate into the heart of the area, the valley of the Cannop Brook dividing it nearly in half.[14]

Considering the Forest in an east to west section, Cannop Brook represents the top of the Caboniferous fold running from north to south while the layer of sandstone emerges on either side, enclosing the Coleford High Delf, Yorkley, Brazilly, Rockey and High Delf coal-seams. These coal deposits

---

[13] Herbert, *VCH Vol. V*, 285.

[14] E. Muriel Poggi, 'The Forest of Dean in Gloucestershire', *Economic Geography*, 6, 3 (1930), 309.

were to prove immensely influential during the period of this study but the Forest's other main mineral resource, iron ore, ensured that the region had been the site of extractive activity since before the Roman period. Writing in 1866, Reverend H. G. Nicholls noted that:

> Numerous other Roman vestiges, on every side of the Forest, may be adverted to ... At Lydbrook, and on the Coppet Wood Hill, at Perry Grove, and Crabtree Hill, all within or near the Forest – the last being situated in the middle of it – many coins of Philip, Gallenius, Victorinus, and of Claudius Gothicus, have been brought to light. We possess indisputable testimony, from Mr Lower's researches in the old iron-making parts of Sussex, that the Romans there carried on metallurgical operations at an early period, and we may claim a like antiquity for our Dean Forest workings.[15]

There is also widely-known archaeological evidence of a Roman temple adjoining the town of Lydney to the south of the Forest.

During the late medieval period, as iron production and timber exports began to expand significantly, Dean's location proved extremely conducive to this growth. In the vicinity of Gloucester to the north-east and close to Bristol (which would experience large-scale growth in the seventeenth century) in the south, the Forest was ideally located, between two navigable rivers. Large amounts of this timber, iron ore, charcoal and coal were also exported by road to the neighbouring counties of Monmouthshire and

---

[15] H. G. Nicholls, *Iron Making in the Olden Times: as Instanced in the ancient Mines, Forges, and Furnaces of the Forest of Dean, Historically Related, on the Basis of Contemporary Records an Exact Local Investigation – 1866* (Coleford, 1981).

Herefordshire. To the north of the central demesne lands, the region stretching from Littledean and Ruardean towards Newnham was well established as a trade route between Gloucester and Monmouth by the late medieval period. The system of roads and routes that met in the vicinity of Littledean was integral to both timber exports from the Forest and the trade of the cloth industry to the east of the Severn. In 1594, the mayor and aldermen of Gloucester described the 'Overs bridge over the Sevearne neere Glouc' as a 'greate and common occupied way'.[16] The archaeological remains of the 'Dean road' - which connected Lea Bailey in the north of the forest to shipbuilders in the south - were long considered to be 'Roman' in origin although local historian and cartographer Gordon Glissold has suggested that this road is more likely to date from the seventeenth century. This observation accords well with evidence of increasing industrial activity during this century. A. R. J. Jurica notes that:

> Its timber and mineral resources have given the formerly extraparochial Forest of Dean a rich and distinct industrial history ... Ore mining and ironmaking, the latter sustained for many centuries by charcoal burning, began in early times. Later much iron ore and coal was taken away by road and river and Forest stone was quarried and dressed for local and distant markets.[17]

---

[16] BL, Lansdowne Vol/76, f. 103.

[17] Herbert, *VCH Vol.V*, 326.

The castles at Chepstow and Monmouth on the Welsh side of the Wye are reminders that the Forest has anciently been the site of the two major crossings between south-west England and south Wales. Not only was Dean well served by the Rivers Severn and Wye, but it also represented the confluence of many overland trade routes, both internal and external to the Forest.

Increasing industrial activity during the seventeenth century, due in large part to its highly controversial nature, has ensured that this region is relatively well documented for the period of study. Changes in crown estate management policy, the increasing value of Dean's timber stores, coal and iron ore, together with the widely perceived assault on customary rights during this period, generated a considerable amount of litigation in both local and central courts. Gloucestershire Archives hold the records of two fifteenth-century sessions of the Mine Law Court together with full and consistent records of proceedings from the late seventeenth century to the court's discontinuance in 1777. While the Verderer's Court and the Swanimote sessions do not relate as directly to the operations of the Forest's extractive industries, their records offer much valuable information regarding popular and local senses of disputes and their implications for the environment in which these people lived and worked. This documentation, in concert with census returns, tax assessments and the records of central courts, provides the basis for the following explorations of custom, industry and popular memory in the Forest of Dean between the sixteenth and nineteenth centuries.

III Dean free miners in context

For obvious reasons, mining industries have long preoccupied historians of industrialisation. Extant documentation of the early coal-mining industries has encouraged examination of both innovation in extraction processes, and the role of large-scale capital investment in funding development and expansion.[18] More recently, historians of the early modern period have demonstrated a concern, not solely with the history of industrial development, but also with ways in which this intensification affected the social structures and cultures of mining communities.[19] Anthropologists and sociologists have made significant contributions to understanding the types of community and belief systems engendered by the specific conditions that characterise mining operations.[20] Martin Bulmer explains that

---

[18] C. Hart, *The industrial history of Dean; with an introduction to its industrial archaeology* (Newton Abbot, 1971); J. Langton, *Geographical change and industrial revolution: coalmining in south west Lancashire, 1590-1799* (Cambridge, 1979); J. A. Jaffe, *The struggle for market power: industrial relations in the British coal industry, 1800-1840* (Cambridge, 1991); C. C. Owen, *The Leicestershire and South Derbyshire Coalfield 1200-1900* (Ashbourne, 1984); W. Ashworth, R. A. Church, M. W. Finn, J. Hatcher and B. Supple, *The history of the British coal industry* (Oxford, 1984-87).

[19] D. Levine and K. Wrightson, *The making of an industrial society: Whickham 1560-1765* (Oxford, 1991); A. Wood, *The politics of social conflict: the Peak Country, 1520-1770* (Cambridge, 1999).

[20] C. Kerr and A. Spiegel, 'The Industrial propensity to strike: An International Comparison', in A. Kornhauser, R. Dubin and A. Ross, *Industrial Conflict* (New York, 1954); S. Lipset, *Political Man: The Social Bases of Politics* (New York, 1963); M. Bulmer, *Mining and Social Change* (London, 1978); R. Godoy, 'Mining: Anthropological Perspectives', *Annual Review of Anthropology*, 14, (1985); J. Nash, *We Eat the Mines and the Mines Eat Us: Dependency and Exploitation in Bolivian Tin Mines* (New York, 1979); D. Warwick and G. Littlejohn, *Coal, capital and culture: a sociological analysis of mining communities in West Yorkshire* (London and New York, 1992); B. Williamson, *Class, culture and community: a biographical study of social change in mining* (London, 1982); M. I. A. Bulmer, 'Sociological models of the mining community', *The Sociological Review*, 23, 1975; N. Dennis, C. Slaughter and F. Henriques, *Coal is Our Life* (London, 1956).

'settlements based on coal-mining are widely regarded as being strong in 'community feeling', 'community solidarity', 'community spirit', or in having 'a sense of community".[21] Suggesting that 'the location of mineral deposits in inaccessible areas gives rise to relatively self-contained communities', Richard Godoy neatly summarises anthropological and sociological contributions:

a combination of low wages, coercive organisation, dangerous but autonomous working conditions, the economic leverage of miners flowing from the importance of mining exports to the health of the national economy, and the physical and social isolation of many mining enclaves underwrites the formation of intense forms of worker solidarity and radical labour movements as well as the growth of new forms of political consciousness. The genesis and growth of radical mining movements is well analyzed in Bolivia, Chile, Mexico, Peru, Nigeria, Zambia, Ghana and South Africa.[22]

By comparison with many of these communities the Dean miners, as will be demonstrated, were far less subject to 'coercive organisation'. Other characteristics outlined by Godoy, however, do reflect the Dean free miners' conditions during the late sixteenth and seventeenth centuries. Godoy notes that 'mining communities tend to integrate surrounding regions into a

---

[21] M. Bulmer, 'Social Structure and Change in the Twentieth Century', in M. Bulmer, *Mining*, 15.

[22] Godoy, 'Mining', 207.

15

single economic sphere', an observation which illuminates the miners' centrality to popular senses of this region during the early modern period.[23] Mining and its related industries were integral to the Forest as an economic unit. Propertied and propertyless, rich and poor, 'ancient' inhabitants and recent migrants were all dependent in many ways on the activities of the mining community.[24]

This book argues that, in addition to their economic influence, this occupational group were integral to resisting encroachment upon local and 'ancient' rights to resources in the Forest. For reasons which will be explained, this was particularly true during the early-seventeenth century. In short, Dean's miners were not only dependent upon rights to the mineral resources, but also upon many of the same customary rights to pannage, estovers, and grazing as the rest of the forest commonalty. Defence of their rights, therefore, meant the defence of practices which sustained many poorer inhabitants in the Forest of Dean. June Nash's work on twentieth-century Bolivian tin miners is illuminating as she attempts to explain 'the solidarity of miners as a work force'. 'In most modern industrial societies', she states that:

> the home life of the workers is physically separated from the job. The motivations and activities of the domestic unit are antagonistic to those of the work group. The shared consumption drives of the family

---

[23] Ibid., 207.

[24] C. Hart, *Royal forest: a history of Dean's woods as producers of timber* (Oxford, 1966); C. Hart, *The free miners of the Royal Forest of Dean and Hundred of St. Briavels* (Gloucester, 1953); B. Sharp, *In contempt of all authority: rural artisans and riot in the west of England, 1586-1660* (Berkeley and London, 1980); C. Fisher, *Custom, Work and Market Capitalism: The Forest of Dean Colliers, 1788-1888* (London, 1981).

cultivate conformity to a given job structure, while the shared work conditions promote a sense of alienation and hostility to the company. In the mining community, the contradiction between home life and work life is less evident. Houses are often an extension of the mine buildings and it is hard to see where administrative buildings end and where the workers' housing begins. Workers families share the same basic conditions as the miners.[25]

Nash surmises, then, that the working lives of these Bolivian tin miners were barely distinguishable from the lives of their families and the environment that supported them. The situation was evidently similar in seventeenth-century Dean.

This integration questions traditional distinctions between occupational and wider customary use of forest lands and this is the focus of Chapter Two. Chapter Three builds upon this analysis, exploring the central role of Dean's mining community in protecting local rights to forest resources in the 1620s and 1630s. The appropriation of local festive custom in the symbolism of these Skimmington riots highlighted a common culture that was being fragmented through the activities of royal favourites and other external interests. Chapter Three asks how this symbolism called upon local gentry to assume their traditional paternalistic role in preventing such encroachment. Concerning the 'communal celebrations' of the Bolivian mining communities, Nash observes that:

---

[25] Nash, *We Eat the Mines*, 87.

These are occasions for expressing community solidarity and continuity with the past. They are also the times when conflicts are dramatised and transformations made explicit. Rituals from the pre-conquest can reinforce identity of a people in such a way as to strengthen their resistance to external domination. The same ritual acted out in a changed historical context can have a new meaning.[26]

Chapter Three, therefore, explores the radical implications of calling upon conservative festive customs in the changing context of the Forest of Dean during the 1630s.[27]

During the sixteenth and seventeenth centuries, these local, small-scale and customary operations were characterised by the fiercely protected autonomy of its mining community. Due to the 'ancient' and peculiar nature of their customary rights, this tenacious mining community enjoyed a remarkable level of freedom in regulating their trade.

Describing the history of lead mines of the Mendip Hills, J. W. Gough reproduces a legal taxonomy of early modern English extractive operations. He explains that:

---

[26] Nash, *We Eat the Mines*, 126.

[27] D. Underdown, *Revel, riot and rebellion: popular politics and culture in England, 1603-1660* (Oxford, 1985); M. Bristol, *Carnival and theater: plebeian culture and the structure of authority in Renaissance England* (New York and London, 1989); M. Harris, *Carnival and other Christian festivals: folk theology and folk performance* (Austin, 2003); C. Humphrey, *The politics of carnival: festive misrule in medieval England* (Manchester, 2001); M. Bakhtin, *The Bakhtin Reader: selected writings of Bakhtin, Medvedev and Voloshinov* P. Morris (ed.) (London, 1984); P. Stallybrass and A. White, *The politics and poetics of transgression* (Ithica and New York, 1986).

from the legal point of view the mines of England have fallen into three main classes, first, mines of the precious metals, which were royal perquisites, secondly, mines the rights in which went with the ownership of the land where they were situated, and thirdly, mines in certain 'free-mining districts', such as the Stannaries, where mining rights were governed by a special local constitution; Mendip it has been generally held, while its constitution was admittedly less complete than that of the Stannaries, falls into the third of these categories. It is obvious that in many respects this is true, but the evidence already quoted goes to show that there was a strong tendency on the lord's part – and a tendency which met with a large level of success – to reduce Mendip to the status of the second class, in which the lord of the soil himself was sovereign over the conditions in the industry.

Gough demonstrates that proportions of extracted lead payable to the Lord of this area in Somerset were increasing during the sixteenth century. This trend apparently reflected the nascent tendencies of a localised, gentry-lead capitalism.[28] Those who mined the Thievely lead field in Lancashire during the early seventeenth century also worked under conditions dictated by the 'lord of the soil'. An early seventeenth-century 'Commission For Working the Mines' contrasts instructively with the operations of the Dean free miners. Dated 28 May 1629, this commission granted special rights to 'our trustie and welbeloved subiectes Sir Raff Ashton baronet, Richard Shuttleworth esqr, Roberte Holte esqr, Nicholas Towneley esqr, Savill

---

[28] J. W. Gough, *The Mines of Mendip* (New York, 1967), 109-10.

Radcliffe esqr and Roger Kenyon gent'. The commission gave these gentlemen:

> full power and aucthoritie upon your survey thereof to give such orders and direccions from tyme to tyme in the premisses for the furthering of our service advanceinge our profits and well ordringe of the said mynes and all miners and workers therein as you shall finde meete and requisite upon anie occacion happoninge.[29]

R. Sharpe France examined a 1632 document designed to fix wages in the Derbyshire lead field together with a 'Notice taken of the proceedings touchinge the ordering and governing of Leadmynes etc' recorded at 'Workesworth in Com. Derbie, 22, 23 et 24 Aug, 1630'. This document suggests that the miners of this region looked enviously to the organisation of the free-mining industry in Derbyshire's Peak country as a system which offered more desirable occupational terms.[30]

Andy Wood describes the lead miners of the King's Field in the Peak country, noting their fierce sense of autonomy and the pugnacious assertion of customary mining laws through litigation in the local barmote or, on occasion, through open confrontation. Even this mining community, however, was subject to the scrutiny of local manorial lords through the 'lot and cope' system. Wood explains that:

---

[29] R. Sharpe France (ed.), *The Thievely Lead Miners 1629-1635*, Lancashire and Cheshire Record Society 52, (Preston, 1947), 1-2.

[30] Ibid., 81.

The owner of Newton Grange took one fifth of the miners' ore as lot payments at that time, as did the owner of Steeple Grange. The exaction of such high rates of lot payment effectively reduced the miners to the status of wage labourers. Hence, free miners from the King's Field described the workforce in such manors as 'labourers' or 'servants'. No formal right of free mining existed within these arbitrary jurisdictions'. The lord appointed the barmaster, whose actions went unregulated by any barmote. Rates of lot and cope [dues taken by the manorial lord] were not fixed by custom, but were variable and determined by the lord.

Not all of the Peak manors had such stringent lot payments levied upon their mining operations but all were subject to the 'lot and cope dues' and these rendered their industry subject to the interests of other parties.[31]

The mining industry in the Forest of Dean was less constricted. The Dean miners' customary *Laws and Privileges*, which were first codified in 1612, state clearly that no 'straunger' of 'whatsoever rank' was to come into the mines. The Crown received their share of the ore extracted from its wastes and demesne lands in Dean directly through the appointment of the 'King's man', a fifth miner who was to work on behalf of the King.[32] Unlike the Peak country then, rates and dues were firmly fixed by custom and, significantly, the operations of this industry were less open to the scrutiny

---

[31] Wood, *Social Conflict*, 121.

[32] Hart, *Free Miners*, 40.

of external capital interests than other English free-mining industries. In 2007, the interviewee described the function of the long discontinued Mine Law Court in the Forest of Dean. He explains that, because of disputes over who had laboured the most to uncover rich coal seams, the miners:

> used to quarrel with one another. So, to finish up ... the free miners got together and they agreed to form their own law court, just like the court today, twelve members of the jury and instead of having a judge, they used to have the constable of St. Briavels, that is the man that used to have to attend every time if there was any trouble caused ... well they still pinched one another's coal and then when these court cases were brought up the constable of St. Briavels had to attend and whoever was proved to be in the wrong, had to compensate the other miner.[33]

The share taken by the 'King's man' was also known as 'law oare' and implied the right of Dean's miners to hold their own court which exercised a complete monopoly of jurisdiction over their industry. Chapters Three and Four examine the Mine Law Court and the miners' *Laws and Privileges* in greater depth.

Lewis's second category of mining operations described a system in which local manorial lords and industrial gentry dictated the terms of production. The free miners of Dean seem to have operated with a remarkable level of autonomy by comparison with similar industries in England during the late medieval and early modern period. This book, therefore, considers the

---

[33] 72 year old free miner of the Forest of Dean. Interviewed in 2007.

particular conditions that pertained to this industry and the working lives of miners. As such, it examines ways in which the nature of mining informed the relation between this occupational community, their environment, and local senses of the past. It is argued that this underpinned local resistance to the many-faceted changes that occurred during the seventeenth and eighteenth centuries.[34]

IV Industrial intensification and social change, c. 1560-1680

This study addresses longer term changes and continuities in the organisation of popular collective memory in the Forest of Dean between the sixteenth and nineteenth centuries. The primary focus, however, has been on those developments that occurred between 1560 and 1680. This period witnessed great change, not only in the intensity of industrial

---

[34] The complex technical nature of efficient mining, and the importance of local knowledge, lent this occupation a peculiar resistance to attempts by large capital investors to gain a foothold or impose large scale control over the operations of Dean's mining industry. The growth of demand for coal produced in Dean was related to the very rapid and significant growth of Bristol during this period. Jurica notes that whilst regular ore mining change underwent a downturn, 'the coal industry on the other hand expanded in the 18th century. New pits and levels were frequently opened. Some of their names, such as Long Looked For, Pluck Penny and Small Profit, reflected the speculative nature of the industry, which until David Mushet published a survey of the strata in 1824 relied on personal knowledge of the geology of the outcrop ... In the later 18th century many miners were too impoverished to pay their gale rents and most lacked the money needed for the pumping and winding machines necessary for deeper working. Coal pits remained shallow and once flooded were abandoned in favour of new workings ... By the 1770s two or three crank-driven pumps had been installed in the coalfield. The first mine to use steam power for pumping was a drift near Broadmoor known in 1754 as Water Wheel Engine and later as Oiling Gin. A steam engine was set up there, perhaps as early as 1766, by a group of foreigners, who in 1776 surrendered a major share in the mine to a company of miners'. N. M. Herbert (ed.), *A History of the County of Gloucester: Volume V. Bledisloe Hundred, St Briavels Hundred, The Forest of Dean* (Oxford, 1996), 330-1. See also Hart, *Industrial History*; Hart, *Free Miners*; W. Maurice, *A pitman's anthology* (London, 2004); A. Campbell, *The Scottish Miners, 1874-1939* (Aldershot, 2000); I. Tyler, *Thirlmere Mines and the Drowning of the Valley* (Keswick, 2005); H. Beynon, A. Cox and R. Hudson, *Digging up trouble: the environment, protest and open cast mining* (London, 2000).

activity and the size of the region's population, but also in perceptions of local industrial and common rights. It is important, initially, to establish some idea of the scale of this growth and examine reasons behind it. Increasing displacement of the rural poor during the late-sixteenth century attracted many to forests in the hope of supplementing their income with the less restricted common lands of the royal wastes and demesnes.[35] Dean appears to have been no exception. An in-migrating population appear to have sought the by-employments generated through increasing demand for the products of the Forest's mining and smelting industries. John Hatcher explains:

> When late Elizabethan and early Jacobean men took stock of the changes which had taken place in the provision of fuel within their lifetimes, they marvelled at the progress of coal 'from the forge into the kitchen and the hall', and from an esoteric combustible into 'a commodity so common and useful that people cannot live without the same. They gloried in its ascent from being a despised substance fit only for the hearths of the destitute into a commodious mineral utilized by 'Noblemen, knights, country and common people' alike. Whereas once coal had been of little moment it was now regarded as 'one of the most important commodities of the realm' and Newcastle was feted as the new Peru, its prosperity founded upon black gold.[36]

---

[35] Underdown, *Revel, Riot and Rebellion*; J. Thirsk, 'Seventeenth century agriculture and social change', *Agricultural History Review*, supplement 18 (1970).

[36] Hatcher, *British Coal Industry*, 53.

Hatcher suggests that 'a growth in national output of more than tenfold between 1550 and 1700 is a strong possibility'.[37] It is sensible to assume, then, that employment opportunities related to both the coal and iron industries increased sharply in areas like the Forest of Dean during the late sixteenth and seventeenth centuries.

Figure 1   Population growth in St. Briavels hundred, 1563-1672

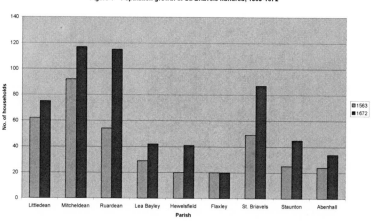

Figure 1 demonstrates the growth in population of most parishes within St Briavels Hundred between 1563 and 1672.[38] The Bishops' Census of 1563 and Hearth Tax returns for the later seventeenth century both assessed the

---

[37] Ibid., 47.

[38] GRO, D383; A. D. Dyer, and D. M. Palliser (eds.), *The diocesan population returns of 1563 and 1603* (Oxford, 2005).

household and, thus, offer consistent records for comparison. The most complete Hearth Tax returns are from 1672 but omit exclusions on grounds of poverty for the parishes of English Bicknor, Clearwell, Bream and Coleford. Any analysis of population shifts in the Forest during the late-sixteenth and seventeenth centuries must acknowledge these shortcomings. The obscurity of the extra-parochial central demesne also presents a significant hindrance which was as frustrating for contemporary authorities as it is for the modern historian. The correlation of Figure 1 and the map of early parishes in Dean, however, suggests that most recorded growth in population was within parishes towards the north of the Forest.[39] While most of these parishes increased in size during this period, Ruardean apparently doubled in size by 1672 and was, by all accounts, a heavily populated industrial village by this point.

Between 1563 and 1672, Littledean increased from sixty households to seventy five. Littledean, like Ruardean, also sat towards the north east of the Forest. Most parishes that adjoined the northern peripheries of the royal wastes experienced this kind of growth across the seventeenth century. Mitcheldean grew from ninety two households in 1563 to 117 in 1672, Abenhall from twenty four to thirty four, and Lea Bailey from twenty nine to forty two. As suggested, records for English Bicknor defy accurate analysis but Stanton to the east of this parish swelled from twenty five households in 1563 to forty five in 1672. This is not striking expansion but these figures do suggest a general pattern of growth. Ruardean, meanwhile, experienced a substantial population increase of more than one hundred per

---

[39] Such growth was primarily experienced in 'Mitcheldean gale', the region to the north that was commonly referred to as that 'below the woods'; this in itself poses questions regarding the idiosyncratic geographical orientation of inhabitants during this period.

cent during this period. An expansion in population and industrial by-employments make it unsurprising this area was the scene of most controversy in the Skimmington riots between 1628 and 1631 as examined in Chapter Three. To gain a more nuanced reading of Ruardean's growth, crude decadal patterns have been gleaned from parish registers. Figure 2 shows the number of baptisms per decade while Figure 3 shows the surplus of baptisms over burials during the same period, revealing an approximation of population growth patterns within Ruardean between 1560 and 1630.

Figure 2   Total baptisms per decade, Ruardean, 1560-1640

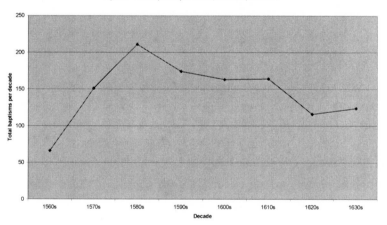

Baptisms in this parish were increasing most dramatically during the 1570s, the 1580s and the 1590s. By the end of the 1570s, the parish clerk had registered almost three times as many baptisms as he had in the preceding decade and this figure had increased further to 211 during the 1580s. The figure still ran at 174 into the 1590s. Figure 3 demonstrates that much of this increase was counteracted by higher mortality rates but at no point did the number of burials exceed the number of baptisms. Ruardean clearly sustained a pattern of consistent population growth during the late sixteenth and early seventeenth centuries, some from increase in resident families and some from in-migration.

Figure 3   Surplus of baptisms over burials, Ruardean, 1560-1640.

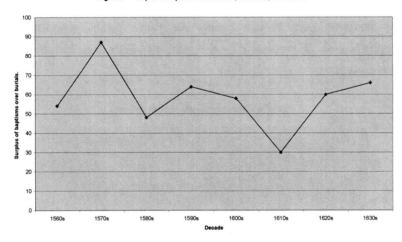

As noted, during this period Dean was exporting large amounts of ore and cinders for blast furnaces in the neighbouring counties of Herefordshire and Monmouthshire.[40] Several trading routes linked Gloucester, Hereford and Monmouth around the northern edge of the forest and all of these met in the parish of Littledean. Clues in northern Dean's present-day landscape and these commercial networks suggest that much of the sixteenth- and seventeenth-century in-migration was linked to employment generated by

---

[40] Herbert, *VCH V.*, 328.

the increased trade in cinders and ore.[41] Several other northern parishes would also, presumably, have benefitted from their proximity to the major routes that connected Gloucester, Monmouth and Hereford with the Forest. This is not to suggest that mining and its associated employments were not significant towards the southern edge of Dean but there appears to have been more variation in commercial activity at the start of the seventeenth century. For example, thirteen sailors, including five members of the notorious Gethin family, lived in Hewelsfield, to the south of St. Briavels parish and close to the navigable River Wye and the ports of Bristol and Chepstow. The region's expanding extractive and processing industries dominated trade and by-employment in Ruardean and neighbouring parishes. In 1608, eleven miners, one collier, eighteen nailers, sixteen labourers and two pinners lived and worked in Littledean. Mitcheldean was home to fourteen labourers and one nailer, nine labourers and four miners lived in Stanton, eleven labourers and one miner in English Bicknor, while the population of Ruardean included one collier, nineteen labourers and six nailers.[42]

---

[41] TNA, MR 179.

[42] J. Smith, *Men & Armour for Gloucestershire in 1608* (Gloucester, 1902). The term 'labourer' is thought to have been interchangeable locally with 'miner' in many official records.

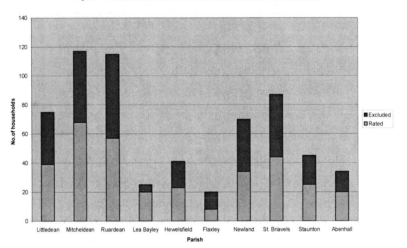

The 1672 Hearth Tax returns, clearly demonstrate the poverty of many inhabitants in these industrial parishes as shown in Figure 4. More than half of the residents of Littledean and Flaxley were excluded from tax assessments on grounds of their poverty while at least forty per cent were excluded in Mitcheldean, Ruardean and Stanton. Taking a slightly broader view of what might have constituted poverty during this period, only the southerly parishes of St. Briavels and Abenhall had more than twenty per cent of inhabitants recorded with more than two hearths. These industrial villages adjoined the northern edge of Dean's extra-parochial wastes. The available statistics for in-migration suggest a fluidity which undermines any pretence of 'timeless' stasis as implied by customary ideals. They also demonstrate that increasing numbers of families in these communities depended on access to the resources of an 'open' forest. Jurica estimates that during this period '100 families depended on mining ore or coal'.[43] This may well have been the case but the records suggest that these families would have been living side by side with many others that counted upon the common rights that the free mining community strove to protect. The protests of miners examined in Chapter Three were integral to the interests of these poorer foresters.

V Custom and popular memory

The influence of custom was ubiquitous in late medieval communities. These customs ranged from a coherent body of legal uses which governed industrial and commoning rights to the seasonal festivals, community norms, shaming rituals and traditions which both ordered and lubricated social interaction. It therefore represented a cultural space that was essential to negotiation and renewal of the 'politics of the parish'.[44] The one common element of all customary practices was a high regard for, and a conscious effort to maintain continuity with, the past and the legitimating evidence of precedent. In this sense, custom represented an interface between present practice and ancestral traditions. The embodied and practical nature of custom or *lex loci* in its idealised sense, a local law that was held 'nowhere but in the memory of the people' and perpetuated in their activity, suggests

---

[43] Herbert, *VCH V.*, 328-9.

[44] K. Wrightson, 'The Politics of the Parish', in A. Fox, P. Griffith and S. Hindle (eds.), *The Experience of Authority in Early Modern England* (Basingstoke, 1996), 10-46.

a certain type of historical memory. As *jus non scriptum*, custom operated through the shared knowledge of all in the community, although the testimony of older, settled, men of relevant occupations was often privileged in resolving conflict. The inclusive nature of parochial custom and its dependence upon knowledge of an intensely local past, then, implies a sense in which the study of custom during the early modern period is the study of popular memory. There is one glaring limitation to the study of custom in this respect. This is primarily an exploration of Dean's free miners and resistance to industrial encroachment and the vast majority of sources, by definition, offer a masculine view of this area and local senses of the past. There is much important work to be done on the ecclesiastical court records which would reveal the agency of women as guardians of popular memory in a way which may, perhaps, have been less directly related to industry in the Forest but which was no less significant for that.

Many local customs, particularly those that governed access to material resources, came under attack from interests that sought to gain exclusive ownership during the later sixteenth and seventeenth centuries. The strong and inclusive sense of the past engendered through the day-to-day experience of local customary practice and the interrelation of social and economic life would, in many areas, prove to be an effective organising focus for tenacious resistance. R. H. Tawney observed that:

> before the great agrarian changes of the sixteenth century begin, there has been a period - one may date it roughly from 1381 to 1489 - of increasing prosperity for the small cultivator. We have emphasised the evidence of this upward movement which is given by the growth among the peasantry of a freer and more elastic economy. We have

watched them shake off many of the restrictions imposed by villeinage and build up considerable properties. We have seen how the custom of the manor still acts as a dyke to defend them against encroachments, and to concentrate in their hands a large part of the fruits of economic progress. In that happy balance between the forces of custom and the forces of economic enterprise, custom is powerful, yet not so powerful that men cannot evade it when evasion is desired.[45]

As Tawney spoke, rather optimistically it must be said, of a balance between economic enterprise and custom, he outlined a burgeoning conflict between the forward-looking impulses of competition and the security perceived by many in the past-oriented 'immemorial routine' of communal agriculture.

Local customs were a major focus of antiquarians such as John Aubrey since the sixteenth and seventeenth centuries, largely with the aim of preserving knowledge of regional folk cultures that were perceived to be under threat. These efforts continued during the eighteenth century and into the nineteenth, many of these later 'collections' apparently inspired by romantic notions of a 'picturesque' rural poor. Tawney's interpretation, published at the beginning of the twentieth century, is distinctive in its recognition of custom as a force for engendering popular political consciousness. He described custom as a resource which could legitimate resistance against innovation contrary to the authority of antiquity. Here, then, is the root of the somewhat paradoxical phenomenon that E. P.

---

[45] R. H. Tawney, *The Agrarian Problem in the Sixteenth Century* (Harrington, 1912), Chapter IV: The Peasantry.

Thompson described as a 'rebellious traditional culture'. Keith Wrightson confirms that:

> The defence of custom was 'quintessentially local politics'. As the now numerous accounts of such local struggles should make clear, localised customary consciousness was just as much a form of political consciousness as the knowledge of national affairs fostered by a developing print culture.[46]

To the historian, customs are most visible in conflict over resources or when appropriated in the legitimation of riot and protest. Records of these events have provided valuable material for the study of early modern culture but too keen a focus on these episodes risks defining custom negatively, by reference to what it is not. If one considers only occasions on which disputes arose over boundaries, rights to graze cattle, or enclosure, there is a danger of understanding early modern local custom as a reactive, backward-looking culture defined through its resistance to encroachment. This would overlook the positive assertion and expression of local cultural codes that informed the ordinary day-to-day life of millions of people in the name of custom and tradition.

Thompson described custom as *praxis*, as the consciously willed actions through which ideology or theory is transformed into meaningful collective activity. He explained that 'At the interface between law and agrarian practice we find custom. Custom itself *is* the interface, since it may be

---

[46] Wrightson, 'Politics of the parish', in P. Griffiths, A. Fox and S. Hindle (eds.), *The Experience of Authority in Early Modern England* (Basingstoke, 1999), 24.

considered both as praxis and as law. Custom's original lies in praxis'.[47] While this is pertinent to the harder core of legal codes that governed access to resources, the same can be said of the cultural codes, norms and traditions that constituted local custom in its penumbral extent. Many popular customs were attached to baptisms, weddings and funerals. Similarly, rituals such as parish wakes and ales, the rush-bearing processions of Plough Monday or the Easter 'election' of the Lord and Lady of Misrule, were central to maintaining the conviviality of local *communitas* and formed an integral strand of efforts to support the poor of the parish. The customary rituals of rogation and beating the bounds affirmed the spatial continuity of local communities through time, while tithe payments and the customary layout of church pews were elements, among others, that ensured social hierarchies were never far from the mind of the church-attending parishioner. Custom, then, was not simply a rhetorical trope used to garner support for the protection of local traditions against a burgeoning 'logic of capitalism'. In a far more positive sense, it was an organising force that embodied continuity between a local community and its past, between a behavioural ideal and the reality of social and industrial interaction.

Through custom then, the late medieval local community ordered its daily activity in line with a particular understanding of the past held intersubjectively by its members and articulated in their rituals and practices. This inclusive model of collective memory illuminates many aspects of early modern popular political consciousness but is problematic

---

[47] E. P. Thompson, 'Custom, Law and Common Right', in E. P. Thompson, *Customs in Common; studies in traditional popular culture* (New York, 1993), 97.

in its inability to comprehend the contribution of individual thought and action to these processes of social reproduction. This shortcoming has been identified in some of the earliest and most influential work on memory studies. Maurice Halbwachs' work on collective memory, for instance, focuses on the relationship between individual memory and the social group, and seems to imply that the former is unable to function outside the context of the latter.[48] Subsequent work in this field, such as that of James Fentress and Chris Wickham, offers a more dialectical interpretation of the relation between the group and the individual in the construction and perpetuation of social memory. Numerous anthropological studies and comparative histories have added weight to the view that individual and collective memories exist in dynamic and two-way communication.[49] Pierre Bourdieu's notion of *habitus* offers a useful model for conceptualising reciprocal relations between the individual agent and his or her environment. He explains that:

> The *habitus*, a product of history, produces individual and collective practices – more history – in accordance with the schemes generated by history. It ensures the active presence of past experiences, which, deposited in each organism in the form of schemes of perception,

---

[48] M. Halbwachs, *On Collective Memory* (Eng. Trans., Chicago and London, 1992), 223.

[49] Fentress and Wickham, *Social Memory*; S. Foot, 'Remembering, forgetting and inventing: attitudes to the past in England after the First Viking Age', *Transactions of the Royal Historical Society*, 6th series, 9 (1999), 185-200; M. Godelier, 'Infrastructures, societies and history', *Current Anthropology*, 19, 4 (1978), 763-771; A. Collard, 'Investigating 'social memory' in a Greek context', in E. Tonkin, M. McDonald and M. Chapman (eds.), *History and Ethnicity* (London, 1989), 89-103; D. Bertaux (ed.), *Biography and Society: The Life History Approach in the Social Sciences* (Beverly Hills, 1981).

thought and action, tend to guarantee the 'correctness' of practices and their constancy over time, more reliably than all formal rules and explicit norms. This system of dispositions – a present past that tends to perpetuate itself into the future by reactivation in similarly structured practices, an internal law through which the law of external necessities, irreducible to immediate constraints, is constantly exerted – is the principle of the continuity and regularity which objectivism sees in social practices without being able to account for it; and also of the regulated transformations that cannot be explained.[50]

Bourdieu's model of social reproduction describes a reciprocal process whereby the movements of individual actors contribute to the schematic mental and spatial structures, within which, future thought and action may occur. The capacity for agency in the actor is, thereby, accounted for in the potential for mnemonic traces of individual activity to contribute, albeit only cumulatively, to the overall direction of the group. This idea underpins the book's general thesis that, during the period of study, the free miners of Dean were remembered locally for their role in resisting encroachment upon Forest resources.

The first chapter builds upon Thompson's seminal interpretation of *habitus* in the context of early modern England and lays the foundations for this hypothesis by thinking about Dean's landscape as a 'memory palace' which literally stored information that was drawn upon in defence of local custom. This material legal record was often recalled, alongside memories of working in the landscape, to establish continuity of rights and garner

---

[50] P. Bourdieu, *The Logic of Practice* (Eng. Trans., London, 2005), 54.

support for their defence when they were perceived to be under threat. This chapter reconstructs the seventeenth-century forest *habitus* using the evidence of place names, landscape features, the material fabric of buildings as well as contemporary maps and court documents. The collated evidence reveals the overwhelming influence of the mining community in popular memory and perceptions of place. In Dean, miners loomed large in perceptions of the Forest, particularly when defending customary access to resources such as wood, timber and coal. The history of this region, as perceived from 'within', was dominated by the physical and symbolic resonance of the miners and their industry. This chapter also highlights affinities between the synchronic senses of time and space suggested by this type of world-view and those that underwrote the timeless ideal of custom. Chapter One, then, demonstrates that many traditional use-rights in Dean were tied to the royal status of the Forest and memories of dwelling and labouring in this local landscape.

What did these common rights mean to those living in the Forest? Drawing on inventories from the area, Chapter Two explores the material value of these rights to each of the diverse social and occupational groups in Dean. To avoid mistaking an ideal of customary traditions for their reality, this chapter assesses the actual value of these rights to forest inhabitants. Free miners, resident industrial gentry, labourers of mixed employment, and farmers with rights to common all come under scrutiny, together with 'foreigners' seeking the benefits of the forest wastes in the straitened climate of early seventeenth-century England. This, particularly, is crucial to understanding the staunchly localist symbolism of popular protest in the Forest which is the focus of the following chapter. The inventories also offer a more expansive view of the community that depended on rights to common in Dean. The major point of this chapter is that these rights were essential to the livelihoods of a wide section of the forest community and intimately tied to mining rights to the extent that the defence of one was defence of the other.

To defend mining custom, then, was to defend rights to fuel, grazing, and pannage. Chapter Three explores what happened when these factors coincided in antagonism to encroachment by outsiders, particularly court favourites who had been granted rights to prized resources in return for services rendered to the early Stuart crown. There were significant episodes in 1611 and in the years 1628-31, with the mining community central to the organization of both. The first involved a grant to the Earl of Pembroke during which the rioting miners were described as 'Robin Hoodes' by the Earl of Northampton. This chapter initially explores the resonances of this legend at the end of the sixteenth century, asking what Northampton's allusion suggests about the way that this forest community, particularly the free-mining element, was perceived by those who were close to central authority. The second episode offers a view from the other direction. In 1628 the provocation was, once again, a royal grant, this time to Lady Barbara Villiers, wife of court favourite Edward Villiers. The miners were also integral to these sustained and more widely-supported actions, but the duty of leadership fell to John Skimmington, also known as John Williams, a free miner. The leader of the Skimmington riots was named after a socially inclusive shaming ritual that had traditionally articulated collective opposition to breaches of local custom. This was a very apposite reaction, then, to the Villiers' grant and this chapter explores the symbolism of this ritual with reference to the social breadth of groups that depended upon forest custom and who, thus, held a collective interest in opposing the encroachment of court favourites.

The chapter then sets these riots in the context of other local risings in the neighbouring forest of Breydon. These were also led by Skimmingtons and it is argued that these types of 'mythical' leaders allowed disparate local actions to be subsumed as part of a wider threat to authority. These disturbances in the forests of south-west England between 1628 and 1631 were to become known as the Western risings and were clearly perceived as such a threat. The chapter closes by situating these episodes within broader patterns of protest and rebellion in sixteenth- and seventeenth-century England.

Physical conflict and direct action were not the only ways that foresters, mainly free miners, sought to preserve the customs that sustained their livelihoods, confirmed their occupational status, and allowed them to maintain control over their industry. While parties such as the Attorney General and other capital interests began to use equity litigation in attempting to undermine local custom, foresters responded with counter suits in the same courts, at once adopting and legitimating these formal and centralised legal processes. Chapter Four considers the transition within the Forest from local, and predominantly oral, legal senses to the increasing influence of a national written law. Foregrounding the agency of this local population in their use of equity litigation, this chapter reveals that the extension of central court jurisdiction was, in many respects, a locally driven process. The influence of these courts, however, went further than popular litigation. Towards the end of the seventeenth century, records suggest that the Mine Law Court consciously moved to emulate the methods of the central courts. Contrary to many teleologies of English state formation, the evidence from Dean implies that the move towards an accepted unitary idea of the law was very much a two-way process. The Mine Law Court presents an object study in the meeting of local senses of the law, oral and written evidence, and various attempts to apply a national and unitary legal code to the 'dark corners of the land'. This chapter, then, charts the increasing dependence of the court and mining culture upon the written record and a narrowing of popular legal memory. The written collection of records and decrees, known locally as the 'Book of Denis', upon which miners' legal defence had come to rest was apparently stolen in 1777 and the court was subsequently discontinued.

The disbandment of the Mine Law Court left traditional forest rights vulnerable to external interest and the common law. Indeed, the year after the court was disbanded, we see the first common-law prosecutions of miners for 'theft' of timber which had 'anciently' been their customary right. Chapter Five sets these prosecutions in the context of eighteenth-century criminal justice reform, tracing the legal changes which favoured the protection of private property and, by which, many traditional customary rights were redefined as crimes. The chapter ties this change to shifting 'ways of seeing' the Forest and a divergence in spatio-temporal perceptions which underpinned common access, on one hand, and exclusive ownership on the other.

In 1831, the Forest witnessed a series of widespread protests against enclosure that gained huge support under the leadership of Warren James, the son of a free miner. The final chapter analyses these 'riots', which took the form of disciplined work, and drew their support from James' call for the free-mining community to 'open' the forest and reassert their traditional rights. In many respects this action would have been recognisable to those who protested against royal grants during the seventeenth century. In the call to protect common rights under the leadership of miners and the appeal to custom through the evidence of the local landscape, the disturbances of 1831 represented strong continuities with older traditions of popular protest. In other significant respects, however, Warren James was clearly influenced by national patterns of protest and held connections beyond his local culture. This episode, therefore, presents a useful study which complicates narratives that imply sharp distinctions between older 'conservative' and newer 'radical' idioms of protest in eighteenth- and nineteenth-century England. Overall, this book charts the influence of the written record on popular collective memory in this royal forest and examines the economic, social, cultural, and political implications of this shifting context.

Chapter One

Landscape, popular memory and the free-mining community

A Custom which hath obtained the force of a Law, is always said to be *Jus non scriptum*, for it cannot be made or created, either by Charter or by Parliament, which are Acts reduced to Writing, and are always matter of Record: But being only matter of Fact, and consisting in Use and Practice, it can be recorded and registred no where but in the Memory of the People. For a Custom taketh beginning and groweth to perfection in this manner. When a reasonable Act once done is found to be good, and beneficial to the People, and agreeable to their nature and disposition, then do they use it and practise it again and again, and so by often iteration and multiplication of the Act, it becomes a Custom; and being continued without interruption time out of mind, it obtaineth the force of a Law. So that Custom in the intendment of Law, is such an Usage which hath obtained *vim Legis*, and is *revera*, a binding Law to such a particular place, persons and things wherein it is concerned.

S. Carter, *Lex Custumaria: or, a Treatise of Copy-hold Estates* (London, 1696), 25.[51]

---

[51] S. Carter, *Lex Custumaria: or, a Treatise of Copy-hold Estates* (London, 1696), URL: http://eebo.chadwyck.com/home Date accessed: 23/05/2008.

I Custom and oral traditions in early modern England

In his seventeenth-century treatise on the origins and perpetuation of custom, Samuel Carter outlined a legal tradition rooted in *'Jus non Scriptum'*, that was recorded 'no where but in the memory of the people'. His idealised account engages with the fiction that customary law was transmitted only through oral tradition. Carter pointed to the effect on this legal tradition when captured in the written record and isolated from the process of lived experience from which he suggested it had grown.[52] Just law, he argued, could not be generated by 'Charter or by Parliament' as these were merely 'Acts reduced to writing', while custom 'taketh beginning and groweth to perfection' through 'Use and Practice'. The flexibility of oral testimony would make the memories of past uses less likely to contradict present practice as many customs were subject to constant and seasonal variation. The written record of the statute or deed, on the other hand, constituted a fixed linear record which the owner of private and exclusive property rights could produce as evidence of unambiguous and exclusive ownership. It is a commonplace, however, that 'oral' and 'literate' modes of legal memory during this period were neither discrete nor opposable in any sense, but existed in a complex and mutually sustaining interplay.[53]

---

[52] A 1652 law suit referring to the first recorded sale of a mining gale within the forest also mentions mining rights being 'reduced into writing' TNA, E126/5, f. 274.

[53] For debates on the differences between oral and literate modes of communication, see R. Finnegan, 'Literacy versus Non-Literacy: the 'Great Divide? Some Comments on the Significance of Literature in Non-Literate Cultures', in R. Horton and R. Finnegan (eds.), *Modes of Thought: Essays on Thinking in Western and Non-Western Societies* (London, 1973), 112-44; W. Ong, *Orality and Literacy: The*

This chapter suggests that custom's representation as a body of unwritten law aided the efficacy of a legal system which was able to accommodate multiple and coincident uses. Thompson noted that:

> during the eighteenth century one legal decision after another signalled that the lawyers had become converted to the notions of absolute property ownership, and that (wherever the least doubt could be found) the law abhorred the messy complexities of coincident use-right.[54]

The chapter demonstrates the embodied nature of local custom in the Forest of Dean during the sixteenth and seventeenth centuries and examines the functional aspects of this flexible code in smoothing the operation of this legal system. It especially considers the accommodation of multiple use-rights which were evidently so problematic for the legal system described by Thompson. As he implied, this system increasingly acted to support exclusive notions of property ownership.

Although in many respects an ideal, the diffuse and malleable nature of unwritten custom left this legitimating force open to appropriation by those at all levels of the social order. Archaic and collective notions of property rights, it seems, proved more difficult to extinguish in the great forests of England during the eighteenth century. In these areas, Thompson explains,

---

Technologizing of the Word (London, 1982).

[54] E.P. Thompson, *Whigs and Hunters: the origin of the Black Act* (Harmondsworth, 1977), 241.

'the foresters clung still to the lowest rungs of a hierarchy of use-rights'.[55] While a number of claimants to common rights may have been clinging to the lowest rungs, they were making claims on the same basis as those at the highest reaches of this hierarchy. In this context, the early modern assault on custom can be linked to a wider division of cultures which characterised a number of English communities, often inculcating a separation of world-views which underwrote perceptions of property tenure. In many areas of southern England early agrarian capitalism was marked by the emergence of yeoman farmers with larger holdings and an increasing tendency to employ wage labourers.[56] Historians have argued that this economic division was often accompanied by a process of social and cultural polarisation.[57] The impulse to improve farmland and notions of private ownership that emerged among this middling group resulted in a loss of commons and wastes upon which the latter group often depended.[58]

---

[55] Thompson, *Whigs and Hunters*, 240.

[56] J. Whittle, *The Development of Agrarian Capitalism: Land and Labour in Norfolk, 1440-1580* (Oxford, 2000), 23.

[57] K. Wrightson, 'The Social Order of Early Modern England: Three Approaches', in L. Bonfield, R. M. Smith & K. Wrightson (eds.), *The World We Have Gained: Histories of Population and Social Structure* (Oxford, 1986), 177-202; K. Wrightson, 'Estates, Degrees and Sorts: Changing Perceptions of Society in Tudor and Stuart England', in P. J. Corfield (ed.), *Language, History and Class* (Oxford, 1991), 30-52; H. R. French, 'Social Status, Localism and the "Middle Sort of People" in England, 1620-1750', *Past and Present*, 166 (2000), 66-99; H. R. French, *The Middle Sort of People in Provincial England, 1600-1750* (Oxford, 2007).

[58] B. Frazer, 'Common Recollections: Resisting Enclosure 'by Agreement' in Seventeenth-Century England', *International Journal of Historical Archaeology*, 3, 2 (1999), 75-99.

Focusing on the relation between popular collective memory and local legal systems, this chapter outlines characteristics of the world-view which sustained idealised notions of customary social and industrial relations. In short, the following delineates the popular *habitus* of early modern Dean.

Customary law in this period was dependent on the dialectic relation of both oral and written evidence.[59] The pretence of custom as unwritten law suggests certain foundational characteristics of a culture in which oral traditions are more likely to have prevailed. Customary practice within the Forest of Dean was subject to historical change, particularly through the reification of the written record, yet those who claimed 'ancient' rights continued to appeal to this timeless ideal of unchanging and continued practice. Despite apparent inconsistencies, this was an ideal with obvious importance to early modern foresters. This chapter presents a systematic analysis of the synchronic ideals which supported these customary perceptions of the Forest, explaining the relation between this type of thought and the efficacy of legal practice. Discussing attempts to understand the mentalities of historical subjects, or 'history from within', Malcolm Gaskill suggests the major difficulty 'that so much of [this type of thought] is expressed in action and concrete symbolism' and is therefore difficult to retrieve.[60] This chapter attempts to recover traces of this experience to build a picture of the idealised relation of local custom to

---

[59] A. Wood, 'Custom and the social organisation of writing in early modern England', *Transactions of the Royal Historical Society*, 6th Series, 9 (1999), 257-69; A. Fox, 'Custom, Memory and the Authority of Writing', in P. Griffiths, A. Fox and S. Hindle (eds.), *The Experience of Authority in Early Modern England* (Basingstoke, 1999), 89-116, 110.

crown authority. It outlines key functional and cultural features of this malleable system to examine the transmission and recall of use-rights in a predominantly oral culture.

II 'one of his Ma(ies)ties auncient Forrest'

In 1613, John Sallens of Blakeney complained that the Earl of Pembroke and his servants would 'soon destroy the forest' by taking excessive amounts of wood from 'divers partes of the said Forrest for the making of Iron'. His main concern seems to have been the loss of common rights which, he assumed, would be caused by this destruction. Sallens, a yeoman, claimed that he and other inhabitants of the Forest of Dean 'have had used and enioyed the said Forrest and the woods and wastes of the same as belonging to their ancient messuages lands and tenements common of pasture and herbage' as the 'kings Maiesties tenants and suitors to the courte and castle of St Brevills'. Legitimating these rights, he invoked the 'statut called Charta de Foresta' made by King Henry III, and pointed to the 'pasture, herbage, estovers, houseboote' which had been enjoyed 'al the time whereof the memorie of man is not to the contrarie', according to 'the government of the swanymote and attachments within the said Forrest'.[61] *The Charter of the Forests* was issued in 1217 to control unrestrained

---

[60] C. R. Hallpike, *Foundations of primitive thought* (Oxford, 1979), 64. Quoted in M. Gaskill, *Crime and mentalities in early modern England* (Cambridge, 2000), 17.

[61] TNA, E112/82/300.

afforestation, a process through which an area was removed from the jurisdiction of the common law and brought under that of forest law. The charter directed that 'no swanimote shall henceforth be held in our kingdom except three times a year.... when our agisters meet to agist our demesne woods and ..... when our agisters ought to receive our pannage dues; and at these two swanimotes foresters, verderers and agisters shall appear'.[62] Sallens appealed to a statute that was designed to limit the spread of afforestation as it had confirmed the Forest's special legal status, thus recognizing the value of this exceptional jurisdiction in confirming customary rights to forest resources for the inhabitants of Dean.

In 1905 J.C. Cox defined a forest in the legal sense as 'an extensive waste land including both woodland and pasture circumscribed by metes and bounds within which the right of hunting was reserved exclusively to the King'. 'This territory', he explained, 'was subjected to special laws – forest laws – by local as well as central ministers'.[63] Introduced from Normandy after the Conquest, forest law ensured that any area brought under its jurisdiction was placed outside the common law of the land. John Manwood's *A treatise and discourse of the lawes of the forrest* (1598) described the ideal character of a royal forest. This 'Territory of wooddy ground' should be 'stored with great woods of coverts for the secret abode of the wild beasts, and also with fruitfull pastures for their continual feed'.

---

[62] H. Rothwell, (ed.), *English Historical Documents, Vol. 3, 1189-1372* (London, 1975), 337-40.

[63] J. C. Cox, *The Royal Forests of England* (1905), Ch. 1. URL: http://www.archive.org/stream/royalforestsofen00 coxjuoft/royalforestsofen00coxjuoft_djvu.txt Date accessed: 14/09/2010

This was significant to wider patterns of governance, argued Manwood, because:

> If a forrest of the Kings be carefully and diligently loked unto, kept, and preserved, as it ought to be, by good and profitable officers, which have the charge and care thereof committed unto them, then there doth grow unto the King by a forrest..... these benefits, that is to say: first the plenty and increase of Deare, as well for the provision of venison for the kinges court, as also for the princely delight and pleasure of the Kinges hunt for his recreation, when his grace is wearied with the burden of cares in matters of common weale.[64]

This passage suggests direct association between central government and forest officials such as verderers and agisters. Manwood aligned the benefit of the commonweal directly with the preservation of a landscape designed to attract and retain deer, ensuring that the King would be able to relieve his mind from the pressures of public life. In Dean, venison and vert, beasts of the chase and their habitat, were the responsibility of the verderer and his agisters as they worked to survey the woods, manage the agistment of cattle, and oversee the prosecution of trespass. In a general sense, therefore, the management of this royal forest aimed to sustain an environment conducive to royal leisure pursuits rather than maximizing profit from the exploitation of its resources. This type of use contributed to the perceived profligacy of Dean and its commoners in the context of late Elizabethan England. Any environment primarily intended to sustain deer-hunting was

---

[64] J. Manwood, *A treatise and discourse of the lawes of the forrest* (London, 1598) URL: http://eebo.chadwyck.com/home   Date accessed: 14/08/2009.

incompatible with enclosed lands or large areas of commercial spoliation and, thus, held obvious benefits for those who sought to exploit common grazing and fuel rights.

According to Sallens, this royal forest afforded inhabitants a set of customary uses peculiar to this environment. The activities that defined this area as a royal forest also implied customary senses of this region which sustained common uses of its resources. Manwood's treatise suggests a congruence between ancient forest and the 'timeless' nature of custom. He noted that, apart from the New Forest 'there is no other forest in England, whereof the beginning or making can be shewed, neyther by the Chronicles, Histories, nor Record, so auncient are all the other forests of the land'.[65] How, then, did these customary and 'timeless' senses of the region relate to royal authority in the minds of its inhabitants?

Manwood explained the local idiosyncrasies of these legal systems, noting that 'Lawes of the Forest are called particular Lawes, for that, although they be generall to all forrests alike, yet they are particular Lawes, in that they are proper to forests, and not to any other places'.[66] Before 1066 a large tract of woodland and waste land in Dean had been reserved for royal hunting and had survived into the modern period as one of the principal Crown forests in England, the largest after the New Forest. The name 'Forest of Dean' was recorded from c. 1080 and seems to have been taken from the valley to the north-east of the area, where a manor called Dean

---

[65] Manwood, *Lawes*, 6.

[66] Manwood, *Lawes.*, 7.

was the administrative centre of the Forest in the late eleventh century. The *Victoria County History* for the region states that in the thirteenth century its bounds were 'the two rivers [Severn and Wye], [from where] it extended northwards as far as Ross-on-Wye (Herefs.), Newent, and Gloucester; it then included 33 Gloucestershire and Herefordshire parishes, besides a central, uncultivated area which the Crown retained in demesne'.[67] Revised bounds, perambulated in 1300, but not accepted by the Crown until 1327, reduced the extent of the forest to the royal demesne and fourteen parishes or parts of parishes, mainly in St. Briavels hundred. The language that recorded the second perambulation illustrates the way that the area was regarded in official record during the fourteenth century. Noting the exclusion of 'Hualseffeld with woods and plains', the physical and active nature of the boundary is suggested in the verb 'errat' meaning, in this context, 'to wander' or to 'go astray'. According to the official account, the meets and bounds 'begin at the bridge which is called Ledenbreeg'. From there, the border leads 'through the royal way', up to the village of Sewent 'thus proceeding through the middle of the village of Sewent up to the bridge which is called Abrigge and then from that bridge up to a certain place which is called Corstleyefforde'.[68] A familiarity with the area would have been necessary to engage with these perambulations. By contrast to the abstracted and bird's-eye representation of a map, it would have been difficult to gauge the extent of the forest without physical knowledge of the

---

[67] Herbert, *VCH, Vol. 5*, 285-94.

[68] TNA, E32/284. Errors in the perambulation of the Forest of Dean (1327).

places described. The implications of this active and embodied description of space within the Forest are considered further below.

As well as the natural limits of the landscape, Dean's boundaries generally aligned with those of St. Briavels Hundred which, in turn, closely traced the periphery of the region's coal and iron fields. The hundred was divided into six administrative bailiwicks, or walks, and regular court sessions at St. Briavels castle heard disputes over access to woodland resources and related issues of forest law. The administration of the royal demesne land of the Forest from the late medieval period was established to enforce forest law in defence of the venison and vert, together with regulating the mining and ironmaking industries. This administration centred on St. Briavels castle and manor and was headed by a royal appointee who served as constable. Forest administration below the constable was staffed by various categories of foresters, the principal ones holding office by tenure of surrounding manors. The forest system was enforced by an attachment court, presided over by verderers, who were officers of royal forests, and by the regular forest eyres. As well as regulating the use of wood or land for more direct industrial purposes such as ironworks, the verderer's court was involved in the regulation of customary rights such as estovers, ploughbote, housebote, pannage and common grazing on forest waste lands.[69]

Complementing this system of local courts, the Mine Law Court was directly responsible for protecting the body of customary law which regulated mining within the Forest. This court held a strict jurisdictional

---

[69] J. Neeson, *Commoners: Common Right, Enclosure and Social Change in England, 1720-1820* (Cambridge, 1993), 313-15.

monopoly over the industry by ancient custom. In 1646, Thomas Yorke, Henry Machen and Robert Reed told the Court of the Exchequer that 'there was & tyme out of mind hath ben a cort called by the name of the Mine Law Court in which all Conflictes Trespases & differences whatsoever betwixt miners and Quarriers their said mines within the said Forest ought there to be herd & determined and not elsewhere'.[70] Disputes were heard and orders ratified before its jury, which was made up of twelve, twenty-four or forty-eight free miners according to the particular circumstance. These miners were inhabitants of the Forest born within St. Briavels Hundred, acquiring through birth the customary right to mine the King's demesne.

Mining for iron ore and the associated iron-making industry were anciently established in Dean. During the seventeenth century, the emphasis on iron extraction changed in reaction to an expanding national demand for coal. Despite constant attempts by outside parties to gain an interest in this increasingly lucrative industry, it remained under the tight regulation of the Mine Law Court until its discontinuance in 1777. The jury of free miners was, by definition, made up of those brought up in the 'mysteries' of the trade, contrasting sharply with the oligarchic ruling groups gaining a foothold in the regulation of large-scale trade and investment in other parts of England during this period. The deposition of Thomas Wallington, a fifty-two year old miner of Littledean, indicates contemporary perceptions of the characteristics of a free miner. In 1638, he recalled that:

---

[70] TNA, E112/183/220.

54

He hath knowen for the space of Thirtie yeares that the custome and usage hath bin that that person which is or hath bin borne & educated in the said hundred of St Brevills hath & may digge & sincke pitts for the finding and discovering of Oare & Coales in any ffree houlders grounds within the premisses of the sayd hundred and sayth that hee this deponent hath not bin interrupted or debarred by any free houlder ffrom his work in any such pitts wherein he hath laboured to finde Oare and Coales duringe the space aforesaid [71]

Wallington's deposition outlined the educational processes whereby a Dean free miner learned the customary practices of his trade and points to the interrelation of the miner and his environment. If a miner was born and had grown up in St. Briavels Hundred he not only had the right to mine, but could transmit this right to his son as long as he was 'borne & educated in the said hundred'.[72] This accorded well with the pragmatic fiction that custom was a timeless body of unwritten and unchanging practices. The Mine Law Court's monopoly of jurisdiction and the restrictions of traditional small-scale mining custom were both, however, increasingly challenged throughout the seventeenth and eighteenth centuries. Despite this, a miner's expertise, intricate knowledge of environment, and popular senses of the locality remained central to the regulation of the industry in this period.

---

[71] TNA, E134/13&14Chas1/Hil16.

[72] Ibid.

The Mine Law Court acted as a corporation for the community of miners, hearing disputes between miners and sought to preserve the system of mining which had purportedly been shaped by customary practice at least since the thirteenth century. Until 1680, the court had no fixed meeting place and was held in different parts of St. Briavels Hundred, in a house or the open air, and occasionally near a particular tree or landmark, indicating an engagement with the mining industry and the spatial relations which informed its operation. Anthony Callowe, a sixty-five year old gentleman of Mitcheldean, deposed in 1625 that 'this court hath bin usually kept in some open space of the Forreste, for that there is noe house or certen place appointed for the same'.[73] In 1656 the court was held at Littledean and later it often met at Clearwell, Coleford, Mitcheldean and Ruardean before settling at the Speech House where it remained until its discontinuance in 1777.[74]

Although these embodied practices may have been less legible to the outsider, the Crown did derive specific profits from the mining industry in the Forest. Economic relations between Dean's mining community and royal government were administered through the Deputy Gavellor, the crown representative in the forest. In 1646, Christopher Tucker of Deane Parva described himself as 'Gaveller and receiver of the rentes and duties due and answearable to his Majestie from the miners in the Forest of

---

[73] TNA, E134/22Jas1/East8.

[74] GRO, D5947/10/1. Schedule of orders, copy mine law orders and mine court proceedings: 1668-1777.

Deane'.[75] The 1673 transcript of the miners' *Laws and Privileges* decreed that 'every week the Gaveller shall visitt the Tuesday the whole mine or at least within two weeks to receive the Customes and dues due to the king aforesaid'. These dues would have included payments from the King's Man, a miner appointed to deliver the Crown's share of ore, and the quarterly payment of a 'Seame of Mine the which is called Lawe oare'.[76] Despite this royal presence in the Forest, the intervention of the government in the mining industry was fiercely limited by custom. This is emphasised in the *Privileges'* by the assertion that 'noe stranger of what degree so ever hee bee but only that beene borne and abideing within the Castle of St. Brevills and the bounds of the Forrest as is aforesaid shall come within the mine'.[77] Despite receiving rents and duties from mining operations, this income was merely part of the existing small-scale trade which had been restricted 'time out of mind' by custom. The Crown, therefore, had no mandate for potential restructuring or improvement, and was thus unable to impose more 'progressive' or efficient methods of exploiting the resources of its forest. This limitation elicited much frustration during the first half of the seventeenth century.

---

[75] TNA, E112/183/220.

[76] Hart, *Free Miners*, 40. The 'King's Man' was a local miner placed in each gale to ensure that the Crown received roughly one-fifth of the produce of each pit.

[77] Ibid., 43.

Earlier records of the Mine Law Court indicate that local knowledge was essential in regulating the industry. The first extant documentation dates from 1469/70 and describes two sessions held at 'Hyll Pitt' near Lydney towards the south of the Forest. These are laconic records, consisting merely of a list of miners' names and corresponding figures for the amounts charged in fine.[78] While written accounts of previous sessions do not survive, the court no doubt convened prior to the appearance of formal records of its proceedings. The scant contextual detail in the 1469/70 sessions suggests that decisions were made based on local knowledge of the industry. Unlike the records of central equity courts, these brief documents were of little use to those unfamiliar with the nature and context of these disputes. As with the fourteenth-century records of perambulation for the Forest, late medieval Dean and its more significant industries were regulated through legal and social institutions that were almost illegible to outsiders.

The obscurity of this region and its customs remained an issue during the early seventeenth century. In 1638, William, Bishop of Llandaff, submitted a bill to the Court of the Exchequer requesting assistance in collecting tithes for the parish of All Saints in Newland. He claimed that a ruling of Edward I had decreed that 'all Tithes newly assarted should pertayne to the said Bishopps Church of Newland (by letters patent) then confirmed by Edw II'. Experiencing difficulties in retrieving the benefit of his customary dues, he complained that 'it is impossible for your said Orator (being a stranger in those partes) to discover what lands have been assarted in the

---

[78] GRO, D6177.

said Forrest[79] The opacity of local customs and practice was a considerable barrier to anyone beyond the boundaries of the Forest of Dean. This was as true of tithe collection as it was of the mining industry, with the expertise required to understand both uses of the landscape depending on detailed knowledge of the environment and its resources.

Local customary practice, in its unwritten form, performed two major functions in supporting the assertion, maintenance and negotiation of common use rights. Firstly, this lack of written trace made it more accommodating to the ambiguities of uses that were multiple and often contradictory. Secondly, this illegibility was integral in preserving local custom from the ambitions of outsiders. The legitimation of these rights depended upon popular knowledge and understanding of the Crown's relationship with the Forest. Several significant dates were regularly invoked in the context of claims to 'ancient' rights in Dean. These included 9 Henry III (The Charter of the Forest), 33 Edward I (statute granting tithes to All Saints church in Newland) and 34 Edward I (the year in which forest perambulations were undertaken). Even this chronological framework varied in its local application. In 1625, a group of miners claimed to have seen 'an ancient deed dated in the reign of King Edward the Second testifying the liberty and privilege of the miners within the Forest'.[80] The earliest known copy of the free miners' 'Lawes and Privilledges', however, was recorded in 1610. It begins:

---

[79] TNA, E112/181/135.

[80] TNA, E134/22JamesI/East. 8.

> Bee itt in minde and Remembrance what the Customes and Franchises
> hath beene that were graunted tyme out of Minde and after in tyme of
> the Excellent and Redoubted Prince King Edward unto ye Miners of
> the Forrest of Deane and the castle of St. Briavells and the bounds of
> the said Forrest[81]

According to this document, mining custom had been in practice since before the memory of man, yet it had also been granted in the reign of King Edward. Perceptions of Dean's mining custom accommodated two co-existing chronological frameworks, without any apparent contradiction.

According to the miner interviewed in 2007, Forest tradition regards these rights as bestowed in return for military service during the early fourteenth century. This version of events is supported by Albert Prince's discussion of the English army in 1327-36. Prince notes the presence of Forest inhabitants, commenting that 'among the foot [soldiers] there were the engineers, artificers, and work-men of various kinds attached to the army. The miners proved extremely useful in siege operations; normally they were drawn from the Forest of Dean'.[82] Local and customary legal senses were certainly capable of accounting for the kind of historical development that Prince describes. Key dates, however, appear to have been structured in accordance with physical experience of the region and recalled when

---

[81] Hart, *Free Miners*, 37.

[82] A. E. Prince, 'The Army and Navy', in J. F. Willard and W. A. Morris (eds.), *The English Government at Work 1327-1336 Vol. I: Central and Prerogative Administration* (Cambridge, Massachusetts, 1947), 332-93, 343.

practice demanded, rather than forming a constant and diachronically ordering presence in Dean's popular *habitus*. This narrative of the forest could apparently negotiate the contradictions of experience in a framework which could comprehend national events without implicating local tradition in a historical chain of causation.

Roland Barthes suggests that 'it is human history which converts reality into speech, and it alone rules the life and death of mythical language... for myth is a type of speech chosen by history'.[83] Explaining the semiological purpose of mythological speech, he stressed its open character but concluded that:

> it is not at all an abstract, purified essence; it is a formless, unstable, nebulous condensation, whose unity and coherence are above all due to its function. In this sense, we can say that the fundamental character of the mythical concept is to be *appropriated*.[84]

In other words, this type of narrative structure allowed for the simplification of a complex history which could be appropriated by many diverse groups in maintaining their foothold on what Thompson described as a 'hierarchy of use-rights'. This was an essential feature of a world-view which could reconcile the ambivalence of collective use by appealing to the

---

[83] R. Barthes, *Mythologies: Selected and translated from the French by Annette Lavers* (London, 2000), 110.

[84] Barthes, *Mythologies*, 110.

'mythologised' and timeless nature of customary forest law, together with popular understandings of monarchy.

While the reality of these relationships was far more complex, this customary ideal provided a malleable legitimating resource for Dean's commoners, carrying significant economic implications. Residence within the bounds of the Forest was keenly claimed by litigants in the Exchequer court. In a mid-seventeenth century equity case, Christopher Tucker confirmed that 'everie Miner dwelling in the said forest and being of the Companie of Miners there might lawfully seeke for and dig and sink a pitt within any the bounds of the said forest'.[85] In 1616, the Exchequer court was told that the inhabitants of Ruddle 'doe desire rather to be within the Forrest than out'.[86] The Tucker dispute highlights the ambivalence of this legitimating resource as his adversaries accused him of acting 'to the greate preiudice of the Common wealth the welfare of which the Complt pretendeth to give color to his uniust vexacion'.[87] Both sides in this dispute were able to argue that their actions were intended for the benefit of the 'Common wealth', the most malleable of early modern state metaphors. The notion of an 'open' royal forest could be deployed in multiple, often

---

[85] TNA, E112/183/220.

[86] TNA, E112/82/300.

[87] TNA, E112/183/220.

contradictory, causes; the flexible and nebulous nature of this ideal was central to its wide and varied use.

Barthes explained that the 'ordinary alibi has an end; reality stops the turnstile revolving at a certain point ... Myth [however] is a *value*, truth is no guarantee for it; nothing prevents it from being a perpetual alibi'.[88] Myth always has an 'elsewhere' at its disposal. Barthes notion that the coherence of mythologised speech depends on its function resonates with Carter's assertion that custom consists only in use and practice.[89] The remainder of this chapter, then, suggests certain modes of collective memory through which the knowledge of custom was transmitted from one generation to the next in a predominantly oral culture.

III The social mediation of local justice

Manwood described forested land as territory 'meeted and bounded with unmoveable markes, meetes and boundaries either known by matter of record or els by prescription'.[90] There is, however, much evidence that the fluidity of territorial markers was a cause of great concern in Dean in the sixteenth and seventeenth centuries. Commanding that 'Thou shalt not

---

[88] Barthes, *Mythologies*, 123.

[89] Carter, *Lex Custumaria*, 25.

[90] Manwood, *Lawes*, 1.

remove thy neighbours meerestone', a *Godlie Sermon* of 1577 suggests that it was actually a more widespread cause of anxiety.[91] The breadth and frequency of this concern has left records which offer an opportunity to examine the conceptualisation of space and its uses according to contemporary customary precedent. Analysis of Exchequer bills suggest ways in which boundaries may have been perceived, transmitted and evidenced by the inhabitants of this region.

The perambulations of the Forest were altered several times during the first half of the seventeenth century. In 1597, Minsterworth parish was excluded from the jurisdiction of the Forest. It is possible that Rodley was also excluded at this point, as by 1623 it was not considered to be within the Forest.[92] An Exchequer case from 1613 illustrates concern over shifting boundaries and disafforestation in the north-east corner of Dean. John Sallens and 'others the Inhabitants' of the Forest were complaining that the villages of 'Ruddle, Rodleighe' and 'Flaxley' were 'auncientlie within the perambulacion meetes & bounds of the said Forrest' but now 'the said Townes of Rodleigh and Ruddle are quite out of the said Forrest, and the perambulacion, limitts & regard thereof'. Appealing to customary ideals, Sallens and the others pleaded that the 'said countie is very populous and the greatest part of its Inhabitants are poore people' who were losing quarrying rights and access to various kinds of estovers through this

---

[91] H. Bullinger, *50 Godlie Sermon III* (1577). Quoted from Oxford English Dictionary URL: http://dictionary.oed.com/entrance.dtl. Date accessed: 23/10/2009.

[92] Herbert, *VCH, Vol. V*, 298.

boundary revision.[93] In 1634, the Forest was expanded to the wider bounds as they were established in 1228 and 1282, but an Act of 1641 restored the bounds of all forests to those in accepted use in 1623.[94] As this retraction was formalised in 1640, John Adeane, gentleman, and others requested that they be allowed to have the privileges and benefits allowable under an Act of Parliament dated 'in the foure and thirtieth yeare of the raigne of King Edward the first'. They added:

> We will moreover that they which have had common of pasture in the Forrest Before this perambulacion was made And they which have bin letten of the said common by the perambulacion aforesaid shall have this common of pasture from hence foorth in the fforrest (as largely & freely) as they were wont to have before ye perambulacion aforsaid.[95]

For those who depended on customary rights as part of their subsistence or occupational strategies, fluctuating boundary markers and perambulations could have severe material consequences.

There was no less anxiety regarding boundaries within the forest. As well as accusations of spoliation being directed at him by John Sallens, Sir Edward Winter, in 1613, found himself the subject of a bill entered by

---

[93] TNA, E112/82/300.

[94] Herbert, *VCH, Vol. V*, 298.

[95] TNA, E112/182/196.

Robert Treswell, surveyor general of the woods. Treswell suggested that Winter and his co-defendants William Kingston and Thomas James 'the better to mayntayne their said uniuste clayme have of late taken and removed the auncyent hedges meanes and boundaries of the same landes and premises'.[96] In 1616 Christopher Hawkins, gentleman of Newnham, complained that William Brayne, William Meeke and Henry Daniell:

> also have digged up and removed the mounds meerestones boundaries and other markes that should sett forth and manifest the certeyntie and contents of the same premisses and having by the destroying and defaceing of the said moundes mere stones and boundaries intermingled the same with theire own landes adioining to the premisses doe now clayme and geeve forth the same to be theire own free land.

On 28th August 1616, Brayne refuted the charge that:

> he hath Digged up or Removed the mounds meerstones boundaries or other markes that should sett forth or manifest the certayntie and contents of the demised premises Or that he hath entermingled the same with his own lands adioyning to the premises in the bill mencioned or any part therof [97]

---

[96] TNA, E112/82/310.

[97] TNA, E112/82/331.

Both of these cases allude to concerns over the manipulation of boundary marks and encroachment in Dean during the early part of the seventeenth century. This indicates anxieties regarding a lack of permanence or consistency in this physical method of record-keeping, certainly by comparison with the security of ownership implied in the fixed and settled record of the deed or map.

Similarly, customary uses of this space were defined by continued practice and evidenced by the spoken word of local inhabitants. In 1593, Thomas Baker explained that he had 'heard crediblie from his ancestors' of their rights to common within the Forest and stated that they had 'lopped treyes ... for all the tyme of his memorie'.[98] In 1618, an Exchequer interrogatory asked each deponent for details of past estovers and also questioned them on how they knew this information. John Hannys, a 53 year old labourer from the north of the Forest deposed that 'he hath credibly heard' of these wood-collecting rights 'by the generall reporte and relacion of ancient men inhabiting within the said Forrest'.[99] In the aforementioned Winter case, Treswell indicated the Crown's dependence on these local and oral transmissions to establish its rights within the demesne lands. He suggested that:

there be yet lyvinge divers aged and auncyent men whose testimonie is requisite for the Manifesting of the same Landes where they bee and

---

[98] TNA, E134/36Eliz/Hil21.

[99] TNA E134/14JasI/Hil8.

67

of his maiesties title to the premmises, who yf they should be decease
before they be examined might eterne to his maiesties greate prejudice
and hurte.[100]

Spoken testimony was evidently problematic for those who found
themselves opposed by a larger group within the community. Benedict Fox,
vicar of Lidney, experienced difficulty in establishing his right to the
collection of tithes and other customary dues. In 1662, he alleged a
conspiracy to obscure 'the exact certainty or exact particulars of the Tythes
and other duties which are severally and respectively due'. He claimed that
he was approaching the Exchequer court for an equitable hearing because
'his witnesses to prove the saide are gone unto remote partes unknown to
your orator'.[101] In the absence of witnesses, Fox apparently felt that he was
left to defend himself against the recalcitrant parishioners of Lydney. The
tensions persisted after Fox's initial complaint, as he regularly made these
kinds of accusations during this period.

The evidence of customary precedent was integral to claims from all social
levels in the Forest of Dean, whether these were representatives of the
Crown, clergymen, gentlemen, miners, yeomen or labourers. A central
body of customary practice determined uses to the material resources of the
Forest, but this core of traditions created a penumbra of norms and
perceptions which held great influence in social interactions. These

---

[100] TNA, E112/82/310.

[101] TNA, E112/403/12.

influenced and were, in turn, structured by patterns of sociality and community relations. Despite the pretence of timeless stasis, this interplay of custom and lived experience inevitably invoked situations in which current use contradicted previous patterns of activity. This ambivalence was difficult to accommodate when uses and rights were fixed and recorded in the written record. Thompson observed that 'the law [in the eighteenth century] abhorred the messy complexities of coincident use rights'.[102] Michael Clanchy's analysis of the transition from oral to written legal record illuminates the situation in seventeenth-century Dean. Clanchy notes that:

> without documents, the establishment of what passed for truth was simple and personal, since it depended on the good word of one's fellows. Remembered truth was also flexible and up to date, because no ancient custom could be proved to be older than the memory of the oldest living wise man. There was no conflict between past and present, between ancient precedents and present practice. Customary law *quietly passes over obsolete laws, which sink into oblivion, and die peacefully, but the law itself remains young, always in the belief that it is old*. Written records, on the other hand, do not die peacefully, as they retain a half-life in archives and can be resurrected to inform, impress or mystify future generations.[103]

---

[102] Thompson, *Whigs,* 241.

[103] M.T. Clanchy, *From Memory to Written Record: England 1066-1307* (Oxford, 1993), 296.

Clanchy, therefore, points to the value of the pragmatic fiction that custom could 'be recorded and registred no where but in the Memory of the People'.[104]

This is not to overlook the role of charters, custumals, court records, decrees and deeds in the transmission of local legal memory. In 1591, Thomas Moorelande, a 71 year old yeoman of Westbury, claimed to 'have common in the saide Forrest under collour of the saide Charter of Rodleighe and not otherwise'.[105] Customary legal rights ultimately depended on the interplay of written records and a complex network of social and industrial relationships, community pressures and the evidence of the physical environment. For this reason, outsiders from beyond the Forest found it almost impossible to interpret, usurp or engage with these legal traditions. Isolating elements of this legal system from its social context was impractical without diminishing its efficacy.

While customary law depended on the interplay of oral evidence and the written record, many litigants pointed to the importance of social relationships and local reputation in the Forest's legal system. In 1582 John Gyes attempted to bring Exchequer proceedings against George Cachemayd and Edmund Cachemayd, both gentlemen, as well as Christopher Bond, John Bond, William Heynes and William Kedgewyn.

---

[104] Carter, *Lex Custumaria,* 25.

[105] TNA, E134/34Eliz/Hil23.

These defendants disputed the legitimacy of equity proceedings, maintaining that:

> the custome of the said mannor of St Brevelles ys that amercyamentes and paynes set & taxed by a Jury sworne at the lawe dayes holden in the said mannor may by the custome of the said mannor be affyred myttygated & dymynished by a Jury called the Contrey.[106]

These defendants preferred justice through the hundredal court of St. Briavels rather than the Court of the Exchequer, as these proceedings were, they claimed, mediated by the entire community designated the 'Jury called the contrey'. As David Rollison notes, the term 'country' in this period referred to a region inhabited by people sharing the same 'cultural characteristics and connotations'.[107] In their dispute with Gyes, the men distinguished between the proceedings of an equity court in which individual deponents were evaluated by deposition, and the operations of the local court system in which the evidence of witnesses was mediated by local custom.

Bypassing the judgement of the hundredal court may have been an intentional strategy of John Gyes, allowing him to appeal to the central court. Local controversy had surrounded an earlier action concerning the Gyes family. In 1574 John's brother, Robert Gyes, was the subject of an Exchequer bill regarding their deceased father, William, the matter of

---

[106] TNA, E112/15/9.

[107] D. Rollison, *The Local Origins of Modern Society: Gloucestershire, 1500-1800* (London, 1992), 15-16.

which was presented by Roger Taverner, royal fee-farmer. William Gyes had apparently been 'called before this court for waistes and spoyles by hym committed within the Forrest and was fyned in the said courte'. These fines, Taverner complained, had still not been paid. To make matters worse, William had also 'contrary to the usage and auncient custom of makinge of leases of such her Maiesties inheritaunces hath proved and gotten wordes putten into the supposed graunt'.[108] This case demonstrates, simultaneously, both the dependence of custom on writing and scepticism over the legitimacy of written records. Despite his father's prosecution for tampering with written evidence, John Gyes preferred to seek justice through the Exchequer court rather than the jury of the local hundred. Not only that but, according to his adversaries, John Gyes sought to avoid community censure and the constraints of social hierarchies as well as the local reputation of his family. From the seventeenth century onwards, appeals to the court of the Exchequer from outlying areas were pursued in ever-increasing numbers, entrenching the hegemony of the equity courts as a centralised legal system. Yet negotiations relating to custom continued to occur in the nexus of local relationships and popular understandings of the law.

Edward Said offered a useful conceptual framework for considering the construction of local solidarities. He explained that:

> A group of people living on a few acres of land will set up boundaries between their land and its immediate surroundings and the territory beyond, which they call "the land of the barbarians". In other words this universal practice of designating in one's mind a familiar space

---

[108] TNA, E112/15/5.

which is "ours" and an unfamiliar space beyond "ours" which is "theirs" is a way of making geographical distinctions which *can* be entirely arbitrary. It is enough for "us" to set up these boundaries in our own minds; "they" become "they" accordingly, and both their territory and mentality are designated as different from "ours".[109]

Documentation from the courts of Exchequer and Star Chamber, together with numerous local court records, suggests much about these types of discursive boundaries. The distinction between 'inhabitants' and 'strangers' is increasingly ubiquitous in litigation relating to disputed customary rights as the records lead further into the seventeenth century.[110]

Complaints from inhabitants of Ruddle in 1613 indicate that, despite the customary pretence of timelessness and stasis, this discursive identity was fluid and contingent. The villagers requested that they be brought back into the Forest following their transition from 'inhabitants' to 'strangers' during the late sixteenth- and early seventeenth-century revisions of forest perambulations. As they highlighted the loss of grazing and fuel rights as a result of this transition their situation attested to the material consequences of this demarcation.[111] Many similar cases suggest that linguistic

[109] E. Said, *Orientalism* (London, 1995), 54.

[110] For attitudes towards strangers and 'foreigners', see J. Selwood, *Diversity and Difference in Early Modern London* (Farnham, 2010); for the period after 1700, see K. D. M. Snell, 'The Culture of Local Xenophobia', *Social History*, 28, 1 (2003), 1-30.

[111] TNA, E112/82/300.

boundaries were constitutive of rights to common and were, in this sense, as real as the 'meerestones' which had been causing Hawkins and Treswell such anxiety. These distinctions reflected perceived pressures on forest resources from an in-migrating labour force which generated anxieties over encroachment on the subsistence strategies of the poor and landless within the forest. These fears were shared by those at all levels of Thompson's hierarchy of rights in early modern local communities. In 1633, Sir Basil Brooke and George Mynne, ironmasters in the Forest, complained that workers in that industry were responsible for vast despoliation and, in particular, that forge owners were:

> setting on worke Welshmen unknowne persons and straungers and others of poore and mean condicions to be their agents and instruments in the said workes and suffering them to make spoyle and wast as in the Informacion is alledged[112]

Brooke and Mynne both owned substantial intersts in Dean's iron industry, perhaps exploiting fears of poor migrant workers to undermine the projects of rival industrialists. That they chose to use this type of language, however, indicates genuine concern over pressures on the linguistic and spatial schema which demarcated customary rights in the Forest.

This is crucial to understanding the miners' role in defending Forest custom which is the subject of the Chapter Four. Discursive and spatial demarcations which sustained mining rights were, in many respects, the same as those which perpetuated the more general customary use of forest

---

[112] TNA, E112/180/66.

resources. These spatial interpretations of custom were not unique to the operations of the free miners, but were essential to the survival of the wider forest community who depended upon access to common resources for subsistence and work. Despite Andy Wood's observation that mining custom within the forest contributed to the expression of a unique occupational identity, then, it follows that this body of law cannot be understood in reified isolation.[113] Mining custom, in fact, represented one component in a complex interplay of discursive and physical activity which perpetuated local perceptions of the Forest. To defend mining rights was, in many ways, to defend the more general notion of 'open' forest. While incompatible with private property and external industry, this ideal united the interests of Forest inhabitants, many of whom apprehended the customary purpose of the area in ways similar to the Dean free-mining community.

The association of common rights and 'open' forest is ubiquitous in the records for this period, not only during the conflict of the 1620s and 1630s, but also in disputes over custom throughout the late sixteenth and seventeenth centuries. In 1574 Roger Taverner once again brought an Exchequer suit against the sons of the late William Gyes, for their father's refusal to 'incoppice' land within the Forest. Taverner argued that Gyes 'had suffered it to lye open and unfenced & not incoppiced to distruction of springe & manifest spoyle thereof'. His language implied a distinction between the type of 'open' landscape which maintained common access to resources, and enclosed or restricted access which accompanied notions of

---

[113] A. Wood, 'Custom, Identity and Resistance: English Free Miners and Their Law c.1550-1800', in Griffiths et al, *Experience,* 249-285.

improving the Forest.[114] Due to the nature of custom, the appeal to 'open' and customary senses of the Forest was evident in the claims of those from all rungs of the hierarchy of use-rights. In 1641, John Adeane and Benedict Hall, both gentlemen, were numbered among twenty defendants to the bill of Complaint of Sir John Bankes, Attorney General. Itemising the customary rights attached to property held within the forest, these defendants stated that they had enjoyed 'lawfull common & taking of necessary bootes & estovers' 'in all the *open* & commonable places of and in the said Forrest'.[115]

The distinction between 'open' and 'closed' forest operated metonymically in articulating two fundamentally incompatible ideologies. The proceedings of the 'Speech Court held at Little Deane the 5th day of October 1637' were very largely concerned with defendants accused of 'cuttinge out of cropps of *sealed* trees'.[116] Projectors who argued for improvement and progress depended on restricting the rights of inhabitants to customary use of resources within the forest wastes. Open access to these spaces was central to the economic actitivies of the mining community. In an assertive outline of these industrial rights, the *Laws and Privileges* of the free miners stated that 'the said Myners may myne in any place that they will as well without

---

[114] TNA, E112/15/5.

[115] TNA, E112/182/196. My emphasis.

[116] TNA, E146/3/29.

the bounds as within, without the Forebodment of any man'. By 1610, therefore, the freem-miners had renounced the official boundaries of St. Briavels Hundred in favour of the more natural limits of Dean's mineral field.[117] This was not simply an industrial claim. Miners and their families were reliant on a holistic customary understanding of 'open' Forest. Like other inhabitants of the Forest, Buchanan Sharp notes that 'miners supplemented the income from their labor by exploiting the forest; they took timber for their pit workings and pastured cattle in the wastes'.[118] Exchequer depositions provide many examples of miners testifying in defence of estovers, various types of 'bote' and other customary uses.[119]

A 1641 petition of the 'Freehoulders Inhabitants and Commoners of the Forrest of Deane' to the House of Lords indicates the extent to which mining rights were entwined with more general uses and customary dues. The petition highlights the common interest of the miners and the rest of the forest commonalty in their need for an 'open' forest. It stated that:

> they the said Inhabitantes and theire Auncestors tyme out of minde some of them by Charter and some by prescription have had and enjoyed in and throughoute the said waste soyle of the said Forrest Common of pasture for theire Cattle Levant and Couchant upon theire

---

[117] Hart, *Free Miners*, 38.

[118] Sharp, *Contempt*, 181.

[119] TNA, E134/22Jas1/East8; T NA, E134/13&14Chas1/Hil16 & T NA, E134/14Chas1/Mich42.

Severall tenementes beinge within the said Forrest Att all times of the yeares (The fence moneth excepted) As also houseboote plowboote and fireboote in & oute of the said woodes and underwoodes as also Pawnage for theire swine accordinge to the Custome of the said Forrest And alsoe liberty & freedom to dig & worke in the said Mynes of Iron Oare & cole according to the Custome of the said Forrest And have used & doe paie unto his Majestie and his predecessors for the aforesaid profites and liberties certaine rentes called herbage rentes, Pawnage Rentes and Galerentes.[120]

The preservation of custom which perpetuated mining rights, therefore, preserved uses that benefited the wider Forest community.

These traditional practices defined the living and working relationships of all groups within the Forest. Tim Ingold suggests that 'tasks are the constitutive acts of dwelling'.[121] He explains that:

one of the outstanding features of human technical practices lies in their embeddedness in the current of sociality. It is to the entire ensemble of tasks, in their mutual interlocking, that I refer by the concept of taskscape.[122]

---

[120] Historical Manuscripts Commission, fourth report, 70; Lord's Journal, IV, 219, 262; House of Lords Records Office, Main Papers, 7009 (June 1, 1641).

[121] T. Ingold, 'The Temporality of the Landscape', *World Archaeology*, 25, 2 (1993), 158.

[122] Ingold, 'Temporality', 158.

His concept of 'taskscape' offers a useful synthesis of landscape and the interactions of those who dwell within it. This is a useful model for interpreting the discursive and physical construction of the early modern locality as perceived from within. Many contemporary court records cite the 'Forest' as shorthand for the accumulated spatial experience of this locality.[123] The mining community, engaging with this space both in its relationship to central government and through the lived experience of the local taskscape, appears to have operated at the nexus of industrial and social relations in Dean. The miners and the poor or propertyless of this area constituted an assertive community of interest as inhabitants of 'open & commonable places of and in the said Forrest'.[124]

Ingold identifies difficulties in quantifying the interaction of human activity and the material environment. He notes that, 'as with a landscape, it is qualitative and heterogenous: we can ask of a taskscape, what it is like but not how much of it there is'.[125] The mining industry needed to be experienced physically to be understood. The legibility of the taskscape was crucial to the operation of the Mine Law Court in controlling an industry which demanded intricate engagement with the local environment. The

---

[123] Concerns over claims to collective rights by virtue of living within or without the forest are very common in the records examined, both in the Exchequer records held at The National Archives, and in more local records held in Gloucester.

[124] TNA, E112/182/196.

[125] Ingold, 'Temporality', 158.

efficacy of its jury depended on their practical knowledge of life within the forest.

This Mine Law Court and its jury resonated with customary perceptions of the area which were grounded in popular experience of the taskscape. Steve Hindle explains that often, 'use of the terms 'the parish' or 'the inhabitants' was a ploy whereby the decisions of *parochiani meliores et antiquiores* could be made to seem rather more representative and consensual than they actually were'.[126] Despite its obvious contradictions, however, the term 'inhabitants' seems to have implied a more representative sense of community in the early modern Forest of Dean than in many other parts of southern England during this period. In spite of presenting themselves as the combined 'common voice' of an area, Wood suggests that depositions presented to equity courts in disputes over collective rights often, in fact, comprised the opinions of the wealthier, settled, male inhabitants of a parish.[127] The Mine Law Court, through the composition of its jury, represented the commonalty of the Forest, although this particular 'common voice' enjoyed more formal expression than was usual for local opinion.

---

[126] S. Hindle, 'The Political Culture of the Middling Sort, c.1550-1700' in T. Harris (ed.), *The Politics of the Excluded, c.1500-1850* (Basingstoke, 2001), 139.

[127] A. Wood, *The 1549 Rebellions and the Making of Early Modern England* (Cambridge, 2008), Ch 3. As mentioned, deponents to the court of the Exchequer present a similar social profile, with the interesting exception of those amongst the mining community who tended towards an increasing engagement with this court as the seventeenth century progressed. Of the thirty-eight traceable deponents to this court between 1662 and 1682, more than two-thirds were rated on two or more hearths in the tax returns of 1671-2. TNA/E134; GRO, 383/1.

This region and its industries were largely illegible from an outsider's perspective. The following section suggests possible ways that the Forest was legible to those who dwelled and worked within it. Customary access to the area's resources was legitimated and regulated through rights which were embodied in the landscape and its uses. The material nature of these rights was, initially, to prove problematic to outside interests wishing to gain a foothold in the region's burgeoning industrial economy. As discussed, this legal memory was purportedly held 'nowhere but in the memory of the people' and extant written records, somewhat paradoxically, point to the important role played by 'ancient men' and the 'Jury called the Contrey' in providing evidence. Although this ideal was a pragmatic fiction, the malleability and efficacy of this system of coincident uses was dependent on the transmission of memory through the oral evidence of inhabitants and the inscription of the material environment. How were these rights and their relation to local histories understood by Dean's inhabitants? The following section sketches several frames of reference through which inhabitants might have perceived the history of their locality and access to its resources.

IV The spatialisation of history

Describing economic expansion and increased population mobility in England during the sixteenth and seventeenth centuries, David Rollison suggests a distinction between the conceptions of space more appropriate to the world view of a minority ruling group on one hand, and the popular spatial perceptions of the masses on the other. He suggests that:

In the minority, space is conceived as an abstract, static and fixed, experienced only by the eye; in the majority, space is a space for movement, involving the whole person, and therefore, potentially, all the senses…….. 'we have two symbolic and anthropological languages of space', ……'scientific' or 'official' thought is invariably of the static, 'map' variety, whereas that of popular is of the moving tour.[128]

The foregoing has described the importance of popular and active understandings of space to the subsistence strategies and cultural coherence of what might be considered a forest community.[129] These fluid perceptions were central to the regulation of industry in the region. Official records relating to this area also actively supported these perceptions during the late medieval period and retained their influence into the seventeenth century. As discussed, the perambulation records of 1327 offered muscular resistance to the scientific grammar of space in their fluid and qualitative directions through the landscape, relating boundary markers and landmarks in succession rather than simultaneously. The phrase *provisum eorundem*, meaning 'to have seen the same', or 'to have sight of the same' describes the physical act of viewing rather than merely recording abstract information. These perambulations imply the interaction of the written

---

[128] D. Rollison, 'Exploding England: The Dialectics of Mobility and Settlement in Early Modern England', *Social History, 2*4, 1 (1999), 7.

[129] By which, I mean those who depended on the claim to residence within the forest limits in legitimation of customary access to its resources.

record and physical experience in communicating the spatial lay-out of the Forest from within.

This interplay was also central to the miner's *Laws and Privileges* which were printed and codified during the early seventeenth century, contradicting their representation as a body of unwritten customs. These articles do, however, demonstrate the embodied nature of mining custom and the perceptions of space appropriate to these characteristics. The *Laws and Privileges* stressed the need for a free miner to have been born within St. Briavels Hundred and to be the son of a miner. This document describes the bounds of the Forest, and thus the land on which they had the right to mine, in language which evoked the local landscape and environment. The 'bounds of the forest' were said to have run 'First betweene Chepstowe Bridge and Gloucester Bridge the halfe dole of Newent Ross Ash Monmouth Bridge and soe farr into the Severne as the blast of a horne or the voice of a man may bee heard'.[130] As land gave way to the river, the marking of boundaries evidently took on greater complexity. With no physical markers available, the miners' privileges were inscribed into the auditory landscape, making explicit the situated and embodied nature of these rights. These auditory markers were contingent on wind direction, weather conditions, and the volume of the voice of a man or the blast of a horn. They were, thus, dependent upon physical experience for their expression. By definition, auditory markers were difficult to represent in abstract records such as maps or tables. As Rollison suggests, popular senses of space depend upon a broader range of experience than those

---

[130] Hart, *Free Miners*, 37.

which can be seen. The forest 'taskscape' needed to be 'felt' or 'heard'. Ingold explains that 'the forms of the taskscape, like those of music, come into being through movement. Music only exists when it is being performed'.[131] A late seventeenth-century bill to the Court of the Exchequer described how the spacing between mines was being determined by the distance that the said miner could throw 'baddel' from his pit. [132] Like many other customary uses, these measurements could only be made through physical experience, and by inhabitants with the skill-sets to gauge them.

While the mining community had to account for wider trading networks in dealing with external interests, the Mine Law Court needed to understand the coherence of this local space as experienced in the daily life of the forest community. As noted, regulation of this industry required a working knowledge of the 'taskscape' into which customary rights were inscribed and, of which, they formed a constitutive element. Rollison identifies a memory technique which is useful in approaching unwritten forms of historical record. Drawing upon anthropological studies and intellectual histories, he suggests that the landscape was literally used to store information. It was, thus, 'a memory palace, so that irrevocably to alter or destroy a land form (as in a mining operation, or in enclosure) was to erase a part of the collective memory'.[133] This analysis contends that mining

---

[131] Ingold, 'Temporality', 161.

[132] TNA, E112 /183/220. 'Baddel' referred to the scree or detritus formed in opening a pit.

[133] Rollison, *Local Origins of Modern Society*, 70.

operations, particularly, could be as effective in constructing or shaping elements of the collective memory.

The case of Thomas Hall, a gentleman of Highmeadows, against Harry Dowle, Thomas Smith and others 'dwellers & inhabitants within the said manner of Staunton' demonstrates the relation between the material environment and collective legal memory. In 1632, Hall submitted a bill complaining that the defendants had entered land known as 'Stanton's Myne the Kedge and Nockows'. According to Hall, the trespassers had:

> broke down the mounds and hedges of the same (it being well & sufficiently fenced) and have cutt downe and carried away five hundred trees there lately growing and have putt into the said woodground and soyle great store of cattle which have eaten spoyled and consumed the Springes and young wood there and have made the same lye open without any fence to the said forrest of dean.

According to Hall, Dowle and the others had gained possession of all written documentation relating to the ownership of this land, and 'pretend that they have some lawfull estate therein, butt refuse to shewe or discover the same'. Hall claimed that these defendants had left him 'Remidiles herein by the strict course of the common law to recover the said writings, deedes, leases and evidences, not knowing the certain dates, or contents of the same nor whether they are contained in bagge box troncke or chest sealed and locked'.[134] With no written evidence of ownership, Dowle and

---

[134] TNA, E112/180/57.

the others claimed common access to this 'open' part of the forest and were able to call upon the more material and collective resources of the local memory palace. They argued that this land could not have been 'laied open' as was alleged in the bill because it had 'layen open' during 'all the time wherof the memory of man runneth not to the contrary'. More than this, they were able to collectively testify that they could not have removed five hundred trees because quote:

> There are few or noe trees thereupon growing but only Shrubbes and bushes and underwoddes and that as they verily believe There hath not byn Fyve hundred Trees thereupon groweing within the memory of man.[135]

Memories of the landscape were regularly cited in testimony defending local custom as the material environment was deployed as evidence of past activity.

Prominent landscape features and memorable fieldnames dominate the Forest of Dean. Compressed within these topograms are the histories and meanings of the local environment, suggesting how Dean's inhabitants understood the world in which they lived and worked. Many of these topograms suggest the profound influence of mining in popular senses of the Forest's history. The Devil's Chapel, the Devil's Churchyard and the Devil's Pulpit are all remains of Roman iron workings and other extractive operations. Dean's industrial history is clearly evident in the names of villages such as Cinderford, Cinderbridge or Coleford. The names of the

---

[135] Ibid.

pits and mines offer myriad possibilities for analyzing the relation between the landscape and local memory. The name 'Pukeputteswey', for example, referred to a goblin-haunted pit, while numerous markers are still known locally by names such as 'Newlyned Myne' and 'Pryors Myne'.[136]

Many 'tumps' and 'meands', small hills formed from the waste products of earlier operations, reflect the place of mining in the history of Dean. Several of these, such as 'Turner's Tump', record the influence of individuals within the forest, as do field names such as 'Keers Grove', 'Martins walle' and 'Edysland'.[137] Towards the north of the forest, near Ruardean, were 'the Pludds', a local name for the remains of open cast mining, while the central area leading from Staunton towards Coleford and Parkend was interspersed with mine workings such as 'Greenes Pitt' and 'Pitcrofte Ruddinges'. These physical memories of past operations cover an area known as 'the Wilderness' or 'the Delves'.[138] In the early modern Forest of Dean, spatial relations were accorded precedence over linear chronology. Traces of mining operations, both ancient and active, dominated the way in which the local environment was imagined and described, in contrast to the statutes and decrees which confirmed exclusive rights of access in Dean during the seventeenth century. These private and

---

[136] TNA, E112/82/310.

[137] TNA, E112/82/310.

[138] Ibid.

royal incursions will be outlined in Chapter Three. In this context, synchronic senses of local space worked to frustrate strictly linear chronologies that underpinned private property ownership.

Writing of the Langalanga people of the Solomon Islands, anthropologist Pei-yi Guo also notes the subordination of time to space. Guo explains that:

> as ancestral beings are thought to have traveled and left evidence on the landscape, their own forms became part of the land, and became fixed in it in a timeless way, so that they still serve as reference points today. The flow of action was fixed by its transmission to landscape.[139]

The past operates to unify cultures, asserts Guo, suggesting that 'the power of stories lies in their reference to known landmarks because they emphasize material and manifest continuity between the present and the past'.[140] This bears obvious analogies with the ritual demarcation of space in early modern perambulation ceremonies. J. J. Fox refers to studies on the 'spatialisation of time', where history is described in terms of landscape, place names and migration paths, a widely observed phenomenon in many cultures. Understood thus, 'irrational' superstitions and non-specific histories seem far more functional and coherent.

---

[139] P. Guo, "'Island Builders': Landscape and Historicity among the Langalanga, Solomon Islands', in P. J. Stewart and A. Strathern (eds.), *Landscape, Memory and History: Anthropological Perspectives* (London, Sterling, Virginia, 2003), 204.

[140] Ibid., 198.

Manwood, in the late-sixteenth century, described forested land as a territory meted and bounded with unmovable marks. This analysis, however, does not imply that these landscapes were beyond processes of historical change. Many of these features were, of course, subject to multiple and shifting interpretations. Field names changed over time and the Bond family papers that are the subject of Chapter Five offer plentiful examples of this. Chapter Four examines an Exchequer dispute over grazing rights on Arlingham Wharf, an area of land that literally shifted along the River Severn due to silting. Drakehord was known by different names locally, reflecting Nicola Whyte's description of mnemonically inscribed landscape features as palimpsests, recording layers of meaning rather than one fixed name or interpretation.[141] As it celebrated the flight of Sir John Winter, fighting for the Royalist cause during the civil wars, Wyntour's Leap would have held different meanings for those with Parliamentarian sympathies. Veronica Strong has written about political competition over the interpretation of monuments from opposing cultural perspectives.[142] This landscape was not unchanging or, in any sense, outside formal history, but this material record of the past did offer a more synchronic interpretation which preserved cultural values over empirical records.

---

[141] N. Whyte, 'The deviant dead in the Norfolk landscape', *Landscapes*, 4, 1, 2003, 24-39; N. Whyte, 'The afterlife of barrows: prehistoric monuments in the Norfolk landscape', *Landscape History*, 25, 2003, 5-16.

[142] V. Strong, 'Moon Shadows: Aboriginal and European Heroes in an Australian Landscape' in P. J. Stewart and A. Strathern (eds.), *Landscape, Memory and History: Anthropological Perspectives* (London, Sterling, Virginia, 2003), 108-135.

The mining community of Dean was involved in the physical and symbolic construction of their local region, and in asserting the place of custom in its history. Church buildings and religious monuments, symbols of community and ecclesiastical authority, dominated the early modern parish.[143] The demesne and wastes of Dean, however, were extra-parochial during this period, and these symbolic landmarks gave way to those associated with the mining industry towards the centre of the forest. The most prominent of these features were the 'scowles', a local term used to describe the remains of mining works, particularly those left by the surface extraction of iron-ore. This process, believed to have pre-dated Roman mining operations in the area, involved removing the visible red ore from the limestone rock formations between which it was found, eventually leaving a pattern of exposed rocks and overhanging tree roots. The resulting mix of deep caverns undercut the more traditional forest floor, creating a distinctive physical environment. These features encircle the northern and south-western circumferences of the area that comprised the central wastes during the sixteenth and seventeenth centuries. In 1866, Rev. H. G. Nicholls explained that it was 'the unanimous opinion of the neighbourhood that these caves owe their origin to the predecessors of that peculiar order of operatives known as "the free miners of the Forest of Dean"'. Mr George Wyrrall, one of Nicholls' contemporaries asserted that 'they were certainly the toil of many centuries'. The scowles, wrote Nicholls:

---

[143] A. Corbin, *Village Bells; Sound and Meaning in the 19th-Century French Countryside* (Basingstoke and Oxford, 1998); B.R. Smith, *The Acoustic World of Early Modern England; Attending to the 'O' Factor* (Chicago, 1999).

have the appearance either of spacious caves, as above Lydney and on the Doward Hill, or of deep stone quarries, as at the Scowles near Bream. Or they consist of precipitous and irregularly shaped passages, left by the removal of the ore or mineral earth wherever it was found, and which was followed down, in some instances, for many hundreds of yards.[144]

These formations ensured that the ancient and 'timeless' nature of the mining industry dominated perceptions of local history among those living and working in the Forest.

Many other landscape features bore witness to the activity of ancient and contemporary mining operations. The iron ore which drove so much early industrial activity in Dean still emerges into the 'Redbrook' towards the west of the Forest. Elizabeth Townley also explains that 'the widespread Roman mining activity of the Dene valley would have produced, not only a landscape of pits and spoil heaps, but a distinctive flora associated with the acidic residues: such as yew, gorse, ferns and bilberries'.[145] This area retained a distinctive appearance, specifically because of the mining industry.

---

[144] H. G. Nicholls, *Iron Making in the Olden Times: as Instanced in the Ancient Mines, Forges, and Furnaces of the Forest of Dean – historically related, on the basis of contemporary records and exact local investigation, 1866* (Coleford, 1981), 3.

[145] E. L. Townley, 'The medieval landscape and economy of the Forest of Dean' (Unpublished Ph.D, Bristol University, 2005), 126.

In 1608, however, a large, detailed map was commissioned by James I in the context of increasing financial exigency. The 'King James map' indicates how this environment may have appeared to Foresters in 1608. From this map, names of settlements and landscape features in early seventeenth-century Dean can be analysed in greater detail. The names of villages and settlements such as Coleford, Cinderford and 'Clowerwall' were the most obvious records of local industrial activity. Included on the map is the town of Staunton towards the west of the forest, adjacent to fields called 'Blaxe Hedge', 'Blaxe Mead' and a large unoccupied space called 'the Blaxe'. This perhaps implies discolouration of the soil from the continued accumulation of cinders produced by the local concentration of iron works. 'Cinder Mead' and 'Upper'/'Lower Cinder Mead' were related to the industry in this way, and suggest that this type of soil discolouration may have characterised parts of the Forest's demesne lands.[146] Less obvious is the evidence provided by landmarks such as Hart's Hill near Littledean which, while apparently recording the history of hunting in the region, is widely thought to consist of slag deposits from earlier industrial activity. The Forest abounded with the remnants of the iron industry and its products. 'Fletch field' and 'Fletchland' which were close to Staunton, referred to the arrows that were produced in great quantities in this area during the late medieval period, as did 'Quarrel Field' which lay towards St. Briavels.

These topograms were significant in transmitting customary rights within the forest. In contrast to the secretive and oligarchic operation of the select

---

[146] TNA, MR 169.

vestries described by Steve Hindle and Paul Griffiths, these popular structures of collective legal memory imply a broad participation in their construction and guardianship; the mining community and their ancestors were, however, more prominent than other forest inhabitants in this regard. [147]

In his study of landscape and memory, Guo notes that topograms 'emphasize material and manifest continuity between the present and the past'.[148] Customary rights depended upon this type of past physical evidence and, in this forest, a large proportion of these memories were generated by the activity of the miners and their ancestors. Bourdieu explains that '*habitus*, a product of history, produces individual and collective practices – more history – in accordance with the schemes generated by history.'[149] This suggests a cyclical dynamic in which the movements of social actors in space contribute to the structural arrangement of that space which, in turn, influences the movements and decisions of those actors.

---

[147] For secondary literature regarding the rise of the 'civil parish' and state formation during this period see Chapter Three. See also P. Griffiths, 'Secrecy and Authority in Late Sixteenth- and Seventeenth-Century London', *The Historical Journal*, 40, 4 (1997), 925-951.

[148] Guo, 'Island Builders', 198.

[149] Bourdieu, *The Logic of Practice*, 54.

By transporting coal and ore from pits to points of sale and through distribution along the Rivers Severn and Wye, this industry was literally constitutive of communication networks in the Forest. The earliest extant records of the Mine Law Court record sessions at a location called 'Hyll Pytt' in 1469/70. Townley identifies an area called 'Hilles' which refers to a 'distinctive, dome shaped hill adjacent to an area of extensive underground iron workings' which, on the 1608 map, is illustrated with converging trackways, indicating a role as a focal point. This territorially distinctive site echoes the siting of Saxon moots, or courts, for community business, providing a suitable location for the fifteenth-century mining court.[150]

The symbolism of the miners is evident in more official and tangible structures at Abenhall church which has a plaque commemorating the miners' participation at Agincourt, or Newland church, home of the fifteenth-century miners' brass. The baptismal font in Abenhall church is embellished with a large miners' coat of arms in light of the custom that a free miner should have been born within St. Briavels Hundred.

Thompson suggested an analogy between Bourdieu's notion of *habitus* and local custom in the context of early modern society. Observing that 'agrarian custom was never fact. It was ambience', he describes:

---

[150] Townley, 'The medieval landscape and economy of the Forest of Dean', 182.

94

a lived environment comprised of practices, inherited expectations, rules which determined limits to usages and disclosed possibilities, norms and sanctions both of law and neighbourhood pressures.[151]

Thompson emphasises the intense localism of this kind of customary environment, stating that the profile of these norms would have varied 'from parish to parish according to innumerable variables'.[152] 'Within this habitus', he suggested:

all parties strove to maximise their own advantages. Each encroached upon the usages of the others. The rich employed their riches, and all the institutions and awe of local authority. The middling farmers, or yeoman sort, influenced local courts and sought to write stricter by laws as hedges against both large and petty encroachments ... on occasion they defended their rights against the rich and powerful at law. The peasantry and the poor employed stealth, a knowledge of every bush and by-way, and the force of numbers.[153]

In Dean, the mining community dominated perceptions of the Forest, particularly when defending customary access to resources such as wood, timber and coal. The history of this region, as perceived from within, was

---

[151] Thompson, *Customs in Common*, 102.

[152] Ibid., 102.

[153] Ibid., 102.

shaped by the physical and symbolic resonance of the miners and their industry. The significance of this occupational community foreshadowed their central role in organising resistance to attacks on common rights in the Forest. Before examining the nature of this protest, Chapter Two looks beyond the customary ideal of 'open' forest to consider the material worth of commoning to inhabitants at every level in Dean.

Chapter Two

Common rights and the forest commonalty

Surveyor: For my selfe have known certain groundes, upon which within this twentie or thirtie yeares was growing great store of Underwood and Timber, and did yearely pay to the late Queene a rent, but now the wood is all gone, the soyle turned to common, and the rent quite lost, and not any paid: and truly more is like to follow in this kind, if the heavie and headlong clamour of the vulgar sort be not (by some advised course of superior officers) moderated in the balance of equity.

R. Church, *An Olde Thrift Newly Revived* (London, 1612), 3.

Those explanations of the world are most authoritative which are founded on the principle of self-evidence. What is self-evident is incontestably true. Established prior to discourse, self-evident truth quite literally 'goes without saying'. The unavailability of self-evidence to critical debate endows it with the unquestionable authority of natural being. Such truth is not constructed, formed, or constituted by discourse, history or society. Self-constituted and exempt from negotiation, it precedes discourse and is more primordial than history.

M. Ryan, 'Self-Evidence', *Diacritics*, 10:2 (1980), 2.

I An ideology of improvement

In 1612 R. Church warned of the 'heavie and headlong clamour of the vulgar sort', echoing contemporary concerns over commoners claiming traditional rights in the forested regions of seventeenth-century England. Chapter One has demonstrated that many common usages in Dean were tied to the royal status of this Forest and memories of dwelling and labouring in the local landscape. The legitimacy of these rights or privileges, then, was linked to the traditional 'way of seeing' the Forest. This world-view was evidently incompatible with the 'improving' ideology of Church's apocryphal surveyor. Free miners, resident industrial gentry, labourers of mixed employment, farmers and 'foreigners' all sought the benefits of Dean's wastes in the straitened climate of the early seventeenth century and, thus, contributed to perceptions that these areas were being mismanaged and illegally exploited. To avoid mistaking an ideal of customary traditions for their reality, however, this chapter assesses the actual value of these rights to forest inhabitants. This illuminates the staunchly localist symbolism of popular protest in the Forest addressed in Chapter Three. The idea of an 'open' forest underpinned usages that were essential to the livelihoods of a wide section of the forest community. These rights, or privileges, were intimately associated with mining rights, to the extent that the defence of the latter was simultaneously defence of the former. The chapter opens by examining the ideological impetus behind moves to 'close' Dean before assessing what 'open' forest meant to commoners who, of course, constituted a very broadly-defined and complex group. This lays foundations for analysis of the diverse and passionate support for miners' protests during the early-seventeenth century.

Published in 1612, *An Olde Thrift Newly Revived* imagines a conversation between 'Master Surveyor', Peregrine the gentleman, 'Master Woodward' and Jenninges the 'poore farmer'. As it promoted the cause of 'projectors' and 'improvers' of the early-seventeenth century, Church's dialogue neatly rehearses many of the central themes of this chapter. Peregrine and the Surveyor offset complaints in defence of local custom against the obvious benefits of the rationalisation and improvement of decayed forest and waste grounds. Expressing his fears, Jenninges warns the group that through 'inclosure.....the king should bee greatly scanted in his pleasure, every man wronged, the poore generally be undone, and all would be in an uprore'.[154] Peregrine, the improving gentleman, suggests that the problem is one of understanding. If the 'headlong clamour of the vulgar sorte' would only abate, he could explain that it was the idea of enclosing rather than the act which was the cause of fear among the commons, and his attempts to increase agricultural and silvicultural profit would provoke much less rancour. 'And though this *name* of inclosing and taking in of Commons and wast grounds be odious to the Communaltie...' he concedes:

> *if they did rightly apprehend it*, that as well the rich as the poore might reape a generall good hereby (as most assuredly they would), no doubt they would importune, that all such decaied Forests, Commons & wast grounds might be taken in[155]

---

[154] R. Church, *An Olde Thrift Newly Revived* (London, 1612), 32. My emphasis. URL: http://eebo.chadwyck.com/home   Date accessed: 28/05/2008.

[155] Church, *An Olde Thrift*, 33. My emphasis. Rollison explains that 'The word 'commonalty' inevitably attached itself to the class of people who shared the condition of being 'common' as distinct from 'honourable'. D. Rollison, *A Commonwealth of the People: Popular Politics and England's Long Social Revolution* (Cambridge, 2010), 95. Those below the level of the gentry in the Forest of Dean are difficult to refer to collectively as the population was diverse and fluid. The claim to be a commoner of the Forest with access to the central wastes and demesnes, however, was ubiquitous in records of protest and litigation. This book will, therefore, refer to this group as the commonalty, the commoners, or the foresters.

Master Surveyor, indeed, suggests that 'the farmer hath spoken well *according to his understanding'.*[156] At the heart of this conflict, to borrow John Berger's phrase, were two competing 'ways of seeing'.[157] Here we have two divergent world views which, when examined, each conveyed a different attitude to the legitimacy of local custom and common rights.

The reality of this cultural and economic division was infinitely more complex than this binary model suggests. Church evidently invoked this Manichean contrast to demonstrate the progressive nature of his model for improvement. Jenninges claims that scientific forest management ultimately leaves the poor with 'nothing but our labours for our hire, which indeed doth greatly discourage all honest men in that kind'. The Surveyor argues that this proletarianisation would be offset because improvement would raise production levels of rural communities to such an extent that everyone, particularly the poor, would benefit from the subsequent increase in wealth.[158] Jenninges is apparently convinced, comparing such counties as 'Kent, Essex, Suffolke, Middlesex …. and divers other Counties' with 'Champaine and open counties'. That 'those inclosed counties' have more

---

[156] Ibid., 35.

[157] J. Berger, *Ways of Seeing* (London, 1972).

[158] Church, *An Olde Thrift*, 9.

100

plenty, argues the farmer, is 'so infallible a truth, as it cannot be denied'. Thus, it seems that Church's rhetorical aim has been achieved.[159]

An Olde Thrift represents the shared local culture of Jenninges and the Woodward as backward and irrational in contrast with Surveyor's broader, progressive vision. The Surveyor attempts 'to lay out highwayes and convenient passages for the country' aimed at the 'encrease of strong and able subjects, whereby the realm shall be much strengthened'.[160] From the end of the sixteenth century, officers responsible for maintaining royal forests were increasingly perceived as outdated and ineffective governors. Richard Hoyle highlights common opinion that many inefficiencies of crown estate management were encouraged by 'the poor quality of supervision by stewards and other Crown officers'. Hoyle adds that 'Stewards were not the only corrupt officers the Crown possessed. Woodwards were notoriously so'.[161] These same tensions arose in a dispute over damage to Dean's resources in the year that *An Olde Thrift* was published. Thomas James, defendant in the case, claimed that the only timber he had taken, other than his 'lawfull' estovers, had been purchased from Charles Jones and William Brown, 'verderers of the said forrest which trees were due to them as fees belonging unto theire office'. Sir Henry

---

[159] Ibid., 38-39.

[160] Ibid., 37-40.

[161] R. Hoyle, 'Shearing the Hog': the reform of the estates, c. 1598-1640', in R. Hoyle (ed.), *The Estates of the English Crown, 1558-1640* (Cambridge, 1992), 204-62, especially 206-7.

Hobart, Attorney General, held a different opinion regarding the benefits of local office, categorically denying that 'any such fees of one oke & one beeche every yeare doe of right belong to the said office of warden or keeper ... of the said forrest'.[162] Government scrutiny of local officers and courts in the Forest of Dean is evident in many seventeenth-century equity cases.

Church's farmer Jenninges also voices concerns over potential legal and social pressures from the more substantial inhabitants of his region. If rights to common were extinguished, who would safeguard the interests of those lower on the social scale? In reply, the Surveyor offers the rational arbitration of equity law which would mediate conflict over resources 'with indifference and conveniencie'.[163] Jenninges fears that equity courts would be unable to comprehend the complexity of social and economic life in these forested areas but the Surveyor is confident that his plans are tenable. The primary tool required for such a transformation is the written record, he claims, unceremoniously dismissing the local culture of the 'plough tale'.[164] The inability of less literate societies to think in progressive terms, according to the Surveyor, is because of their attachment to the context of present necessity. The written record allows for accurate record keeping and longer-term planning. The Surveyor argues that the large timescales involved in growing trees or encoppicing woodland dissuade many from

---

[162] TNA, E112/82/310.

[163] Church, *An Olde Thrift,* 33.

[164] Ibid., 5-6.

investing in arboricultural management. 'In planting young trees or sowing their seedes', he explains, 'they think not to live to reape any profit thereby, during their lives'.[165]

Binary logic of the kind typified in *An Olde Thrift* held wide currency in the rise of empirical thinking during this period, providing a framework within which to categorise experience and observation. Binary thought, of course, aids simplified interpretation of complex phenomena. Stuart Clark points to 'debates about the role of dualistic categories in areas of scientific debate' during the sixteenth century, explaining that these systems were also 'asymmetrical' or 'hierarchical'.[166] As such, not only did this type of binary thinking simplify complex relations, but it also categorised experience through an interpretive paradigm which privileged dominant interests as rational or progressive. In this vein, Church marked a clear distinction between the world-view of those who sought to free land markets from ties of custom, and those whose livelihoods depended on the preservation of local use-rights. The structure of his seventeenth-century dialogue betrays a clear sympathy with the former.

Writing in the late-twentieth century, Raymond Williams indicated the power of oppositional logic in the birth, development and consolidation of an ideology. He suggested that:

---

[165] Church, *An Olde Thrift*, 5.

[166] S. Clark, 'The 'gendering' of witchcraft in French demonology: misogyny or polarity', *French History*, 5 (1991), 426-437.

there is now 'proletarian ideology' or 'bourgeois ideology', and so on, and ideology in each case is the system of ideas appropriate to that class. One ideology can be claimed as correct and progressive as against another ideology.[167]

An Olde Thrift dramatizes the private men of property as progressive and rational, while older systems of forest management emerge as an obstacle to improvement. In its most common sixteenth- and seventeenth-century usage, this term implied 'land improved or rendered more profitable by inclosure, cultivation, the erection of buildings', but also 'the action or process of enhancing' and 'increase, enlargement, growth, development, advancement'.[168]

The Surveyor does eventually address the initial capital outlay required for improvement, but answers these concerns by pointing to growth and increased return on investments. 'It is true', he admits, 'that upon first view or apprehension thereof the labour and charge seemeth somewhat great, but with patience, and upon some few yeares expectancie, the gains will greatly overtop the charge'.[169] In contrast to customary 'ways of seeing' which looked to the past, then, the very concept of improvement implied a forward-looking attempt to anticipate the future. In this sense it was, by

---

[167] R. Williams, *Keywords* (London, 1983), 157.

[168] *Oxford English Dictionary* URL: http://dictionary.oed.com/entrance.dtl Date accessed 12/1/2013.

[169] Church, *An Olde Thrift*, 10.

definition, progressive. The Surveyor ultimately asks Jenninges if he would:

> not thinke it a good and pleasing sight to see a large decayed forest, or wild and ruinous piece of ground, which as it lieth is not worth perhaps five pence the acre, to be now inclosed with ditches and quick set and planted with many yong tres of divers kinds, to prove worth eight shillings or ten shillings the acre: what should I say more.[170]

This resonates with Michael Ryan's theory on powerful and authoritative ideologies, whereby the beneficial nature of improvement, in rhetorical terms, 'literally goes without saying'.[171]

This is not to say these ideas were represented or advertised purely in terms of novelty. The contrary was often the case, as suggested by the name *An Olde Thrift Newly Revived*. Karl Marx was confident that:

> No social order ever perishes before all the productive forces for which there is room in it have developed; and new, higher relations of production never appear before the material conditions of their existence have matured in the womb of the old society itself.[172]

---

[170] Ibid., 38.

[171] Ryan, 'Self-Evidence', 2.

[172] K. Marx, *A Contribution to the Critique of Political Economy* M. Dobb (ed.) (Moscow, 1970), 21.

Joan Thirsk suggested that it has not been 'usual to allow projectors any ideals. The very name became a dirty word in the early seventeenth century, synonymous with rogue and speculator'.[173] Church's dialogue and various schemes for irrigation, damming, drainage, enclosure and improved road systems during the period reveal, not only that many projectors believed that their schemes would contribute to the collective good in various ways, but also that they did not necessarily imply a sharp rupture with the past. The emergence of what can, very generally, be termed 'bourgeois ideology' did not initially signal a break with the old world of common right, but was often conceived as a growth or improvement on or within existing modes of production. Local custom was venerated by many as a tangible link between present practice and the wisdom or experience of previous generations. Far from a 'new kind of industrie', Church's Surveyor offers 'an old thrift newly revived'. Rather than an entirely novel transformation, he proposes careful expenditure and the stricter management of existing systems.[174] He aims to halt a perceived process of decline rather than introduce major innovation to estate management policies.

This emphasis on reinvigorating or tightening existing systems reflects many aspects of Elizabethan and Jacobean estate management and explains concerns with potentially profitable areas like the Forest of Dean. Church's Surveyor offers improvements that are incompatible with local traditions of commoning, but 'self-evidently' beneficial to all. Ryan suggests that any

---

[173] J. Thirsk, *Economic Policy and Projects: The Development of a Consumer Society in Early Modern England* (Oxford, 1978), 17.

[174] Church, *An Olde Thrift*, 9.

truly authoritative ideology should claim origins in nature itself. While Church wrote that 'Trees set by art doe grow sooner and better than wild trees', John Norden, author of *The Surveyor's Dialogue*, was careful to explain that 'Art only growes from nature's working deedes, Which first did sowe in Aristotle seedes'.[175] Speaking on behalf of the Stuart surveyor, Norden thereby implied a horticultural teleology rooted in the natural inspirations of classical philosophy. Rather than breaking with the past, then, surveyors simply employed these 'arts' to improve the productivity of waste grounds.

An Olde Thrift represents an ideal expression of two discrete world-views opposed for rhetorical purposes. Lived experience was far more complex. As will be demonstrated, these two positions were not fixed and opposable ideologies, but fluid and contingent 'ways of seeing' or being. Despite this complexity, at the core of much conflict in the Forest of Dean during the first four decades of the seventeenth century was the fundamental incompatibility of enclosed or improved forest and 'open' forest. The latter term was regularly deployed in defence of traditional rights or usages. Marx observed that the 'distinction should always be made between the material transformation of the economic conditions of production .... And the legal, political, religious, aesthetic or philosophical – in short, ideological – forms in which men become conscious of this conflict and fight it out'.[176] James

---

[175] Church, *An Olde Thrift*, 16; J. Norden, *A Store-house of varieties briefly discoursing the change and alteration of things in this world* (London, 1601), 141. URL: http://eebo.chadwyck.com/home Date accessed 14/09/2009.

[176] Marx, *Contribution*, 21.

Decker attempts to soften this distinction, suggesting that 'I am, therefore I think' more properly reflects the notion that 'subjectivity does not arise merely from the physical ability to think; it grounds itself in the material'. [177] This relation between material experience and ideology illuminates much about the nature of conflict in seventeenth-century Dean. While improvement could be framed as a process of natural development, the idea of an 'open' forest held such broad ideological appeal precisely because it was grounded in the daily experience of foresters and their ancestors. Marc Steinberg recalls Thompson's insistence that 'hegemony was never total and that the common sense of shared experience could rudely interrupt the pontifications of a dominant ideology'.[178] He suggests that lived experience is 'in conflict with imposed consciousness', as people both draw upon and struggle with the weight of their traditions and the forces of hegemony to make collective sense of their world'.[179] The struggle for hegemony between those advocating traditional uses of the Forest and more dominant schemes to improve and close the wastes was to define most major outbreaks of conflict in seventeenth-century Dean.

---

[177] J. M. Decker, *Transitions: Ideology* (Basingstoke and New York, 2004), 15-16.

[178] Ibid., 478; Valentin Volosinov also identified language as the site of political struggle, V.N. Voloshinov, *Marxism and the Philosophy of Language* (Harvard, 1973).

[179] M. W. Steinberg, 'A Way of Struggle: Reformations and Affirmations of E. P, Thompson's Class Analysis in the Light of Postmodern Theories of Language', The British Journal of Sociology, 48, 3 (1997), 471-92.

Antonio Gramsci stressed that the consent secured by bourgeois hegemony is an active consent, not a passive submission.[180] Rather than simple coercion or force, effective leadership is rooted equally in the organisation of consent to a particular political system. Williams asserts that bourgeois hegemony 'is not imposed; rather it is 'negotiated' by unequal forces in a complex process through which the subordination and the resistance of the workers are created and recreated'.[181] Dean's miners were clearly distinct from other groups of labourers and workers, arguably never fully submitting to processes of proletarianisation that characterised many other areas of seventeenth- and eighteenth-century England. Similarly, local industrial gentry and royal grantees do not closely resemble the bourgeois class of investor envisaged by Marx. During this period, though, the Forest of Dean undeniably witnessed a transformation in which the hegemony of capital investment and private property was increasingly seen to threaten a traditional culture of common right, even if this culture was, in many respects, an ideal.

The following chapters outline these processes of negotiation in their material and ideological contexts respectively. This chapter outlines the

---

[180] R. Simon, *Gramsci's Political Thought: An Introduction* (London, 1985); Q. Hoare and G. N. Smith (eds.), *Selections From The Prison Notebooks Of Antonio Gramsci* (London, 1971). I understand the problematic nature of using the term 'bourgeois' in the context of the seventeenth century, but I use it to describe an ideology (or ideological cluster) which embraced the forward thinking principles of private/exclusive property ownership and nationally co-ordinated economic and trading networks. I am thinking primarily of an ideology which constituted itself in opposition to the messy complexity of locally constituted and collective use-rights, against which it attempted to cultivate its own progressive image.

[181] Williams, *Keywords*, 155.

early seventeenth-century assault on custom in the Forest of Dean. Underpinning Chapters Three and Four, it assesses increased contestation of local custom; not only of rights claimed, but also the terms under which they were claimed. It then considers the actual material value of these usages to a broad section of this forest community. In short, this chapter traces the ideological division which informed much conflict in early seventeenth-century Dean and describes the cultural and economic position of the miners which situated them as effective protest leaders. Chapter Three examines how the 'common sense of shared experience could rudely interrupt the pontifications of a dominant ideology', while Chapter Four assesses the role of the mining community in allowing the advance of progressive ideologies in a broader sense.[182]

II An assault on Dean's 'ancient' rights

Chapter One discussed relations between oral tradition, the material environment, and customary practice in the Forest of Dean during the sixteenth and seventeenth centuries. The timeless stasis implied by custom inherited from immemorial tradition suggests a community characterised by consensus and agreement. In reality, it is argued, the hold of local customary practice was partly due to its ability to comprehend the ambivalence surrounding contradictory claims to resources. This situation was complicated by the increasing impact of the written record during the seventeenth century. That, more properly, is the subject of Chapter Four. The following pages consider competing legal jurisdictions in early modern

[182] Steinberg, 'A Way of Struggle', 477.

England and explore custom in two aspects. They analyse *lex loci* as one of several interpretations of legality, but also as a field in which differing systems competed for legitimacy. According to Kate Crehan, one aspect of what 'hegemony means in practice' is 'the power to determine the structuring rules within which such struggles are to be fought out'.[183] The struggles in the Forest of Dean offer an opportunity to examine competition over the determination of structuring rules. They demonstrate both assertion of custom by physical force, and increased formal litigation over contested claims.

The Forest of Dean's legal system consisted of several courts, each covering its own aspect of forest governance or manorial regulation. The hundredal court of St. Briavels was overseen by the constable of the hundred and held more general sessions in the vein of a court baron or a court of pleas. The Verderer's Court heard offences against venison and vert while the Mine Law Court held a monopoly of jurisdiction over the customary mining industry of the forest. These jurisdictions were not spatially distinct and overlapped in many respects. As well as this local complexity, the sixteenth and seventeenth centuries also saw the increasing involvement of central equity courts and other external courts. Extant records suggest that disputes could proceed through more than one court simultaneously.[184]

---

[183] K. Crehan, *Gramsci, Culture and Anthropology* (London, Sterling and Virginia, 2002), 204.

[184] For examples, see TNA, E112/15/9; TNA, E112/82/300; E112/82/310; TNA, E112/181/109; TNA, E112/181/125; TNA, E112/182/194 & TNA, E112/182/196.

This complexity was not simply due to overlapping court jurisdictions. More fundamentally, perceptions of legitimacy were dependent on the differing subjectivities of groups or individuals. At one end of a continuum, *lex loci* constituted a coherent body of use-rights to be defended in local courts. At the other, it consisted of less formal norms and contingent relationships which mediated custom in its social and cultural aspects. In 1620, Robert Witt complained to the Court of Star Chamber that his 'water corne mill' at Flaxley had been illegally destroyed by the defendants and over 'one hundred others'. The defendants accused of this armed attack were far from marginal characters in this community. They included Christopher Hawkins, alderman of Newnham, and attorney in the Court of Common pleas, George Pumfrey, another alderman of Newnham, Thomas Stevens, a constable of Newnham and Henry White, sheriff's bailiff of the hundred of Westbury.[185] The involvement of such substantial inhabitants suggests that, despite Witt's protestations to the contrary, the destruction of his mill had been pursued through legal channels which held a convincing level of legitimacy. To judge by the evidence given to this court, Witt, himself, was not adverse to the use of physical methods of enforcement. In February 1619, according to these records, he and other defendants had held the plaintiff 'in strong duresse & Imprisonment Untill they had most corruptlie & unlawfullie extorted, exacted & receyved of and from your said subiect divers somes of monie to his great wrong, damage and oppression'.[186] The plaintiff's cry of foul play was seemingly ineffectual in

---

[185] TNA, STAC8/304/26.

[186] TNA, STAC8/298/19.

the face of Witt's alleged physical restraint and intimidation. Here, as Crehan suggests, 'hegemony ... clearly involved some very material forces'.
[187]

John Webbe's complaint to the Court of Star Chamber in 1622 demonstrates the relativity of legal senses in the Forest. Webbe, gentleman of Mitcheldean, accused his assailants of attacking him with various weapons, including 'longe picked staffes swords daggers Glaves Javelins forest bills and divers other weapons'. Despite the severity of his accusations, Webbe seems to have been just as concerned with the defendants' confidence in the legitimacy of their actions. He described how they had:

> sett up and erected in the said house of the said Richard Page in Michelldeane aforesaid a Courte and made Justices and officers and a cryer of that Courte in the forme of a sessions of the pease and toke upon them to call in theire courte divers and sundrye persons of good name and quallytie in Michelldeane.

Webbe's account of this alternative session 'of the pease' hints at the effects of social polarisation on different views of acceptable legal practice. Whether or not he understood this court to possess any legitimate authority, he was convinced that it was working 'to the slander and reproche of divers honest and substanciall persons'. Perhaps unsurprisingly, considering the highly rhetorical nature of many complaints to Star Chamber, he structured

---

[187] Crehan, *Gramsci, Culture and Anthropology*, 205.

his testimony to represent this 'Courte' as an inversion of more officially sanctioned legal institutions. His oppositional social thinking is suggested by anxieties concerning the status of these defendants, a group containing six cordwainers, a weaver, a dyer and a labourer, and his concern for the reputation of those 'honest and substanciall persons'.[188] Clearly, Webbe would also have felt physically intimidated in this situation, but this only lends weight to Crehan's sense of the materiality of hegemonic negotiation.[189] James Sharpe discusses a seventeenth-century ballad, *The Brickmakers Lamentation from Newgate*, in which a brick maker is accused of stealing a workmate's bread. The brick-makers decide to hold their own mock court in which:

> A judge, and a jury, and a clark did appear,
>
> A sheriff, and also a hangman was there.
>
> The judge being set and the prisoner brought forth
>
> The plaintiff he there on a brickbat took oath.

Sharpe uses this ballad to demonstrate that 'the law evidently entered the popular mind sufficiently to be, or at least thought to be capable of being,

---

[188] TNA, STAC8/298/13.

[189] Crehan, *Gramsci, Culture and Anthropology,* 204.

represented as a subject for fairly detailed parody'.[190] If John Webbe was to be believed, such fantasies had taken on a far more physical form in the Forest of Dean.

Emphasising that these sessions had been held 'in the night tymes…at or about Twelve of the Clocke in the night', Webbe's complaint looked towards a common elite anxiety regarding visibility of the social order. Paul Griffiths affirms the ubiquity of such anxieties in early modern England. Whilst the offence of 'nightwalking' was becoming increasingly feminized in the metropolitan consciousness by the early seventeenth century, he observes, in more provincial settings it was 'largely a concern about the grave dangers of random movement after dusk and the suspicions to which it gave rise'.[191]

Cultural polarisation and concerns over nocturnal activity also loomed large in Sir Edward Winter's interpretation of mining custom in 1607. As constable of St. Briavels, Winter was embroiled in a dispute with the mining community regarding his occupational claim to take coal from the forest. He complained to the Court of Star Chamber regarding miners' attempts to sabotage these operations by intimidating his employees and destroying his pit. Winter's language attests to the psychological construction of legitimacy and, once again, emphasises the relativity of

---

[190] J. Sharpe, 'The People and the Law' in B. Reay (ed.), *Popular Culture in Seventeenth-Century England* (London, 1985), 244-70, 262.

[191] P. Griffiths, 'Meanings of nightwalking in early modern England', *Seventeenth Century*, 13, 2 (1998), 212-38, 223.

world views which underpinned claims to Dean's resources. He referred to the fiercely asserted rights of free miners, for instance, as 'their pretended customes and liberties'. There was evidently a wide-spread animosity towards his efforts in 'restrayninge and reprehending of them from theire ordenance custome of huntinge and distroyinge your Maiesties game within the said Forrest'. Despite such an obvious motive, Winter attributed a more calculating method of recruitment to Edmund Bond and the other defendants. He suggested that they did 'consult and complott together howe to make your said subiecte odyouse and hatefull to the common people there'. His accusation suggests a distinction between his sense of legitimacy and the beliefs of those on the lower rungs of local society. He claimed that the defendants:

did most slanderously lye and maliciously publishe amongste theire neighbours that the quyet havinge and takinge of the said Cole pitte and coales would prove the certeine and likelyest meanes to bereave them the said enhabitantes of theire pretended customes and liberties within the said Forrest, presuminge upon this plausible suggestion that the common people woulde have tumultuouslie and Ryotousle without further deliberation overthrowen and wasted the saide pitt.

Winter proposed, perhaps very perceptively, that Bond and the others were able to draw support for their actions by linking his mining operation to more general encroachments, highlighting a threat to the 'open' forest that perpetuated local customary uses. He suggested that they had pursued such a course:

well knoweinge that in the myndes of the vulgar sort (of that country especiallye) there is not anything that leaves a deeper impression of hatred and malice then a conceipt once strongly apprehended by them of beinge abridged by any man of such freedoms and liberties as they challenge and doe pretend to have.

Winter's evidence thus constructed an opposition between the legitimacy of the rights attached to his office, and local customs which existed only 'in the myndes of the vulgar sort'.

Winter's stereotyping persisted, describing the alleged 'Ryotors' as 'men of verie lewde conversation and the aptest persons in that countrey to attempt or Commyt any outrage or misdemeanor'. These offences, Winter protested, were not to be suffered in a 'well governed Commonweale', echoing Webbe's fears that they were 'the more heynouse and intolerable in that they were committed and executed in your Maiesties Forrest and that in the night time'. Not only had these defendants unnaturally committed their crimes on a 'Saturdaye betweene eleven and Twelve of the Clocke in the night (when good subiects should be in bedd)', but they were heavily armed and disguised with 'vizards and scarfes', a point that the defendants very strenuously denied. Winter's bill to Star Chamber, then, contrasted his quiet legal possession of rights with the armed and aggressive attempts of the defendants to claim their pretended custom. The apparently legitimate, open and daylight proceedings of his employees were also set against the supposedly unnatural nocturnal activity of this group. Contrary to his language of social description, the defendants contained five yeomen of Newland and two gentlemen including Richard Catchmay 'of late advanced to the Capteynshippe of one of the trayned bandes in that division of the forest'. Sir Richard Catchmay served as Justice of the Peace during the early seventeenth century. According to Winter, they were 'all or the most of them for many years together being knowen to be the most sedytiouse, turbulent and dangerouse spirits of that Countrye'.[192] Winter's apparently strategic testimony worked to construct a series of oppositional relations which ultimately combined to represent him as the conduit of orderly governance while his opponents were cast as a disorderly, hidden and riotous threat. He made this claim to Star Chamber, despite Catchmay's social standing and influence.

It was not only fellow gentlemen that adopted this view of Catchmay. Two decades later, in 1636, a group of quarrymen from the Forest also characterised his behaviour in terms of unconventionality and disorder. Contrasting with the seigniorial dispute between Winter and Catchmay, this complaint was made in more humble, albeit no less rhetorical, terms. The Court of the Exchequer was told that 'Your sayd Orators are all of them poore inhabitants within the precinct or perambulacion of the sayd Forrest'. These plaintiffs, including the widow of a mason, collectively pleaded against the actions of Catchmay as he brought a suit against them at Gloucester County Assizes. Catchmay sought to stop the plaintiffs extracting stone from within areas of the Forest as they claimed was their ancient customary right. They pleaded for this ruling to be overturned as Catchmay's recent enclosure of these areas would impinge on their ability to support their wives and children. The plaintiffs were adamant that they were merely exercising the customary right to break ground which they had enjoyed 'time out of mind'. As they continued to dig stone, Catchmay seems to have decided to make a similarly physical intervention. The quarrymen complained that Catchmay and his accomplices had 'broken in

---

[192] TNA, STAC8/303/7.

118

pieces & spoiled stones that have been dug up', specifically adding that this damage had been done in 'a malicious & riotous manner' and 'at night'.[193] While binary stereotyping was, in many ways, characteristic of a division of cultures in seventeenth-century England, it would appear that it was not only the elite who could emphasise these anxieties in defending their cause.

Sharpe proposes that 'the law as a whole represented an important means of transmitting the wishes and aspirations of authority into the popular consciousness'. In this context, at least, it seems that the negotiation of legal hegemony was a far more reciprocal process.[194] The impression given by evidence from Dean during the late sixteenth and early seventeenth centuries is that the law was not imposed on this community from outside but was, in many ways, culturally mediated from within. Local custom was very much related to a traditional way of seeing or being in the forest as particular world-views supported particular understandings of legality. From the disembodied voices in centuries old legal proceedings it is impossible to determine, with any degree of certainty, whose testimony bore greater veracity. Yet it is evident that during the early seventeenth century in the Forest of Dean, many felt that 'the structuring rules within which such struggles were to be fought out', remained open to interpretation and contestation.[195] Moreover, this contest over legal

---

[193] TNA, E112/181/109.

[194] Sharpe, 'The People and the Law', 264.

[195] Crehan, *Gramsci, Culture and Anthropology,* 204.

ideologies was grounded in the material experience of forest life. These competing ideologies came to the fore in the context of an assault on local custom which was largely inspired by royal grants of forest resources in the opening years of the seventeenth century.

III Private men and the searching the forest.

On his accession to the throne in 1603 James I inherited severe fiscal difficulties from the regime of his predecessor. In May 1602, Lord Treasurer Buckhurst had implored that 'it was fittest to have peace with Spain before we be too far spent, for he [Spain] hath a spring that yieldeth continual supply, his Indies, & we are like a standing water, which war will exhaust & make dry & barren'.[196] As part of an early Jacobean drive to tighten the use of royal demesne lands, many foresters were made to feel increasingly insecure over their common rights.

Post-conquest forest law had been upheld by the Justices in Eyre, a triennial circuit made by royal courts. Since the decline of these sessions in the fourteenth century, royal forests were increasingly managed through an array of swanimotes and local courts which operated under the influence of local gentry. Peter Large concludes that 'the progressive weakening of the Crown's administrative hold during the sixteenth century had effectively handed over the control of many royal forests to their inhabitants'.[197] Many

---

[196] Roger Wilbraham, *The Journal of Sir Roger Wilbraham, Solicitor-General in Ireland and Lord of Requests, for the years 1593-1616*, 49-50. URL:
http://www.archive.org/stream/journalofsirroge00wilbrich Date accessed: 28/1/2009.

legal records from Dean reflect this shift away from the protection of Crown interests by the first half of the seventeenth century.[198]

From the perspective of the Jacobean government, this relative autonomy had allowed rent on Crown estates to remain at lower and outdated levels, avoiding the vast upheavals in land ownership and inflationary growth of the sixteenth century. Richard Hoyle warns against simplistic readings of the efficacy of Elizabethan land sales, arguing that these make 'no allowance for inflation; in real terms the value of the estates was progressively reduced'.[199] By the time James I came to the throne, his regime was struggling against the twin effects of growth and the consequences of late-sixteenth century crown estate management. His administration was left with the task of attempting to squeeze more income from lands which had effectively had the terms of their tenure frozen by the Elizabethan government. Hoyle notes that under Elizabeth, 'customary

---

[197] P. Large, 'From swanimote to disafforestation: Feckenham Forest in the early seventeenth century', in R. W. Hoyle (ed.), *The Estates of the English Crown, 1558-1640* (Cambridge, 1992), 389-417, 389.

[198] While the 'Speeche Courte held at Little Deane' on 20 July 1637, for instance, records only prosecutions for offences against the wood of the forest, Star Chamber cases such as that relating to yeoman 'Robert Yearesly of Highemeadows within the parish of Newland and divers others to the number of five persons at the least' for killing deer 'riotously', suggests that 'poaching' was becoming the responsibility of a centralised legal authority. This case also provides some idea of local tensions which could be behind the recourse to central courts in such prosecutions. It notes that Yearesly had attempted to undermine the local system by telling people that 'William Wyntour of Colford', 'Deputie Constable of your highness Forrest of Deane' and 'Judge of your maiesties courte of St Brevells' was biased and had showed favouritism in his judgements. TNA, E146/3/29, STAC8/304/4. For more examples of this shift see TNA, STAC8/280/29 & STAC8/280/23. R. B. Manning, *Village Revolts: Social Protest and Popular Disturbances in England, 1509-1640*, Oxford, 1988.

[199] Hoyle, *The Estates of the English Crown*, 12.

tenants were offered confirmations of their customs or preferential leasehold arrangements for taking upon themselves the expense of repairing river banks and coastal defences ... without wages'. It was, under James, 'no longer possible (if it ever had been) to alter significantly the terms and conditions by which customary tenants held their lands'.[200]

Uninterrupted use had 'anciently' justified customary access to forest resources but now attention turned to undermining this security of tenure. Many private men of no particular qualification were recruited to carry out searches of 'concealments' which, generally, consisted of land that had been assarted from royal forest without disclosure. In 1613, the aforementioned John Sallens claimed that he had been 'lawfullie seised in his demeasne ... time out of mind' and thus had rights to common in the forest. These usages were in dispute following a royal grant of forest resources made to William Herbert, the third Earl of Pembroke, a prominent figure in this episode. Despite protestations to the contrary, Otho Nicholson claimed that these lands had been assarted but Sallens and his co-plaintiffs still submitted 'themselves & theire estate to his mercy'. Nicholson, the most notorious of these searchers, had apparently promised 'the said Inhabitants that compounded' that they would not lose 'theire Commons, estovers, botes profits or commoddities within the said Forrest'. [201] The quest to uncover defective titles clearly promoted uncertainty. The authority of these searchers was often questionable and regularly in conflict

---

[200] Ibid., 31-32.

[201] TNA, E112/82/300.

with the interests of other private men. For complex and often contradictory reasons, then, these areas were increasingly subject to the scrutiny of the Crown and private speculators.

The thinly veiled recusancy of many resident gentry can only have fuelled anxieties over the Forest of Dean. Christopher Hill identified late sixteenth-century fears of the suspected activities of Jesuits and seminary priests in the 'dark corners of the land'. These areas were feared as potential nests of rebellion and resented for their resistance to the 'civilising process' which was perceived to emanate from London and its surrounding areas.[202] Caroline Litzenberger provides plentiful evidence that Dean was a ripe target for such stereotyping during the late sixteenth century. The Forest had a well established record of absenteeism from worship, and she notes that '45 per cent [of the parishes] lacked any regular catechetical instruction'. Dean was the area of Gloucestershire demonstrating least conformity to Elizabethan Protestantism. Thus, '65 per cent of the parishes lacked both regular sermons and the reading of homilies', explains Litzenberger, while 'a large proportion of the forest parishes still had some undefaced vestige of pre-Reformation piety' and 'used traditional vestments'.[203]

It was not only 'backwardness' in religion or the drive to swell royal coffers that concerned authorities. In 1610 it was remarked that the Forest sheltered

---

[202] C. Hill, 'Puritans and 'the Dark Corners of the Land'', in C. Hill, *Change and Continuity in Seventeenth-Century England* (New Haven and London, 1991), 3-47, especially 9-10.

[203] C. Litzenberger, *The English Reformation and the Laity; Gloucestershire, 1540-1580* (Cambridge, 1997), 136-7.

'such a multitude of poor creatures, as it is lamentable to think so many inhabitants shall live upon so bare provision as upon spoil of the forest woods'. A petition of the 'more respectable inhabitants' in 1622 adopted a more judgemental tone, complaining that 'people of very lewd lives and conversations' were 'leaving their own and other countries, and taking the place for a shelter and a cloak to their villainies'.[204] There can be little doubt that during this period the Forest of Dean was perceived as a 'dark corner'. The region appeared so to central government. Despite the marginal location of the Forest, plentiful mineral and timber resources ensured the economic significance of this region. Dean was therefore of crucial strategic importance to the sixteenth- and seventeenth-century English state. Hill describes contemporary perceptions that private investment was eventually responsible for shining light into these regions.[205] During the early seventeenth century, the Crown and other projectors were acting to blur the division between the public interest of the commonweal and that of private men. Church's opposition between a 'progressive' improving ideology and backward-looking, obscure management of the supposed 'dark corners' was one that held many resonances for the Forest of Dean during the early seventeenth century.

Once again, social practice was far more complex. While these searchers embodied the ideological impulse that sought to undermine the concept of

---

[204] BL, Lansd. MS. 166, fol. 354. Both of these are quoted in Cyril Hart, *The Free Miners of the Royal Forest of Dean and Hundred of St. Briavels,* Newton Abbot, 1971, 174-5.

[205] Hill, 'Puritans and 'the Dark Corners of the Land'', 46.

an 'open' forest, it is important to recognise that it was largely an ideal. The notion of timeless custom was deployed in complex, often contradictory, ways by various groups or individuals claiming Dean's resources. To understand the relation between this ideal and support for seventeenth-century resistance, it is important to look more closely at who was able to exploit traditional management of the central wastes. How many, in this forested region, actually stood to lose through the actions of the searchers and improvers?

IV Popular use of 'open' wastes in the Forest of Dean

A 1668 dispute in the Court of the Exchequer sought to clarify who held legitimate rights to common in the Forest. The case distinguished between those claiming rights attaching to property, those who had assarted land from the Forest, and those who suggested that, since the 1650s, the 'waste grounds of the said Forrest have continued open' as they had 'anciently' been. Specific mining rights differed as they attached to the person through birth and acculturation.

The case was directed at several defendants who lived towards the edge of Dean's accepted boundaries. The court sought to discover which formal rights had been confirmed or compensated in the attempted disafforestation of the 1630s with a view to identifying legitimate access in the 1660s. These defendants offered a picture of the types of formal rights that were understood to have attached to property tenure in seventeenth-century Dean. This case specifically targeted common usages attached to the manor of Rodley as this was not consistently included in official perambulations since the thirteenth century.

The defendants confidently asserted the legitimacy of their claims. They assured the court that compensation offered to those affected by disafforestation in the 1630s could not prejudice or bar them from 'enioying their Antient and undoubted Rights of Comon in the said Forrest of Deane'.[206] Jeremy Dyett, for example, claimed that he was 'seized of an estate in fee simple' in an ancient messuage in the manor of Rodley. Dyett claimed that these lands, which consisted of about thirty five acres, entitled him to 'reasonably keep on all his aforesaid lands and tenements levant and couchant att all tymes of the yeare seaventie commonable beasts'. He also confirmed that 'no parte of his aforesaid lands or Tenements is Assart lands'. Richard Young also held an estate in fee simple as part of the manor of Rodley which, he suggested, allowed him to keep thirty two 'commonable beastes'. Anthony Arnold did not specify his manor of residence but claimed that his 250-acre estate lay 'within the hundred of St Brevills and within the perambulacion of the said Forrest of Deane'. This, he assured the commissioners, entitled him to gather estovers of dead and dry wood together with common of pasture and herbage 'in all the Comonable places in and of' the Forest of Dean. More specifically he claimed the right to keep 'eightie commonable beasts' and 'pannage for hogges in tyme of pannage'. Arnold was also adamant that none of his land had been assarted from the Forest. While these Foresters claimed their rights, they agreed that:

---

[206] TNA, E112/403/8.

divers Cottages and new buildings have been erected & divers Purprestures assarts & other offences have been committed & made in and upon the said Mannors ... And these defendants doe confesse that by such purprestures spoyles offences the said Forrest is much Impayred & that abuse is committed in & upon the woods & wasts of the said Forrest.[207]

The situation before the Civil Wars had clearly been no less confusing. Court records from the early seventeenth century suggest a complexity that illuminates later attempts to uncover suspected assarted lands.

In 1632, Attorney General William Noy issued commissioners from the Court of the Exchequer to examine several properties which had recently been established in the vicinity of Newnham. Tenants of these properties to the north of Dean's central demesne lands were claiming access to the Forest's resources. George Smith of Newnham, for example, held 'in severaltie two parcells of Meadowe and Pasture conteyninge by estimacion seaven acres' which was worth 'fortie shillings yearly'. John Gwilliam held 'one cottage and one Water Mill with garden and sheep coate built thereupon called by the name of Sawbridge Mill in the Forrest aforesaid of cleere yearly vallue of 3 poundes'. This commission named 29 properties and Noy concluded that:

divers messuages Tenements and Mills and Cottages have of late years been made and built uppon the said Forrest and a great part of the same Forrest hath been inclosed by divers and sundry persons and by

---

[207] TNA, E112/403/8

127

them converted to there owne uses to the great annoyance of the said Forrest and as much lie in them to the disherison of his Majestiie of a great part of the said Forrest ... all the aforesaid messuages Cottages Mills and Sheep Coats ben erected and built upon the soile and ground of his said Majestie of the Forrest of Deane and inclosed out thereof .
[208]

Illegal encroachment blurred the boundaries between formal and informal common rights as commoners were claiming rights attached to tenements and messuages within Dean's bounds, but the Attorney General evidently disputed the status of these cottages and other properties.

Chapter Four examines, more closely, the fate of local gentlemen John Winter, Basil Brooke and George Mynne at the Justice Eyre in 1634. Their industrial abuse of Forest wastes supports the contemporary crown view that some of Dean's inhabitants were using customary rights as a way to accumulate private profit from this increasingly valuable royal forest. More pertinently, perhaps, the records of the 1634 Eyre detail the activities of less wealthy cottagers and the way they viewed Dean's resources as well as the exigencies of maintaining an 'open' Forest. The Eyre lists 266 foresters, the majority recorded as labourers, who were convicted and fined for erecting cottages and encroaching on the 'King's Soil of the Forest' in recent years. Many of these presentments included charges for gathering and keeping livestock in less regulated areas of the Forest. William Collys of le Mynde near Littledean and Francis Acton, labourer, also of Littledean, were each presented for building a sheepcote. This was particularly controversial as

---

[208] TNA, E112/180/55.

sheep were not regarded by many to be commonable beasts in the Forest.[209] Five labourers and a coal carrier were all accused of encroaching in the region of Parkend and convicted of pasturing 'pigs and other animals to the grave oppression of the soil and the terror of the deer'. Anne Gibbins of Parkend, widow, was also keeping pigs and other animals by which the common pasture in that region was 'overwhelmed'.[210]

These presentments underline links between increasing industrial activity and the use of Forest wastes by those seeking employment opportunities and the possibility of supplementing their income in this way. In 1614, according to the records of the Eyre, nineteen labourers had erected cottages at Ruardean in an 'unknown fee' at the northern edge of the coalfield, while eight were convicted for the same in English Bicknor, to the north-west of the wastes. The overwhelming majority of those presented dwelled towards the northern part of the Forest where much of Dean's industrial activity was located. In the later 1620s, the area had witnessed major disturbances associated with the enclosure of Mailescott Woods. Many presented were labourers who had built cottages in Littledean, an industrial parish to the north-east of the central demesne, and Coleford, which was located on the central coal seam. The majority, though, were

---

[209] CUL, LL.4.7. Proceedings of the Justice of Eyre held for the Forest of Dean at Gloucester Castle, 1634. This set of documents is actually filed under reference CUL, LL.3.10. The session of the Justice Eyre had, apparently intentionally, recorded indeterminate rulings over the status of sheep as commonable beasts and the exact nature of mining rights. These records are now available in an edited volume with useful commentary on the context of the proceedings. See N. Herbert (ed.), *The Forest of Dean Eyre of 1634*, Gloucestershire Record Series (Bristol, 2012).

[210] Ibid.

held accountable for perprestures on the demesne lands themselves. In 1626, twelve woodcutters were presented for their cottages in Staple Edge, an extra-parochial area adjacent to many of the major ironworks. These records document the scale of damage that each of these encroachers had caused to the King's woodland. John Tompkins, for example had destroyed ten horse-loads of wood in building his cottage, William Beard had destroyed eight horse-loads, and Ambrose Goslyn's cottage had taken one wagon-load. During the previous two years these three wood cutters had consumed 5 s, 5 s, and 10 s worth of the King's woodland respectively.[211]

In May and June 1630, the court heard, fifty nine labourers had erected cottages in the northern and central areas of the extra-parochial demesne lands. Many of these had settled in Soudley and Oakwood which were also close to ironworks in the vicinity of Staple Edge. Several were accused of encroaching on the King's soil in Cannop in the Forest, once again in the region between Ruardean and English Bicknor and relatively close to Mailescott Woods. The remainder of the encroachments in Whitecroft, Bream's Eaves, Wet Wood and Park Forge, were concentrated around the heavily-mined area known as the Delves, close to Parkend, a major centre of mining and iron working. This was to be the scene of major disturbances in the 1830s under the leadership of Warren James, the son of a free miner.

In addition to erecting cottages in the same area, Thomas Phillippes, the elder, was presented for keeping a horse or mare pasturing on the demesne lands, John Edwards for grazing two cows, Richard Millard for keeping two

---

[211] Ibid.

horses, and John Weaver for pasturing two mares. Walter Weaver was convicted of keeping three mares or horses without any warrant while several cottagers in the Parkend region were presented explicitly for keeping pigs to the detriment of the royal forest and its game.

While humbler Forest inhabitants appear to have used the 'open' forest to supplement their income, many of the region's minor gentry apparently manipulated the vagaries of local custom to exploit Dean's resources to their own ends. Richard Hankinson, gentleman of Parkend, stands as a useful and representative example. In the 1634 Eyre, Hankinson was convicted of building a dwelling house at Whitemead Park together with a stable and a barn. By 'pretext of these buildings', the court noted, he pastured his pigs and other animals to 'the serious oppression of those living in the Forest'. He was also charged with pasturing a dairy herd of ten cows to the 'king's loss'. The abuses of more powerful industrialising gentry involved in the iron industry, though, were on another scale altogether. As noted, Chapter Four examines these prosecutions more thoroughly. Several of the largest ironmasters in the Forest were held to account at the 1634 Eyre for spoliation of Dean's demesne lands through exceeding the amount of wood due to them under the terms of their respective grants. Sir Basil Brooke, employer of Richard Hankinson, and his business partner George Mynne, were fined 50, 039 li 16 s 8 d, while Sir John Winter was fined 20, 230 li.[212]

Many tenancies were still being disputed later in the 1630s through plans to compensate those who were losing common rights following attempts to

---

[212] CUL, LL.4.7; Herbert, *The Forest of Dean Eyre of 1634.*

introduce tighter regulation after the Eyre. Sir John Bankes, then Attorney General, led action in the Court of the Exchequer to ascertain who was eligible for compensation and who was not. The lengthiest of these suits, which ran from 1638 to 1639, contained extracts from an Act of Parliament which had been made in the 34th year of Edward I's reign. This was the disputed perambulation that was to cause problems for Rodley's residents in the 1660s. It was decided:

> to be allowed unto them and everie of them the benefit and priviledge of one Acte of Parliament bearing date at the Cittie of Westminster the twenty eighth day of May in the Raigne of King Edward the first of Famous memory which hath these words (vizt) Wee will moreover that they which have had common of pasture in the Forrest Before perambulacion made And they which have bin letten of the said common by the perambulacion aforesaid shall have this common of pasture from hence foorth in the Forrest (as largely and freely) as they were wont to have before the perambulacion aforesaid. [213]

Royal grants to 'outsiders' were not the only threat to traditional rights or privileges. During the 1630s they were also threatened by government moves to enclose large areas of the wastes which aimed, as Bankes would have it, at preserving ship timber for the navy. The evidence of several litigants and the conclusions of the Justice Eyre, however, suggest that exploitation by local ironmasters was causing far more damage than grazing animals. Bankes complained that twenty one defendants had

---

[213] TNA, E112/182/196.

unlawfully entered 'closed' lands with 'horses, carts, waynes and axes' and taken away trees that were fit for ship timber under 'their pretended customs' that 'have bene and are used by them by usurpacion and by connivance of his Majesties officers and not by presripcion'.[214] These defendants assured the court that, by 'prescription tyme whereof the memory of man is not too the contrary', they had paid 'certain Rents called Herbage and Pawnage Rents' to 'his majestie and all his royall progenitors and predecessors'. This, they argued, preserved their right to 'herbage in all the open and commonable places of and in the said Forrest' which were 'belonginge to their ancient messuages lands and tenements within the sayd Forrest as hereafter is set forth'. They also told the court that, in a previous Exchequer decree of 1629, the learned counsel of 'his majestie conceaved that the said inhabitants had right to common and necessary bootes'. The court had apparently ruled that any development of the Forest wastes should leave 'sufficient common for the commoners there'. Foremost in this context were rights of pannage for pigs and 'fyrebote of dead and dry wood' but also, 'for the necessary Reparacions and Redificacions of such their Auncient messuages and dwelling houses', they were to be allowed 'Tymber in the said Forrest by the view and delivery of the foresters and Verderers'.

These commoners were asked to make their claim for compensation by stating the origin of their uses, how they held them, and the amount of rent that they paid to maintain them. The point of this legal action, it seems, was to establish the claims which attached to commonable property, thereby

---

[214] Ibid.

firmly distinguishing between formal rights which would be compensated, and informal uses which would not. As in the earlier case, there was to be 'noe common' for new cottages, newly erected houses, or assarted lands. Bankes' original bill implies that these defendants were in a minority when ranged against the local manorial lords and 'greate' freeholders who, perhaps understandably, were in favour of disafforestation which would allow the development and enclosure of their lands. These defendants, apparently from a lower socio-economic group, still clung to the benefits of their 'ancient' rights to common. Among the twenty one, was William Hayward who held ten acres from Edmund or John Berrow as 'parcell of the said manor of Blakeney' in St. Briavels Hundred, and paid 2d annually 'to his Majesty for herbage'. Robert Younge held two messuages in Blakeney, also from the Berrows, and paid 4d annually for herbage. Edward Worgan who held land in Newland paid 6d for herbage, George Harris of Ruardean paid 2d for the same, while John Gwilliam and Thomas Whooper, also of Ruardean, paid 1d and 2d respectively. As will be discussed, the 4,000 acres offered in compensation was disputed as insufficient acreage. It was also claimed that this allocation was in a remote corner of Dean, but that it also failed to take account of many within the forest who exploited the lack of surveillance to graze their stock and collect resources from the land.

Royal grants of the 1620s and 1630s restricted the access of those who were unable to prove their claim to customary rights; these attempts to limit uses of the Forest provided the context for the 1630s and the Skimmington riots. These disturbances, which authorities perceived as part of the Western rebellion between 1628 and 1632, are the subject of Chapter Three. The point, here, has been to establish the material dependence of many in this region on what they understood as customary access to Dean's resources, which in turn explains many aspects of the broad and determined support for the miners' actions. What, though, can we infer about the number of commoners who might have been dependent on the smaller-scale and less formal use of the Forest wastes and demesnes. Who really stood to lose from attempts to 'close' large areas of the forest?

Ecclesiastical probate inventories offer at least a glimpse of more humble inhabitants than the local gentry, large estate holders, and substantial cottagers. Produced by officers attached to the church courts when a person died intestate, they record household possessions and livestock assessed as part of the total estate. Unfortunately, these records do not offer any basis for a sound, quantitative, analysis of these inhabitants as the inventories were recorded sporadically and their survival has been even more subject to chance. Some areas of the Forest are better represented than others, and the same can be said for chronological continuity. They do, however, offer a more qualitative sense of the types of households and activities that characterised different parts of the Forest. Mitcheldean, for example, is notable in these inventories for its almost total lack of 'commonable beasts' or livestock of any kind, probably reflecting its position as the major market town in this part of Dean.[215] The rest of the Forest presents a different picture for the seventeenth and early eighteenth centuries.

An overwhelming number of inventories from the Forest record significant quantities of livestock. Mitcheldean aside, only those whose estate was valued at less than 10 li generally owned no animals. There are exceptions

---

[215] GRO, D149.

even here as George Worgan of Coleford, whose estate was valued at 7li 7s 4d on his death in 1703, left seven store pigs while John Morgan of Woolaston died in 1714 leaving two ponies and a colt which amounted to almost half the value of his estate.[216] 381 inventories survive for the Forest and surrounds between 1600 and 1730. Of these people, thirty seven died leaving an estate of 10 li or less and only six of these left livestock of any sort. A significant proportion of these foresters died leaving an estate estimated at between 10li and 30li. All of these left several animals and, in fact, it was often the ownership of these which had pushed the value of the estate above 10 li, emphasising the importance of the 'open' Forest to those at this economic level. For this group, livestock of one type or another constituted approximately thirty per cent of their estate as valued on average. It is difficult to imagine, in fact, that those with estates of 10 li or less did not view Dean's wastes as a source of dead wood for fuel, herbs, or other dietary supplements. Even, or particularly, among this group with more modest means, then, the enclosure of these lands would presumably have had a significant impact. Walter Partridge of Newland died in 1663 and left an estate valued at 19 li 14 s including two small beasts, eleven sheep and six swine, while Thomas Rives of Coleford died in 1704 leaving one horse, twenty pigs and twenty four sheep which accounted for approximately a third of his 29 li 12 s estate.[217] The inventories are replete with these kinds of examples but, taken as a whole, they also build an

---

[216] GRO, D149/1703/77 & GRO, D149/1714/3.

[217] GRO, D149/1663/227 & GRO, D149/1704/1704/136.

interesting, if impressionistic, picture of variation between different areas of the Forest.

The inventories that survive for Mitcheldean suggest a population employed in service trades. Of the twenty one sets extant for the years between 1600 and 1730, there was a tailor, a baker, a clockmaker, a baker, a saddler, a mason and a cordwainer. Only two of these households were recorded with livestock. Ann Nash left four cows and one heifer in 1670 while John Butcher, the baker, left one heifer and two pigs in 1714. The inventories offer a very different picture of Ruardean and Littledean which bordered the northern periphery of Dean's wastes and were closely associated with the mining industry, iron founding, and related by-employments. Practically every household in both parishes had a variety of livestock counted in the value of the estate. Of the fifty surviving inventories for Ruardean, only six list no livestock which appears to correlate directly with lack of means. Most of those listed held estates of between 10 li and 30 li. There were one or two exceptions such as Thomas Arkell who died in 1715 leaving an estate of 333 li in which were numbered twelve cows, six 'yonge beastes', five 'yearlings', and five horses. Far more typical were foresters like Anthony Smart who left an estate of 18 li 0 s 8 d including three cows, two calves, one heifer, a horse and twelve sheep, or Henry Yearsley who left an estate valued at 18 li 12 s in which were three cows, four young cattle, one mare, four sheep and two small pigs.[218] Two colliers are recorded, and it is likely that these were involved in the trading of coal rather than mining alone. This was reflected in the large numbers of horses, mares, and colts owned by Thomas Harris and Richard Jelfe. Both also held several sheep,

---

[218] GRO, D149.

pigs and other cattle. This contrasts with William Dawes who was a ground collier, working on the periphery of the mining industry. He left nothing but clothes, a bedstead and two pewter dishes when he died in 1700.

Littledean was very similar. Of the twenty five surviving inventories, only six do not mention working or grazing animals. Three free miners are listed as residents of Ruardean. Anthony Andrews died in 1702 and left five horses, two mares, four colts, two calves and three pigs. Thomas Mountjoy died in 1710 leaving seven horses, two cows, and twenty seven sheep. While Richard Wood left no livestock in 1712, the impressionistic evidence of these inventories implies the importance of common usages to those associated with the more industrial aspects of Dean's economy.[219] This is certainly apparent when Ruardean and Littledean are compared to areas with a more diverse or market-based economy such as Mitcheldean.

The commoners of Dean during this period, then, constituted an extremely complex, and often internally competitive, group that depended upon or appropriated 'open' wastes and the associated ideal of timeless rights to common in this royal forest. The evidence suggests that, while the claim to ancient custom was an ideal in many senses, the usages implied in this view of the forest were materially crucial to industrialising gentry, more 'middling' farmers, those who claimed formal rights attaching to property tenure through manorial custom, and poor labouring cottagers who exploited the lax management of wastes to supplement their income. Very

---

[219] GRO, D149.

significantly, of course, the free-mining community had a vested interest in maintaining an 'open' Forest.

Seventeenth-century legal records and inventories offer plentiful evidence that Dean's free miners were not only dependent on customary mining rights. They also claimed other usages such as estovers and grazing rights. It seems that this generated a strong community of interest between them and other groups in this complex and often contradictory forest commonalty. A 1619 Exchequer bill questioned Baynham Throckmorton's ability to regulate customary wood allowances in his capacity as Constable of St. Briavels Hundred. The plaintiff, Sir Henry Yelverton complained about the amount of wood that had been removed under 'a pretended custom' but seemed particularly concerned about that taken by free miners. Yelverton called for increased supervision, suggesting that:

> according to an ancient Custom Claymed by them in that behalf that befor any tymber be taken by them for the purposes and uses aforesaid they should shewe their need and make theire demands thereof at the speache or Forty daies court to be holden for the said Forrest and when anie such demands have been made of tymber as aforesaid.

Throckmorton responded by denying that he 'hath not allowed timber to foresters, strangers & contrey men who have no right to it ... without restraining or punishing them'.[220] Both miners and a wide variety of commoners held a vested interest in maintaining traditional rights that were tied to the idea of an 'open and cominable' forest.

---

[220] TNA, E112/82/343.

The community of interest would have been consolidated by the miners' need to maintain an 'open' forest in order that they might exercise their right to mine in any part of Dean's demesne lands except for churchyards and orchards. Thomas Wallington, a free miner whose evidence appeared earlier, made this plain to the Exchequer court in 1637. He claimed that they:

> May digge and sinke pitts for the finding and discovering of Oare and Coales in any free houlders grounds within the premisses of the sayd hundred and sayth that hee this deponent hath not been interrupted or debarred by any free houlder from his worke in any such pitts wherein he hath laboured to finde Oare & Coales.[221]

There is much evidence to suggest that miners depended on estovers and grazing rights as much as, if not more than, other commoners in Dean. Ultimately, the miners' need to sink pits anywhere that they found coal or iron ore preserved the idea of an 'open' royal forest and its associated privileges. This enabled them to draw wide support in defending their occupational custom as this, by definition, worked to maintain the traditional access of others. Chapter Three explores the dynamics of this broadly-supported and tenacious resistance.

---

[221] TNA, E134/13&14Chas1/Hil16.

Chapter Three

Protest, social drama and popular memory in the Forest of Dean, c.1550-1640

It may be said in conclusion that the diviner occupies a central position with reference to several fields of social and cultural relationships. He acts as a mechanism of redress and social adjustment in the field of local descent groups, since he locates areas and points of tension in their contemporary structures. Furthermore, he exonerates or accuses individuals in those groups in terms of a system of moral norms. Since he operates in emotionally charged situations such norms are restated in a striking and memorable fashion. Thus he may be said to play a vital role in upholding tribal morality. Moral law is more vividly made known through its breach. Finally, the diviner's role is pivotal to the system of rituals of affliction and antiwitchcraft/sorcery rituals, since he decides what kinds of rituals should be performed in a given instance, when it should be performed, and sometimes who should perform it. From the Ndembu point of view, the diviner is a man who redresses breaches in the social structure, enunciates the moral law, detects those who secretly and malevolently transgress it, and prescribes remedial action both on the social-structural and cultural levels.

V. W. Turner, *Dramas, Fields and Metaphors: Symbolic Action in Human Society* (New York, 1974), 241.

I 'The wild humours of those Robin Hoodes'

Victor Turner's work on social drama in the Ndembu culture of Zambia offers significant insights into the leadership of popular protest in pre-industrial England. His analysis of the diviner's role in indentifying, articulating and redressing a breach of moral law bears important analogies with the organisation of popular resistance in the Forest of Dean. This chapter brings Turner's notion of social drama to bear on the free miners' role in redressing breaches of custom during the early seventeenth century. These miners, it has been established, were part of a wider community that had traditionally depended on a complex set of common rights accommodated by royal forest management. As discussed, the seventeenth century witnessed a two-pronged assault on this forest custom from both changing Crown policies and novel opportunities for private projectors, several of whom were members of the local gentry. These encroachments not only impeded the exercise of mining custom, but also disrupted common rights to grazing and fuel. As foresters, the miners were as dependent on access to these resources as their right to mine for coal and ore. Two of them, Christopher Bond and Thomas Worgan, were arrested following the 1612 disturbances which are discussed below. As they languished in the Gatehouse jail in Westminster, their plea for an expeditious hearing centred on concerns that 'their harvest & other affairs were lying all to losse & spoile for want of their libertie'.[222] This reliance, and their symbolic position within the forest commonalty, it is argued,

---

[222] TNA, SP 14/69 f. 32.

foreshadows their heavy involvement in organising resistance to the enclosure and privatisation of forest wastes.

The following pages explore the conjunction of protest, folklore, occupational identities and popular memory. In a context of national transformation, this nexus can reveal how the remembrance of landscape and labour governed the way this local community understood itself and its place in the world. In Turner's terms, the miners' position left them ideally situated to recognise, articulate and redress a breach of moral law. Two episodes that occurred in the early seventeenth century are the primary foci. The first disturbance, in 1612, was the consequence of a royal grant to the Earl of Pembroke which allowed him novel and exclusive access to resources from an area of Dean's woodlands. The 'Skimmington riots' of 1628-31 followed a similar pattern of resistance when Sir Edward Villiers, brother of court favourite George, was granted possession of Mailescott Woods, an area towards the industrial north of the Forest. This chapter builds on Chapter Two, initially sketching the specific context in which the common rights of royal forests became subject to concerted scrutiny. It then moves to a dramaturgical and sociological reading of the two larger-scale riots provoked by this competition for resources. Both of these episodes are notable for their expressions of folkloric language and performance. D.R. Woolf argues for the declining influence of folklore in the language of use rights after 1600. The reasons for this, he expands:

lie not only in changing attitudes to historical evidence, but also in the widening division between learned and popular cultures in the seventeenth and early eighteenth centuries.[223]

During the first episode, rioters were described by the Earl of Northampton as 'Robin Hoodes' while the second series of disturbances were led by John Skymington, a figure that took his name from a local shaming of south-west England. These incidents were very different in nature, the former an expression of elite anxieties while the latter represented a popular call to local and traditional solidarities, but both seem to have emerged from the epistemological world described by Woolf.

Taking folklore as a shared symbolic resource which can articulate mythologised and simplified versions of local histories, this chapter explores early modern traditions of protest in two ways. It analyses what the first incident suggests about the way that those in authority perceived the 'forest cultures' of England at the beginning of the seventeenth century, while considering what the second series of episodes can reveal about popular ideologies of protest in seventeenth-century England. In short, this chapter explores relations between collective action and shared material experience in early modern Dean.

Chapter Two described an early-seventeenth century assault on custom in the Forest of Dean. The consequent insecurity over long-established rights forms the backdrop to the Earl of Pembroke's royal grant in 1611. Under the terms of his grant, Pembroke was allowed 12,000 cords of wood and

---

[223] D. R. Woolf, 'The "Common Voice": History, Folklore and Oral Tradition in Early Modern England', *Past & Present*, 120 (1988), 26-52, 27.

£33.6s.8d per annum towards enclosing this area for twenty-two years. Nobody was to take ore, coal, wood, timber or cinders from the Forest without the earl's permission.[224] This encroached upon local custom at all levels of the social scale and, quite predictably, generated considerable tensions in Dean. In 1612, the Earl of Northampton, as lord lieutenant of Gloucestershire, reported the disorder caused by Pembroke's grant. This mining and cutting, he said, had caused 'some fifteen desperate knaves' to set fire to piles of cordwood, after which they danced around the fire crying 'God save the King'.[225] He explained that:

> they still walk the wood with weapons and oft I hear weak shot; they call their neighbours cowards for not assisting them; they give out that they look for more help; the Justice has given order for their apprehension but the country favour them [226]

Northampton stressed the benefits of local gentry regaining control from the 'odious' Pembroke. These forest residents, he suggested, were more capable of tempering the 'wild humores of those Robin Hoodes'.[227]

---

[224] N. M. Herbert (ed.), *A History of the County of Gloucester: Volume V. Bledisloe Hundred, St Briavels Hundred, The Forest of Dean*, (Oxford, 1996), 363.

[225] TNA, SP14/70/49.

[226] By his use of the term 'country', I assume that Northampton referred to the local plebeian population.

[227] TNA, SP14/70/49.

Roger Manning and Cyril Hart agree that these 'Robin Hoodes' were probably members of the free mining community.[228] As mentioned, two of those arrested for these disturbances, Christopher Bond and Thomas Worgan, were certainly free miners. An Exchequer suit of 1613-14 lends further credence to this interpretation. An order issued by the court in January 1613 had dealt a potentially devastating blow to the mining community, confirming their custom only 'of charity and grace, and not of right'.[229] The Earl of Pembroke's complaint suggests that the miners' immediate reaction was to continue working. He was aggrieved that the miners had 'by pretence of title of common and of Estovers in the said Forrest' and directly against the terms of his grant, 'taken libertie to themselves to cut down, waste and spoil his Maiesties wood ... at their wills and pleasures'. Worse still, they had 'wrongfully entered the said Forrest' and 'unlawfully ... digged and gotten great store of iron mynes, ore and sinders'. Pembroke suggested that iron and coal had been 'taken and carried to the rivers of Severn and Wye to be transported into the realm of Ireland and to divers ironworks and other places without the licence or consent of your Suppliant and against his will'.[230]

The 'Mynors' replied with a comprehensive account of their ancient rights which, they asserted, had 'been allowed unto them .... by all the time

---

[228] Manning, *Village Revolts*; C. Hart, *The Forest of Dean: New History, 1550-1818* (Stroud, 1995).

[229] TNA, E126/1, fol. 270 r.

[230] TNA, E112/83/411.

146

whereof the memory of man is not to the contrary' and had also 'been allowed before the Justice in Eyre and also at the Courts of Justice holden in King Edward the Thirds tyme before the Constable of the said Forrest and Steward of the Castle of St Brevells'. In more immediate defence, they countered accusations that they had been evading the terms of the grant to sell their product in Ireland, explaining that they 'would starve if they were to rely on the custom of Pembroke's works'. These free miners claimed that they were:

> able by their labours to get sufficient iron ore and myne for the complainants works within half a year which the complainants forges and mills will hardly spende and work out within one year after as the other half year your defendants and the rest of the mynors shall be voyde of worke and thereby have not means to maintain themselves and their charges.[231]

Pembroke's royal grant caused considerable disruption to Dean's traditional customary practices. The 'timeless' custom which had allowed miners to seek coal and ore in different parts of the royal demesne lands was incompatible with the Earl's attempts to control mining and the flow of trade in and out of the forest. The occupational flexibility and independence which had apparently been theirs for centuries was stifled by the imposition of Pembroke's directives. This was not only a concern in respect of their occupation, the miners pleaded, but their families and dependants were also endangered. The grant thus had a social as well as an economic impact, as its implications extended into households and domestic contexts.

---

[231] Ibid.

Brian Manning interprets Northampton's statement as a suggestion that the 'miners of Dean were no better than 'Robin Hoodes".[232] While there is little doubt that Northampton was genuinely concerned about this disorder, evidence suggests that he might actually have been making a more subtle comment on the shared culture of these miners and local resident gentry. In doing so, Northampton referenced a tradition which implied the co-operation of these two groups in preserving forest custom.

Mark Ormrod suggests that the Robin Hood legends portray the forested areas of late medieval England as regions which challenged the spatial dominance of monarchic authority.[233] In the 'greenwood' royal authority depended, at least in part, on the negotiation of obscure local power structures. These tales were noted for the versatility of their eponymous hero, providing those at all levels of late medieval and early modern society with entertainment and a complex means of self-reflection and legitimation. Woven from various strands of oral and written tales originating in the twelfth or thirteenth centuries, these stories defy sterile distinctions often drawn between popular and elite cultures.[234] There is no doubt that the Earl of Northampton was familiar with the tradition represented in the tales. Lower on the social scale, *The Cobler of Caunterburie* (1590) recalled 'olde

---

[232] Manning, *Village Revolts*, 276.

[233] W. M. Ormrod, 'Law in the Landscape: Criminality, Outlawry and Regional Identity in Late Medieval England' in A. Musson (ed.), *Boundaries of the Law: Geography, Gender and Jurisdiction in Medieval and Early Modern Europe* (Aldershot, 2005), 7.

wives that wedded themselves to the profound histories of Robin Hood'.[235] The sixteenth-century editor of a widely circulated medical text noted that 'every boy and knave has access to these books, reading them as openly as the tales of Robin Hood'.[236] A. J. Pollard confirms that 'a most significant moment in the development of the Robin Hood story was the drawing of five of these separate tales together in the fifteenth century into a compilation called the *Gest of Robyn Hode*, in which a single connecting narrative was supplied'.[237]

This narrative was exemplified in a 1590 broadsheet, the *Iest of Robin Hood*.[238] A forest yeoman here, as in other renditions, Robin was a familiar

---

[234] W. J. Ong, *Orality and Literacy: The Technologizing of the Word,* London and New York, 2000; A. Fox, *Oral and Literate Culture in England, 1500-1700* (Oxford, 2000); S. Niditch, *Oral World and Written Word: Ancient Israelite Literature* (Louisville, Kentucky, 1996); M. Harris, *Carnival and other Christian festivals: folk theology and folk performance* (Austin, 2003); A. Fox and D. Woolf (eds.), *The spoken word: Oral culture in Britain, 1500-1850* (Manchester and New York, 2002); J. Goody, *The Interface between the Written and the Oral* (Cambridge, 1987); J. Goody *The Logic of Writing and the Organisation of Society* (Cambridge, 1989); A. Wood, 'Custom and the social organisation of writing in early modern England', *Transactions of the Royal Historical Society*, 6th series, 9 (1999), 257-69.

[235] Fox, *Oral and Literate Culture in England,* 40-2.

[236] Thomas Raynalde, (ed. and trans.), *The Byrth of Mankynde, Otherwyse Named the Womans Booke, Newly set forth, corrected and augmented* (London, 1545), f. D verso.

[237] A. J. Pollard, *Imagining Robin Hood: the late-medieval stories in historical context* (Abingdon, 2004), 4.

[238] *A Merry Iest of Robin Hood, and his life, with a new play for to be plaied in May-games. Very pleasant and full of pastime.* (London, 1590), URL: http://gateway.proquest.com/openurl?ctx_ver=Z39.88-2003&res_id=xri:eebo&rft_id=xri:eebo:image:17475 Date accessed: 22/5/2010.

figure to both gentle and common audiences. His expertise with bow and arrow exemplified the martial training and hunting that characterised both groups. The *Iest* assumes the right of these foresters to use violence in achieving the aims of local justice. The language of the ballad narrates their encounters in terms comparable to chivalric codes of honour. As if describing a rout in battle, the text relates how Robin's men 'drew out their bright swords, that were so sharp and keene, and laid it on the Sheriffes men, and drove them down by deene'. This code of honourable violence against outsiders evokes more common ground between elite and popular cultures in the forested 'dark corners' of the land. It is widely accepted that popular protest in this period was shaped by 'forms of militia organisation, in which every man aged between 16 and 60 was legally required to take part'.[239] The *Iest* represents Robin and his men as a well-trained local band. The text notes that 'Robin ... bent a good Bowe' and the story is littered with references to training and discipline. Comparing the royal retinue with Robin's own following, the king even reflects privately that 'His men are more at his bidding then my men be at mine'.[240]

These tightly organised and well-armed local militias were not without precedent. In his analysis of Jack Cade's revolt, for instance, Montgomery Bohna describes the expression of violence grounded in a customary right

---

[239] A. Wood, 'Collective Violence, Social Drama and Rituals of Rebellion in Late Medieval and Early Modern England' in S. Carroll (ed.), *Cultures of Violence: interpersonal violence in historical perspective,* (Basingstoke and New York, 2007), 99-116, 101.

[240] *A Merrie Iest of Robin Hood and his life* (London, 1590).

to bear arms as a way of registering political opinion.[241] The foresters of Dean were extremely well armed and trained during the early sixteenth century. The military muster for Gloucestershire in 1522 listed weapons presented within St. Briavels Hundred. The foresters themselves produced 121 daggers, 112 swords, 114 glaives, thirty-one sallets, eighteen Forest Bills, twenty-two hauberks, thirteen horses, sixteen harness, seven horse and harness combinations, eight shields, five gorgets and one lance.[242] More than two-thirds of those listed possessed weaponry, while these figures only include those adult males deemed fit for military service. Early-seventeenth century court records are replete with evidence of armoury in the Forest.[243] Even allowing for the rhetorical nature of Star Chamber proceedings, the *Iest*'s representation of organised and violent resistance within forest communities apparently reflects the extent of weaponry in the late medieval and early modern Forest of Dean.

Compared with the experience of miners in Dean, this fellowship of 'merry men' seems closer to an idealisation of the social relations that underpinned customary usages in the Forest. These folk tales represented a shared culture comprised of commoners and local gentry in the forested regions of England, Robin and his men embodying the intermediate type of sylvan yeoman or artisan. As will be explored, this idealised and mutually

---

[241] M. Bohna, 'Armed Force and Civic Legitimacy in Jack Cade's Revolt, 1450', *English Historical Review*, 118 (2003), 563-82.

[242] R. W. Hoyle (ed.), *The Military Survey of Gloucestershire 1522* (Stroud, 1993).

[243] For examples of this see TNA, STAC8/156/15, TNA, STAC8/298/13 and TNA, STAC8/178/27.

supportive hierarchy was central to the symbolism evoked by Dean's Skimmington riots of the late 1620s.[244] Relations between the commonalty and gentry of the forest regions were far from convivial, particularly in the early seventeenth century. Miners were apparently as central to this forest culture as the folkloric Robin Hood was to early modern mythologies of the 'greenwood'. These legends vividly evoked the obscurity of the 'greenwood' from an outsider's perspective. Unlike the Sheriff, we are told that Robin and Little John know the paths 'each one'. In similar fashion, the free-mining community symbolised local knowledge of this region and its taskscape. They occupied a key cultural position which, as argued in Chapter One, articulated memories of laboring and living in this landscape, thus offering an effective focus for attempts to preserve this traditional way of life.

Tales of Robin Hood circulated traditionally among all levels of late medieval and early modern English society, mythologising the fierce localism and collective mentalities of forest communities. Northampton apparently thought that local gentlemen best understood the assertive popular communalism that had been provoked by the crown grant to Pembroke. The resistance of foresters and local relations between gentry and commoners were ostensibly grounded in a shared culture of collective use-rights that were incompatible with the exclusive property of the 'private man'. Conflict between these opposing world-views was to erupt more extensively in the late 1620s. Northampton's folkloric appropriation suggests much about elite concerns over social relations in the Forest

---

[244] D. Underdown, *Revel, Riot and Rebellion: Popular Politics and Culture in England, 1603-1660* (New York, 1987).

during the early seventeenth century. Elite and vernacular interests coincided in the later Skimmington riots of 1628-31 in the Forest, underlining the interaction and conflict between local gentry, the forest commonalty and parties viewed as outsiders.

II The Skimmington riots

The Skimmington riots serve as another reminder that ideological opposition to 'improvement' was very much grounded in the material conditions of Forest life.[245] The methods of production which characterised many improving projects in seventeenth-century England implied fundamentally different social structures to those in the Forest. Communities dominated by the large market farmers of the lowland arable regions, for example, tended towards nucleated settlement. In this type of village, land holders and wage labourers often lived in close proximity and, thus, interacted with their neighbours on a daily basis.[246] In many of these areas, higher concentrations of material resources in fewer hands allowed for production on a scale which signalled a significant break with smallholding traditions. This change in scale, coupled with the privatisation of land ownership and the alienation of many smallholders from their land,

---

[245] For the sake of clarity in this chapter, I will refer to the unrest in the Forest of Dean from 1628-31 as the Skimmington riots, but the leader as John Williams, also known as Skymington, in accordance with how he is described in contemporary documents. The ritual itself will be referenced as skimmington or riding skimmington.

[246] K. Wrightson, and D. Levine, *Poverty and Piety in an English Village. Terling, 1525-1700* (Oxford, 2001).

meant that an increasingly proletarianised workforce often lived in concentrated settlements that suited the requirements of increasingly wealthy large landholders and farmers. Joan Thirsk describes the open communities of some arable districts. She suggests that they complemented the 'closed' villages, providing a labour pool for the wealthier farmers that inhabited the latter.[247] In these material conditions, labourers no longer needed to live on the land for these areas to be agriculturally productive. Their terms of employment and habitation were largely tied to the sale of labour rather than any meaningful tenure of the fields that they worked.

By contrast, Thirsk outlines more traditional household-based industries of the pastoral regions, explaining that:

> Pasture farmers lived in isolated farms and hamlets as well as in villages, and the population was thus more widely scattered than in the arable lowlands. Manorial courts could not exercise close surveillance over their tenants, and tenants generally held their land by freer tenures. In many of these dispersed areas of settlement, moreover, it is noticeable that the population consisted of one class only; the poor and rich did not always live cheek by jowl, as in the nucleated villages.[248]

There is evidence of considerable in-migration to the Forest of Dean during the late sixteenth and seventeenth centuries, particularly in regions such as

---

[247] Thirsk, *Seventeenth-Century Agriculture and Social Change*. 165; Underdown, *Revel, Riot and Rebellion*.

[248] Thirsk, *Seventeenth-Century Agriculture* , 167.

Ruardean and its immediate vicinity, an area which was rich in mining and associated industries. Many landless and vagrant poor were thus attracted by the extensive commons and wastes of these more pastoral, forested areas. The coincidence of in-migrating poor and rising coal prices, suggests that migrants were encouraged as much by opportunities for employment in Dean's expanding extractive and manufacturing industries. Thirsk notes that pastoral regions were usually characterised by small-scale family farmers and that 'the common pastures were a community asset available to all' but also that 'another key to the success of this way of life' were the additional methods available to supplement a living.[249] Records suggest that these additional methods were prevalent in the Forest of Dean.

Dean supported many employment opportunities related to the coal and iron industries. The 1608 survey of Able and Sufficient Men in the Forest lists miners, colliers, oresmiths, apprentices, nailers, cutlers and pinners as well as many other occupations derived from exploitation of the Forest's wood and timber.[250] As described in Chapter One, this activity was recorded throughout Ruardean in related place names such as 'Turner's Tump', 'Cinder Hill', 'Nailbridge', 'Smith's Way' and 'The Pludds'.[251] Thirsk warns against regarding such industrial occupations as by-employment,

[249] Ibid., 170.

[250] J. Smith, *The names and Surnames of all the able and sufficient men in body fitt for his Ma(ies)ty's service in the warss, within the county of Gloucester ... 1608* (Gloucester, 1980).

[251] Herbert, *VCH, Vol. V.*, 232-3. TNA, MR 179.

arguing that 'they were not accidental or subsidiary, secondary or a miserable makeshift. They were an integral part of the pastoral way of life'.[252] It would appear that the large numbers of poorer inhabitants in the Forest did not represent a group which had been entirely alienated from their means of production. These areas could sustain large communities of poorer, landless inhabitants through trades and occupations which did not entail direct subordination to wealthier employers. Records also imply relatively free access to pasture on Dean's commons and wastes, conditions which indicate a relatively autonomous and assertive commonalty. Furthermore, these groups, alongside the miners, depended upon common access to 'open' forest and the various resources which, protesters claimed, had been regarded as collective property since 'time out of mind'. It was this 'open' forest that was under threat by royal grants to Villiers and other court favourites.

At 10am on the morning of 25 March 1631, Robert Bridges sat at home with his family in Bicknor, an industrial village towards the north-east of the Forest of Dean. He described how their house was marched upon by a group of inhabitants from their village and from Stanton, Newland and Coleford. The band numbered at least five hundred and 'did march with two Drummes two Coulers and one Fife and in a warlike and outragious manner did assemble themselves together Armed with gunnes, pykes, halberds and other weapons'.[253] After threatening to 'pull downe Bridges'

---

[252] Thirsk, *Seventeenth-Century Agriculture and Social Change*, 172.

[253] TNA, SP16/188/20.

156

howse', they 'went into the ground called Mailescott, and there did extreamly beate certain Colliers being in the said Grounds and one other person being a Strainger'.[254] Bridges was an agent of the Villiers family, favourites of the Caroline court who, in 1625, had been granted mineral rights in Mailescott Woods, an area of Dean adjoining Bicknor. Disregarding 'timeless' Forest custom, this royal grant aroused great anger. While aspects of the disturbances were violent, there were no fatalities and the so-called rioters were apparently careful to maintain order in their 'ranks'.

Under the terms of the 1625 grant, Sir Edward Villiers gained 500 acres known as Mailescott woods in the Forest of Dean 'for good services done'. [255] The grant of Forest resources to an outsider would have been an unpopular proposition in any situation, as was evident from the disturbances that followed Pembroke's grant. Yet Villiers' grant was particularly inflammatory. Not only was it made to an outsider to be 'held as of his Mannor of Eastgreenewiche'[256] in Kent but, upon the death of Sir Edward, the land fell under the administration of Sir Giles Mompesson who was acting on behalf of Lady Barbara Villiers. Mompesson was a projector who had 'acquired a very evil reputation' through what his adversaries

---

[254] Ibid.

[255] TNA, SP16/257/94.

[256] Ibid.

described as his 'reckless audacity'. [257] He appears to have wasted no time in enclosing the land at Mailescott and setting men to work in digging or sinking coal pits.

An Exchequer decree of 1628 further granted quiet possession of Mailescott to Lady Villiers and had, significantly, distinguished formal rights related to property tenure from the less formal custom of the propertyless.[258] Privileging exclusive ownership attached to the enclosure of common land, this decree hardened lines of division between private interest and common right in the Forest. A large proportion of this community stood to lose essential resources if the 'open' forest were to be enclosed. Once again, evidence implies that resistance to this privatization was led by free miners.

In direct violation of the 1628 decree, a number of inhabitants of the forest continued to mine and to pasture cattle on this land. Buchanan Sharp notes that at their prosecution:

all of the defendants, as inhabitants of the hundred of St Briavels, asserted that they had the right to common of pasture *and the right to mine in the wastes of the forest* ... [stating] flatly in their answer to the Attorney General that they would not be bound by an Exchequer

[257] S. Lee, 'Mompesson, Sir Giles (1583/4 - 1651 x 63)', rev. Sean Kelsey, *Oxford Dictionary of National Biography*. URL: http://www.oxforddnb.com Date accessed: 14/1/2008.

[258] TNA, E125/4, fols. 50-54 & E112/179/28.

decree that recognised *the right of the King and his grantees* to enclose Mailescott and other lands in Dean.[259]

Mailescott and other lands named in the 1628 decree had their enclosures destroyed in the riots that ensued, during protests associated with the loss of mining rights in this part of the Forest. Before the enclosures could proceed, Lady Villiers had to make one concession – to 'permit the mining of iron ore in Mailescott Woods as freely as before the decree of 1628'. This concession did not bring these disturbances to a close, but it seems that once the miners' demands had been satisfied only minor riots persisted.[260] This bears two interpretations; either anger at the enclosures had dissipated or, more likely, the mining community had been the organisational focus of larger scale resistance. The larger-scale incident at Bridges' house is significant in this context. Among the marching group was John Williams, who was also known as the mysterious Skymington, an alias that appears to have held great regional significance. His occupation was recorded as 'labourer', a description which was interchangeable locally with the term miner.

During March and April 1631 in Dean, enclosed lands were thrown open by large numbers of rioting commoners led by John Williams. In 1612, the Forest's 'Robin Hoods' had been careful to accompany their 'disorderly' actions with shouts of 'God Save the King', thus aligning themselves with

---

[259] B. Sharp, *In Contempt of All Authority: Rural Artisans and Riot in the West of England, 1586-1660* (Berkeley, 1980), 206. My emphasis.

[260] Sharp, *In Contempt of All Authority,* 206.

the best interests of the Jacobean commonwealth. In 1631, the direct interests of the Crown together with local landowners and industrialists were generally avoided which further suggests efforts to maintain the legitimacy of these actions.

The level of support for those involved in the 1631 disturbances was clearly demonstrated by fierce animosity borne towards those responsible for Williams' arrest. Williams was 'finally captured sometime in March of 1632 by William Cowse, one of the King's forest officers'.[261] On Sunday 8th April, both Cowse and his accomplice William Rolles, were leaving church in Newland when they were assaulted by a large group of parishioners. During this affray, both pistols belonging to Cowse and his contingent were discharged. Justices of the Peace, Sir Richard Catchmay, Sir Robert Cooke knight and Charles Bridgeman esquire, professed that:

> Wee coulde by no means discover what was the first occasion of the Affraye, whether the under sorte of people were provoked by seeing those twoe persons in the Company of Mr Rolls & Mr Cowse whoe had done the good service of apprahending him whome they commonly called Skymington, or that they were provoked by these wordes uttered by Mr Rolls cominge out of Church (where are the Hawkins-es the Ryoters).[262]

These Justices were unsure whether the anger of parishioners had been provoked merely by the presence of Williams' captors or by the fact that

---

[261] TNA, SP16/188/20.

[262] TNA, SP16/215/57.

they had attended church in hope of apprehending more suspects as they worshipped. Whatever the precise catalyst, the arrest of Williams was evidently a deeply unpopular act. Cowles and Rolles implicitly acknowledged this, arriving at church prepared to defend themselves against the parishioners of Newland. According to the local Justices, these parishioners had simply 'repayred to Church in an orderly manner to heare devine service without any expectacion of meeting as is Conceived with Mr Rolls Mr Cowse & the rest of their Companye'.[263]

The anger in this parish suggests a keenly felt sense of collective interest in this forest community. The difficulty encountered by forest authorities also points to the neighbourly relations that informed the moral economy of Dean, certainly when this way of life seemed to be threatened.[264] In November 1631, the sheriff of Gloucestershire wrote to the Attorney General describing problems entailed in recruiting the local population to his searches for 'John Williams called by the name of Skymington.[265] The opening passage of the sheriff's account is worth quoting at length. Upon receiving a warrant from local Justices:

---

[263] Ibid.

[264] E. P. Thompson 'The moral economy of the English crowd in the eighteenth century', *Past & Present*, 50 (1971), 76-136.

[265] TNA, SP16/203/36.

to apprehend some of the late Riotors in the Forrest of Deane wheruppon my undershereife with 120tie men by me provided, passed over the River of Sevearne late in the night with an Intent to take the said offendrs, and for that purpose watching all night, repaired (before the breake of the day) towards the howse of one John Williams called by the name of Skymington, thinkinge to have caught him in his bedd, But beinge discovered by some of the Inhabitants of that place, they only apprehended two of the offendors, and soe retired for that tyme, which with a woman brought in at the next Sessions, was all the Service could be done upon that warrant.[266]

As with the Robin Hood legends, neither the sheriff nor his men were comfortable searching in this terrain. Faced with the opaque nature of this region, the sheriff noted that due its landscape of 'hills, woods myne pitts and colepitts where they dwell the apprehending of them becomes very difficult and must be effected only by policy and never by strength'. Until the efforts of Cowle and Rolls bore fruit a few months later, it seems that this policy was unsuccessful. The sheriff ordered a 'Callinge together of the Trained bondes of the Forrest' in the hope that he could arrest those suspects known to be trained soldiers. He also tried to entice Williams' neighbours with the promise of a large reward, but the foresters were reluctant to betray the leaders of these riots, often tipping them off in advance of his searches. The sheriff complained that he had searched from 'place to place that day, parte of that night, and the next day where the

---

[266] Ibid.

Riotors dwell', but upon arriving at their respective homes he had been informed that they had fled into Herefordshire and Monmouthshire.[267]

The symbolism of these riots suggests much about solidarities and conflicts within this forest community. As rioters attempted to pull down the fences erected by Mompesson, they acted:

> by sound of drum and ensigns in most rebellious manner, carrying a picture or statue apparelled like Mompesson and with great noise and clamour threw it into the coalpits that the said Sir Giles had digged.[268]

Given the nature of these disturbances, it is no surprise that the leader or leaders were commonly referred to as 'John' or 'Lady Skymington'. This action was, it seems, was framed in the idiom of popular shaming rituals.[269]

David Underdown notes that a skimmington was also 'a ritual action against the chosen target: to 'ride skimmington' was to take part in a demonstration against the skimmington in the pejorative sense'. Like the folk hero Robin Hood, however, the name skimmington had a variety of meanings within early modern popular culture. It could refer to the target of a shaming ritual,

---

[267] Ibid.

[268] Ibid.

[269] For further work on the symbolism of early modern popular crowd action, see J. Walter, 'Gesturing at authority: deciphering the gestural code of early modern England', in M. J. Braddick (ed.), *The Politics of Gesture: Historical Perspectives,* Past and Present, Supplement, 4 (Oxford, 2009), 96-127; D. Underdown, "But the shows of their street': Civic Pageantry and Charivari in a Somerset Town, 1607', *Journal of British Studies,* 50, 1 (2011), 4-23.

the act itself or, as in the case of Dean, to the leadership of a protest. This ambivalence allowed separate risings to subsume themselves as part of a wider and more general action and, importantly, it obscured identities. The rioters in Dean, it seems, were riding Skimmington against the particular interests of the Villiers family. Invoking customary social roles, the Skimmington rioters foregrounded a hierarchy of use-rights that had been jeopardised by the 'improvement' of the forest. In this hierarchy, different social groups had always occupied different rungs but they were, at least, on the same ladder. As the 1628 decree concerning Mailescott drew a distinction between informal usages and private property rights, so too did it drive a wedge through this sylvan culture. The skimmington seems to have been an appropriate response to this violation of Forest custom. Through the ritual grammar of the skimmington, the rioters highlighted a breach of customary norms represented by the increasing interest of outsiders in the regulation and ownership of forest resources. Rachel Bonney remarks that anthropologists have 'recognised the importance in 'primitive' societies of folklore as an educational tool for the transmission of cultural traditions, values, and histories from one generation to the next'.[270] Just as the Robin Hood legends could imply a behavioural model for every inhabitant, these rituals also articulated a particular version of Forest history, a tradition steeped in paternalism, common right, shared labour and a fierce tenacity in defending this lifestyle. This simplification obscured much conflict, but it was an ideal that implicitly called upon local gentry to do their duty and stop the Villiers family's attempts to dominate collective resources. There is

---

[270] R. A. Bonney, 'Teaching Anthropology Through Folklore', *Anthropology & Education Quarterly*, 16, 4 Teaching Anthropology (1985), 265-270.

much evidence to suggest that early modern labouring people thought of rebellion as a collective act of petitioning.[271] Local gentry were, however, involved in seventeenth-century attempts to 'improve' the Forest. Perhaps, however, they were still regarded as the most effective group to petition in the cause of preserving Forest custom.

The customary version of Forest history was heavily idealised but, articulated in the form of the folk hero Skymington, it was flexible and could, therefore, accommodate contradictory interests in the cause of fostering broad solidarities. Chapter One examined Barthes' work on the open character of mythological speech which describes a 'formless, unstable, nebulous condensation' ideally suited to appropriation as it only gains unity and coherence through its specific application or function.[272] The mythologised folk hero offers a simplification of complex relationships and histories. Skymington presented an ideal, a flexible tradition which could look beyond the antagonisms of everyday forest life to garner support for collective action. This loose folk memory was incompatible with the strict historical record of private property ownership represented by equity decrees, deeds and other written documents. The economic and cultural distinctions between common rights and private property were tied to different ways of seeing forest history which were held up in relief by the symbolism and actions of rioters in early-seventeenth century Dean.

---

[271] Wood, 'Collective violence', 109.

[272] R. Barthes, *Mythologies: Selected and translated from the French by Annette Lavers* (London, 2000), 110.

Sociologists have highlighted the dramaturgical and performative aspect of everyday actions. Erving Goffman posited that people in a social context 'dramatize' their actions to manage the way that they are interpreted by others. Central here is his concept of 'front' which he explains as a range of standardized expressive mechanisms that people adopt in suggesting a generalised and intersubjective view of situations. For Goffman, 'front' relates primarily to 'setting', or the spatial location of action, while the notion of 'personal front' refers to the 'manner' and 'appearance' of performance.[273] The two concepts explain ways that action can suggest a generalised reality, emphasising the most desirable aspects of behaviour. These insights offer useful ways of interpreting the significance of John Williams' adopted alias, his cultural position as a free miner, and the ritual symbolism of the Skimmington protest against Bridges and Mompesson in the contested area of Mailescott Woods.

During the first years of Charles I's personal rule, Underdown suggests, 'Skimmington briefly becomes a folk hero, similar to Robin Hood or to 'Captain Cobbler' and 'Captain Pouch' in earlier peasant risings, regarded as able to redress all sorts of popular grievances.[274] The records of sixteenth- and seventeenth-century protest give us the names of many figures, real and imagined, who appear to have performed the twin function of drawing support for, and declaring the cause of, popular risings. Many of these famously assumed the rank of captain. The Lincolnshire Uprising and

---

[273] E. Goffman, *The Presentation of Self in Everyday Life* (London, 1990), 30-34.

[274] Underdown, *Revel, Riot and Rebellion,* 110-11.

the Pilgrimage of Grace of 1536 were partly inspired by Captain Cobbler (shoemaker Nicholas Melton of Louth, Lincolnshire) and various figures named Captain Poverty. Early seventeenth-century grievances produced Captain Pouch (also known as John Reynolds of Desborough, Northamptonshire), Captain Dorothy Dawson in Yorkshire, and Captain Ann Carter in Maldon, Essex.[275]

Naomi Tadmor's work on the social context of sixteenth-century biblical language implies links between these popular folkloric leadership tropes and Church liturgy. She suggests that the rank of Captain drew on the language used to describe Christ, producing strong scriptural connotations of both exalted leadership and faithful service.[276] Following M. L. Bush, she observes that Captain Poverty was seen to represent both the commons and Christ.[277] In this context, a captain symbolises the three-fold project of serving true religion, demonstrating obedience to the King, and preserving

---

[275] J. Walter, 'Grain riots and popular attitudes to the law: Maldon and the crisis of 1629', in J. Brewer and J. Styles (eds.), *An Ungovernable People: The English and their Law in the 17th and 18th Centuries* (London, Hutchinson and Rutgers, 1980), 47-84; B. Capp, *When Gossips Meet: Women, Family, and Neighbourhood in Early Modern England* (Oxford, 2003), 316-7; J. Walter, 'Reynolds, John'. *Oxford Dictionary of National Biography* (online ed.). Oxford University Press. doi:10.1093/ref:odnb/67261 Date accessed: 14/09/2012.

[276] N. Tadmor, *The Social Universe of the English Bible: Scripture, Society, and Culture in Early Modern England* (Cambridge, 2010), 131-136.

[277] Tadmor, *Social Universe of the English Bible*, 150; M. L. Bush, 'Captain Poverty and the Pilgrimage of Grace', *Historical Research*, 65: 156 (1992), 17-36.

balance within the commonweal.[278] While drawing support and signifying the cause of a protest, the figure of the Captain also served to cloak rebellion in political and religious conservatism.

The most conspicuous of these figures was Captain Poverty associated with the Pilgrimage of Grace in 1536. The first reference to this figure was in a letter of revolt and articles issued by rebels in the north of England. Ostensibly protesting against Thomas Cromwell's planned Dissolution of the Monasteries, their grievances covered a more complex range of social, economic and agrarian grievances. While several leaders adopted the guise of Captain Poverty, the mantle was apparently first assumed in Richmondshire. An eyewitness, John Dakyn, recalled that 'in the time of the insurrection I heard a simple poor man they called Lord Poverty say he would die in the matter; and I suppose none knew more of the matter than he, such is the rudeness of the people'.[279] During the Cumberland uprising, Penrith cathedral hosted the controversial Captains' Mass attended by Captain Poverty, Captain Faith, Captain Pity and Captain Charity.[280]

---

[278] Rollison identifies 1381 as the 'true birth of the age of the commonweal'. Rollison, *A Commonwealth of the People*, 147.

[279] 'Henry VIII: March 1537, 26-31', *Letters and Papers, Foreign and Domestic, Henry VIII, Volume 12 Part 1: January-May 1537* (1890), 786. URL: http://www.british-history.ac.uk/report.aspx?compid=103367 Date accessed: 22 July 2013.

[280] Bush, 'Captain Poverty and the Pilgrimage of Grace', 17-36; R. W. Hoyle, *The Pilgrimage of Grace and the Politics of the 1530s* (Oxford, 2001).

The articles of these bands sought to preserve Christ's true religion and the commonwealth, a twin concern which found its expression in Captain Poverty and his accomplices. Bush locates this cultural idiom in the tradition of *Piers Plowman*, particularly the fifth and sixth chapters of Langland's original text which described a pilgrimage of grace against the destruction of the commonweal.[281] Like the character of Piers, Captain Poverty represented both Christ and the commons simultaneously challenging and confirming the social order. This figure firmly asserted the existing hierarchy while temporarily asserting commoner leadership with the aim of redressing an imbalance in the commonweal. David Aers explains the post Black-Death religious context in which the original *Plowman* text was produced. He describes how 'the Church evolved a theory in which poverty was very far from being a mark of God's special disfavour ... it was a commonplace assumption that the pauper would seem to have been created and placed in the world for the sake of rich man's salvation'.[282] It seems that the figure of Captain Poverty was called upon as the folkloric embodiment of this exegetical theory, drawing authority for intervention in matters of the commonwealth. Many of the 1536 pilgrims were anything but paupers, but this only serves to demonstrate the malleability of this folkloric symbolism. Some of the real identities behind these figures are known, others are not, and a number are the product of literary imagination. The significant point is the tendency for early modern

---

[281] Bush, 'Captain Poverty and the Pilgrimage of Grace', 17-36.

[282] D. Aers, *Community, Gender, and Individual Identity: English Writing, 1360-1430* (London and New York, 1988), 21.

protest to focus on these kinds of symbolic leaders, real or imagined, suggesting popular cultures that were attuned and accustomed to thinking collectively in terms of allegory and folklore.

These traditions did not only derive from literary models. The *Piers Plowman* text grew out of a wider cultural context and wider forms of intersubjective experience in medieval England. These allegorical displays of community values were also associated with the processions of feast days and holy days perceived to be under threat in 1536. The performance of mystery and morality plays were a regular feature of community life and popular interaction with church liturgy and guild fraternities.[283] The most well-known of these plays, *Everyman*, is an allegory populated by such characters as Good-Deeds, Angel, Knowledge, Beauty, Discretion, and Strength.[284] Other morality plays introduced figures such as Justice and Equity and were attached to religious festivals, marking significant holidays as they were enacted by guilds and other bodies.[285] These performances often involved the entire community and took the neighbourhood or local environment as their setting, imbuing significant places with symbolic

---

[283] P. M. King, 'Morality Plays', in R. Beadle (ed.), *The Cambridge Companion to Medieval English Theatre* (Cambridge, 1994), 240-64.

[284] A. C. Cawley, *Everyman and Medieval Miracle Plays* (London, 1956; reprint, London, 1990).

[285] S. Beckwith, 'Ritual, Church and Theatre: Medieval Dramas of the Sacramental Body', in D. Aers (ed.), *Culture and History, 1350-1600* (Detroit, 1992), 65-89.

significance.[286] These semiotic traditions of late-medieval intersubjectivity applied to the Skimmington protests in Mailescott Woods. The nature of these disturbances thus underlines Goffman's assertions about the significant spatial dimension of dramatised social actions.

Adam Fox has described the pervasiveness of theatricality in the everyday lives of early modern English men and women.[287] These traditions of community theatre embedded a familiarity with reading allegorical representations that were spatially-situated and articulated shared moral concepts. Moreover, during the sixteenth and seventeenth centuries, there appears to have been a familiarity with acting upon these theatrical models. The symbolism of protest reveals embedded traditions of community theatre, literary inheritances, and scriptural tropes that underpinned the dramatisation of action. Returning to Goffman's notion of 'front', Skymington as folk leader highlighted a threat to the region's shared cultural values and the perceived assault on ancient forest custom.

---

[286] S. Beckwith, *Signifying God: Social Relation and Symbolic Act in the York Corpus Christi Plays* (Chicago and London, 2001), 36-37.

[287] A. Fox, 'Ballads, Libels and Popular Ridicule in Jacobean England', *Past & Present*, 145 (1994), 47-83.

IV Social drama and broad patterns of allegiance

Despite their local nature, these riots should be interpreted in the context of wider disturbances outside the Forest and across the south-west of England. The Western Rising of 1628-31 was largely a protest against the enclosure:

> of the three Royal Forests of Gillingham in Dorset, Braydon in Wiltshire and Dean in Gloucestershire, but it derived its unity from the leadership of the mysterious Lady Skimmington … apparently the pseudonym of a certain John Williams who, although he possessed influence on both sides of the Bristol Channel, probably received the name from Wiltshire followers, for it is from an old custom of that county that it is derived.[288]

That so many suspected rioters took refuge in Dean's neighbouring counties, together with their threats to call upon 500 Monmouthshire men, suggests that popular political communication extended beyond the physical limits of this particular forest. Underdown is confident that the three 'Lady Skimmingtons' of Braydon and John Williams of English Bicknor in Dean were, in fact, separate people. A 1631 entry in the *Calendar of State Papers*, however, suggests Williams' influence on other communities in the south-west of England during this period. Several of these were in forests which had been the subject of more extensive disafforestation than the projects in Dean. The *Calendar* entry for 23 June recorded the recollections of William Gough, suspected leader of disturbances on the 'New-Gained Grounds' of Lord Berkeley at Frampton

---

[288] D. G. C. Allan, 'The Rising in the West, 1628-1631', *The Economic History Review*, New Series, 5, 1 (1952), 76.

and Slembridge to the east of the River Severn. According to Sir William Guise and Nathaniel Stephens, Justices of the Peace, Gough had been drinking with some other soldiers when conversation turned to:

what Skimmington had done for the Forest of Dean, and of the stirs in the Forest of Brayden, they agreed that if the country would allow victuals and other content to Skimmington and his company, they would come to Frampton and Slimbridge, and throw open the new enclosures.[289]

Whether or not Williams was physically present in any other disturbances which have been taken to constitute the Western Rising, knowledge of his activities influenced inhabitants of other forested areas in this region which experienced similar assaults on local custom. Gough's testimony suggests a close relation between the organisation of the trained bands, the mining community, and resistance to disafforestation within Dean and, it seems, across a wider area. The communication structures of local militias could also transmit news of popular resistance. Underdown notes that 'there were long traditions behind the foresters' forcible defence of common rights'.[290] Assuming the guise of John Skymington, Williams was able to articulate the target of local grievances while simultaneously allowing multiple risings in this region to subsume themselves under a common leadership in the minds of the local population.

---

[289] TNA, SP16/194/60.

[290] Underdown, *Revel, Riot and Rebellion,* 110.

The skimmington ritual and, by extension, the leadership of John Skymington, symbolised a breach of custom that was central to the world-view of local inhabitants and which had allowed them access to forest resources since a 'time out of mind of man'. The riots thus highlighted the wedge which was being driven through an, admittedly idealised, forest community by enclosure. Broadly speaking, this was a division between those who had tenure of property and those who depended upon less formal access to forest wastes. Calling on ancient custom in this manner, rioters were able to foreground the hierarchy of use rights which they felt was being lost through 'improvement' of the forest. Victor Turner provides a theoretical model which complements Goffman's work on symbolic social action, illuminating the nature of these disorders and the role of the Skymington figure. His notion of social drama conceptualises the context in which John Williams' dramaturgical performance sought to broadcast the initial breach to the most potent effect in drawing support. According to Turner, 'a moral law is more vividly made known through its breach'.[291] This clearly describes the impact of seventeenth-century attempts to improve and enclose Dean; Williams' attempt to redress this breach raises important questions over the miners' role in steering a course between subsequent compromise or permanent division in the Forest over the following two centuries.[292] The second phase in Turner's model is characterised by mounting crisis:

[291] V. W. Turner, *Dramas, Fields and Metaphors: Symbolic Action in Human Society* (New York, 1974), 37-42.

[292] Wood, 'Collective violence', 107.

during which, unless the breach can be sealed off quickly within a limited area of social interaction, there is a tendency for the breach to widen and extend until it becomes coextensive with some dominant cleavage in the widest set of relevant social relations to which the conflicting or antagonistic parties belong.[293]

This illuminates the broad alignment of those resisting innovation, not only in Dean, but also other forested areas in the south west of England. This breach seems to have pitched improving and customary ways of seeing against each other in a manner which highlighted horizontal patterns of affiliation and collective interest across a wider area than is usually to be expected in seventeenth century England. This conflict had engendered a cleavage in the 'widest set of social relations' relevant to these two conflicting ideologies. Underdown explains that:

> In their resistance to disafforestation and fen drainage, in their demands for the enforcement of traditional market regulations, the common people of England were expressing a set of values deeply rooted in their culture, which also had important political implications. Behind the regional differences ... there was a political culture shared by people in all areas, a culture whose elements included assumptions about the permanent validity of ancient laws and customary rights, and about the existence of appropriate modes of government in church and state.[294]

---

[293] Turner, *Dramas, Fields and Metaphors*, 37-42.

[294] Underdown, *Revel, Riot and Rebellion*, 119.

Although not inspired by class antagonism in a modern sense, the geographical spread of these forest riots clearly generated much anxiety in central government. Sharp notes that, despite their relative lack of violence and staunch localism, 'the government regarded the disorders which compose the Western Rising as insurrections threatening the good order and stability of the state'.[295]

A tangible fear persisted that these forest riots could prefigure a major rebellion of the type which had begun to seem less feasible in other parts of England towards the end of the sixteenth-century. It is widely accepted that a decline in large-scale rebellion was due, largely, to the withdrawal of an emergent middling group that had traditionally led the more sizeable uprisings of the late medieval period.[296] Evidently, the country's 'dark corners' were still feared as potential nurseries of large-scale rebellion. These areas were a different proposition; in the forests of south-west England, the distinctive survival of large-scale protest depended on Dean's free miners performing the organisational role that had traditionally been adopted by middling groups in other regions.

This chapter has examined the role of the mining community in organising and articulating resistance to the breach of custom in Dean during the early

---

[295] Sharp, *In Contempt of All Authority*, 96.

[296] For example, see A. Wood, *The 1549 Rebellions and the Making of Early Modern England* (Cambridge, 2007); J. Walter, 'A 'Rising of the People?' The Oxfordshire Rising of 1596', *Past and Present*, 107, 1 (1995), 90-134.

seventeenth century. The following chapters explore the types of redressive or remedial procedures that Turner suggests characterise attempts of local and central authorities to seal these breaches. They examine the extent to which new types of social and legal organisation either worked to reintegrate the disturbed social group or recognised an irreparable schism between the contending parties. Examining the agency of different groups, Chapters Four and Five argue that the process of sealing the breach was, in the Forest of Dean at least, a more nuanced and dialectical process than suggested by Turner's model.

During the sixteenth and seventeenth centuries, this marginal region became central to the designs of the Crown and other capital interests. The consequent assault on Forest custom provoked a series of disturbances which seriously tested the power of local authorities. Two of these incidents were notable for their invocation of folkloric tropes. The first was on the part of concerned authorities, while the second was an expression of the solidarities which underwrote the most threatening resistance between 1628 and 1631. These allusions differed in nature, but this chapter argues that both were drawn from an epistemological world in which folkloric references were imbued with political significance at all levels of the social scale.

In 1612, the Earl of Northampton's characterisation of rioters as 'Robin Hoodes' suggests the way that local authorities viewed these peripheral forest cultures during the early seventeenth century. These inaccessible and obscure regions enjoyed a particular relation with the Crown, but this relation engendered a tenacious culture which could only be overseen by local gentry familiar with this way of life. In this light, Northampton's allusion may be interpreted not only as a genuine concern for the preservation of order, but also as a comment on the intrusion of court favourites into autonomous 'country' regions and a recognition of the influence that the mining community held over life in the Forest of Dean. While these two expressions of folklore were made with very different intentions, and emerged from opposite ends of the socio-economic and political spectrum, both belong to the same epistemological world in which mythical figures articulated shared collective values. Northampton argued for the power of local gentry to restore order. Nearly twenty years later, the Skymington figure embodied a custom which was intimately tied to a world-view that, at least nominally, acknowledged this hierarchy. This hierarchy, of course, implied the paternal duty of local gentry to maintain order in the face of encroachment by outsiders. Significantly, the interests of local gentlemen who were undoubtedly complicit in attempts to improve the Forest were carefully avoided during the physical and symbolic violence of these riots.

The free miners were clearly central to local perceptions of the past which underwrote traditional claims to resources at a time when local custom was under assault from local interests. This vision was integrally linked to the symbolism of protest in the 1620s. A folkloric reading of the Skimmington riots emphasises the performative aspects of early modern popular protest. In a dramaturgical sense, the folk hero John Skymington emerges as a figurehead embodying collective values and garnering support by projecting a simplification of complex and often conflicting relationships. This type of folk culture also, it is argued, worked to transmit these values and traditions of protest from one generation to the next. John Williams, as a free miner, clearly articulated memories of living and labouring in this traditional 'open' forest. In the context of early seventeenth-century England, these two episodes illustrate the continuing and multivalent political relevance of folkloric language and action throughout the social hierarchy. The somewhat polarised reception of the Skymington figure, however, throws into relief cultural and economic divisions that were becoming more pronounced in the Forest of Dean during this period. The following two chapters examine the nature of attempts to seal this breach of custom. Chapter Four, in particular, considers the ideological shifts that underpinned changing industrial relations in the Forest of Dean towards the end of the seventeenth century.

Chapter Four

Shifting legal mentalities in the Forest of Dean, c.1630-1660

Originally, I set out to understand why the state has always seemed to be the enemy of 'people who move around' ... efforts to permanently settle these mobile peoples (sedentarization) seemed to be a perennial state project ... the more I examined these efforts at sedentarization, the more I came to see them as a state's attempt to make a society legible, to arrange the population in ways that simplified the classic state functions of taxation, conscription, and prevention of rebellion ... how did the state gradually get a handle on its subjects and their environment? ... the standardisation of weights and measures, the establishment of cadastral surveys and population registers, the invention of freehold tenure, the standardisation of language and legal discourse ....seemed comprehensible as attempts at legibility and simplification. In each case, officials took exceptionally complex, illegible, and local social practices, such as land tenure customs or naming customs, and created a standard grid whereby it could be recorded and monitored ... these state simplifications, the basic givens of modern statecraft were, I began to realize, rather like abridged maps. They did not successfully represent the actual activity of the society they depicted, nor were they intended to; they represented only that slice of it that interested the official observer ... thus a state cadastral map created to designate taxable property-holders does not merely describe a system of land tenure; it creates such a system through its ability to give its categories the force of law.

J.C. Scott, *Seeing Like a State: How Certain Schemes to Improve the Human Condition Have Failed* (New Haven and London: Yale University Press. 1998), 2-3.

I Popular agency and state simplifications

Prior to the late 1660s, the only extant record of the Mine Law Court in the Forest of Dean consists of three membranes pertaining to sessions held at 'Hyll Pytt' in 1469 and 1470.[297] The paucity of written documentation reflects the importance of local knowledge and community relations to the operation of mining law during the fifteenth, sixteenth and early seventeenth centuries. These papers list only names and corresponding fines with no record of offence, which gales were granted, or the names of jury members, suggesting the illegibility of the mining industry to outside parties in this period. A bundle of documents collated during the 1780s, by contrast, indicate that the situation was very different by the end of the seventeenth century. The 'Schedule of Orders and proceedings of the Mine Law Court' details 'Fourteen Original Orders written on Parchment marked numbered and dated as follows' running from 1668 to 1737. The bundle also contains 'An old Paper indorsed "Bounds of the Miners" much damaged and very imperfect but appearing to have been a Copy of the Laws and Customs of the Miners printed in 1687'.[298] There are also 'Seven

---

[297] GRO, D6177/1.

[298] GRO, D5947/10/1.

Original Orders for raising money written on paper dated as follows and tied up with the Proceedings of the Mine Law Court of the respective years of their Dates'. The first of these sessions was held on 30 April 1706. The final document in the bundle is marked 'Mine Law Court 26 August 1777 ... There has been no court holden for the miners since this day which is a great loss to the Gaveller and causes various disputes amongst the colliers'. [299] As Dean's free miners attempted to preserve their traditional industry, it is argued that by the end of the eighteenth century this dependence on the written record was a significant factor in the collapse of the Mine Law court.

The late seventeenth and eighteenth centuries thus witnessed increased documentation of the mining industry, a process which helped to render Forest life legible to outside interests. Following reconstitution of the Forest Eyre in 1634 which signalled Crown attempts to revive medieval forest laws, Dean was the subject of multiple commissions, surveys and equity court actions. The latter aimed generally at disafforestation and compensation for inhabitants losing customary rights as a consequence of this improvement. In 1635 a warrant of commission was granted to Henry, Earl of Holland and 'others for disafforesting the forests of Dean and Essex', while the same year, Sir Charles Harbord, the Surveyor General for the Crown, produced a record of the 'Particulars of Cannop House and lands in the Forest of Dean'. [300] Between 1637 and 1639 several surveys,

---

[299] GRO, D5947/10.

[300] Bodleian Library, MS Bankes 55, fol. 50. & MS Bankes 60, fol. 22.

commissions, petitions and Exchequer actions were generated relating to disafforestation, while this decade also saw the appointment of John Broughton, the Forest's first deputy surveyor. The essence of Scott's cadastral state vision is reflected in the transition from management of the Forest by regarders to the appointment of a surveyor, an office which implies a more actively quantified assessment of these lands. The increasingly comprehensive documentation of the mining industry suggests more scrutiny from the 1670s onwards. An Exchequer interrogatory from 1684, for instance, directed the commissioner to ask deponents whether they were:

> well acquainted with any lawes or Customes or pretended lawes or Customes of the Quarriemen in the Forrest of Deane [and] have they any lawes or Customes or any Jurisdicion ... to make any laws [and] are they governed by all or any of the pretended lawes or Customes of the Colliers. How come they to be so governed and by what means and under what pretence, doe the Quarrymen and Colliers and Miners derive theire Custome from an antient Inquisicion or from any and what other authority have you seen the same or a copy thereof.[301]

The questions contained in interrogatories such as these indicate that the nature and legitimation of mining rights were subjected to closer examination from the mid seventeenth century.

By the end of this century the Forest was rendered more penetrable and legible to outsiders. Scott observes that the state 'creates such a system

---

[301] TNA, E134/35Chas2/Mich40.

through its ability to give its categories the force of law', implying a unidirectional and deterministic model of state enlargement.[302] The evidence from this region suggests a more reciprocal process. Even if this local community did not intentionally work to inscribe themselves in the early modern English state, this does not preclude the exercise of agency on their part. Scott does attribute agency to the centralising state, partly through the unintentional consequences of its actions. The process by which Dean's free-mining industry became increasingly legible during the course of the seventeenth century, however, bears many similarities. Philip Cassell highlights the importance 'of connecting unintended consequences of action with institutionalized practices' in studying processes of social reproduction whereby cultural and economic traditions are transmitted from one generation to the next.[303]

Evidence suggests that the free miners, attempting to preserve their occupational rights through heavier documentation and the use of equity courts, unintentionally rendered their industry more legible. That these rights required 'open' forest linked the struggle of the mining community to that of the propertyless and poor foresters as well as those who claimed rights by prescription. The mining community, it has been argued, were the focus of efforts to resist the early seventeenth-century assault on common rights. The Exchequer case of 1684 suggests the expedience, to the Quarrymen at least, of claiming that their occupational rights were

---

[302] Scott, *Seeing Like a State*, 3.

[303] P. Cassell (ed.), *The Giddens Reader* (Basingstoke, 1993), 92-101.

governed by the miners' court.[304] To understand the mining industry, embedded in the social life of the region, was to read the taskscape which perpetuated 'pretended Custome'; this, in turn, obstructed attempts to improve and rationalise forest management. This chapter argues that the Mine Law Court was the focus for collective memories which sustained the self-perceptions of this community, particularly its capacity for resisting the projects of external interests. In their regular trade through external networks, this court operated at the nexus of local and national senses of community, legality and, thus, identity. William Sewell discusses the problems of collective agency, noting that it 'entails an ability to coordinate one's actions with others to form collective projects to persuade, to coerce'.[305] The mining community of this forest played a central role in coordinating the defence of traditional practices and, judging by the reputation of John Williams alias Skymington, was popularly regarded as an organising focus for this type of collective action. This chapter considers the implications of the Mine Law Court's increasing legibility during the seventeenth century.

In his work on collective cognition, Paul Dimaggio considers the relation between institutions and the capacity for agency. 'Culture is fragmented among potentially inconsistent elements', he suggests, describing how this limited coherence can inhibit collective activity. Dimaggio claims that the

---

[304] TNA, E134/35Chas2/Mich40.

[305] W.F. Sewell, 'A Theory of Structure: Duality, Agency, and Transformation', *The American Journal of Sociology*, 98, 1 (1992), 1-29.

capacity for agency of any given community or social group is, to a large degree, dependent on the 'thematization of clusters of rituals and schemata around institutions'.[306] He thus outlines a functional aspect of institutions in generating interpretive schema which allow for a broad coherence of meaning and, thereby, the motivation for action in a collective context. He describes these 'institutional logics' as 'sets of "material practices and symbolic constructions" which constitute "organising principles" and are "available to organisations and individuals to elaborate"'. DiMaggio adopts Friedland and Alford's taxonomy of institutional practices including those of capitalism, the state, democracy, family, religion and science, noting that 'each entails a distinctive logic'.[307] Friedland and Alford suggest that these institutional logics are 'symbolically grounded, organizationally structured, politically defined and technically and materially constrained'.[308] In the Forest during this period, it seems that the institutional logics of action pertaining to both nascent capitalism and the state, both of which shared many features, were incompatible with those of the free-mining community and their court. In contrast to the abstracted axioms, linked routines and rituals of these external institutions, the logic and symbolic constructions of

---

[306] P. DiMaggio, 'Culture and Cognition', *Annual Review of Sociology*, 23 (1997), 263-87, 277.

[307] R. Friedland and R. Alford, 'Bringing society back in: symbols, practices, and institutional contradictions', in W. W. Powell and P. DiMaggio (eds.), *The New Institutionalism in Organizational Analysis* (Chicago, 1991), 223-62.

[308] Ibid., 223-62.

the Mine Law Court were embedded in popular life within the Forest, as demonstrated by the rituals of the Skimmington riots.

Sherry Ortner suggests a useful distinction between the capacity for collective action which can be attributed to the Dean miners compared with that of most subordinated groups. She explains that:

> The agency of (unequal) power, of both domination and resistance, may be contrasted with the second major mode of agency noted earlier, that of intentions, purposes, and desires formulated in terms of culturally established "projects". This agency of projects is from certain points of view the most fundamental dimension of the idea of agency. It is this that is disrupted in and disallowed to subordinates.[309]

The tenacity with which the mining community continued to assert and practice their ancient mining custom throughout this period dismisses any idea that they were disallowed a capacity for agency in the pursuit of projects.

Defending 'open' forest against encroachment was only one aspect of the free miners' agency. To consider only reactive collective action risks misunderstanding the more sustained activities that contributed to the Forest taskscape. It is misleading to assume that the only conflict in this region was due to the forest community defending their common rights against encroachment. The seventeenth century gave rise to increasingly intricate disputes between the mining community and local gentry, between

---

[309] S. Ortner, *Anthropology and Social Theory; Culture, Power, and the Acting Subject* (Durham, New Jersey and London, 2006), 144.

local gentry and royal favourites, and between commoners and favourites. Disputes similarly occurred within the mining community, and between the broader forest commonalty and various groups of in-migrating cottagers. The negotiation of power rarely consisted of straightforward relations of domination and resistance, but rather involved multiple and competing logics. The most fundamental lines of conflict seem to have been drawn between the incompatible logics of private capital accumulation and the burgeoning state, on one hand, and the communitarian ideal of many commoners on the other. DiMaggio's notion of logics provides a vocabulary for discussing cultural conflict as a confrontation between inconsistent logics of action.[310] Processes of social reproduction in early-seventeenth century Dean were embroiled in a complex network of relations that were both intended and unintended consequences of various logics of action.

Each type of institutional logic informed a different mode of negotiation. The reintroduction of the Eyre in 1634, the physical petitioning of the Skimmington riots and increasing recourse to equity courts were prominent examples. The events of 1628-31 represented a clash of competing ideologies as formal litigation confronted the more physical forces of traditional protest. Church clearly understood this dynamic as a conflict between 'the balance of equity' and 'the heavie and headlong clamour of the vulgar sort'.[311] The spoken and written record intertwined in complex ways in both local and centralised legal processes. During the 1630s in

---

[310] DiMaggio, *Culture and Cognition*, 277.

[311] Church, *An Olde Thrift Newly Revived.*

Dean, however, there seems to have been a decisive shift in favour of the written legal memory of equity courts over the verbal and synchronic recall of the 'countrey' in evidencing customary rights. The following sections unravel some of this complexity to gain a more balanced understanding of the legibility of this industry and the forest community from the 1670s onwards. It thus seeks to demonstrate the reciprocal and cyclic nature of agency and legal process in a context of state formation. In short, this chapter examines transformations of consciousness attendant on the increased prevalence of the written record in the Forest of Dean.

II 'Acts reduced to Writing'

In 1638 Thomas Wallington described growing up in the Forest as an education. The 52 year-old free miner's deposition also reveals the embodied nature of Dean's customary practices, particularly those of the mining industry, at the start of the seventeenth century. These rights were certainly less documented than they appear to have been by the eighteenth century. Wallington's socialisation was as essential to his occupation as apprenticeships were to many urban artisanal trades during this period. Late nineteenth-century inquiries into the nature of Dean's mining industry, although later than this study, highlight the importance of this experience for anyone who sought to make their living as a miner. In 1883, the government mines inspector noted that:

a colliers work cannot be learnt in a day; it is only after long experience that a man can master the difficulties of his occupation, and to the old hands we must look to initiate and instruct the younger men who are working with them.[312]

During the Quarrymen's dispute of 1684, William Worgan, a 64 year-old labourer of Newland, affirms that these rights could not simply be bought and sold, but were inculcated, he claimed, through the process of growing up in the Forest. He told the court that he had:

> heard and believeth that the said defendents were borne within the perambulacion of the said Forrest and bred upp under their parents or other Quarrie men there for that he hath known them from their Infancie, and may clayme a right of digging & workeing stones in the said Quarries and sayeth yt the right of ye said Quarries have gone from the fathers to the sonnes being borne within ye perambulacion of ye said Forrest.[313]

As Wallington suggested, the legitimacy of his rights were very much grounded in physical experience. The Skimmington riots indicate that when these rights were threatened legitimate methods of redress were similarly physical.

Paul Connerton emphasises the embodied aspect of collective memory and its inter-generational transmission in cultures that retain a high oral residue. Foregrounding the significance of somatic practices, he notes that:

---

[312] Report of the Mines Inspector, South Western District, 1883 (PP XIX, 1884), 273, quoted in Fisher, *Custom, Work and Market Capitalism,* 63.

[313] TNA, E134/35Chas2/Mich40.

Many forms of habitual skilled remembering illustrate a keeping of the past in mind that, without ever adverting to its historical origin, never-the-less re-enacts the past in our present conduct. In habitual memory the past is, as it were, sedimented in the body.

Discerning two distinct aspects of social practice, Connerton identifies sets of incorporating practices. These are present in everyday interactions between people, he suggests, indicating that transmission can occur 'only during the time that their bodies are present to sustain that particular activity'.[314]

Wallington's seventeenth-century deposition and Connerton's modern notion of incorporating practices support the idea that the forest *habitus* was both constituted by, and constitutive of, the activities of its inhabitants. Wallington described an unchanging cycle of interaction between the acting subject and his environment. The synchronic characteristics of this ideal are outlined in Chapter One, but the forest community and the customs that defined it were subject to diachronic change. A major catalyst was the increasing prevalence of the written record, reflecting the inscribing practices that Connerton contrasts with incorporating practices. He describes how modern technologies of print, encyclopedias, indexes and computers all 'require that we do something which traps and holds information, long after the human organism has stopped informing'.[315] This

---

[314] P. Connerton, *How Societies Remember* (Cambridge, 1989), 72.

[315] Connerton, *How Societies Remember*, 73.

disembodiment suggests that the written record would have generated increasingly abstracted understandings of rights, particularly by comparison with customs and traditions that were sedimented in the human body and its practices. Connerton's work illuminates how the defensive use of the written record worked to sever the free miners' rights from the physical practice of mining.

The Earl of Pembroke's grant in 1611 and the activities of searchers during the first two decades of the seventeenth century evidently challenged traditional senses of legitimacy. The increasing scrutiny of customary practice appears to have inspired the first written statement of the miners' *Laws and Privileges* in 1610. Cyril Hart notes similarities between this copy and the first printed version of the *Laws and Privileges* which had been 'Written out of a parchment roll now in the hands of Richard Morse [Deputy Gavellor] of Clowerwall' in 1673. Hart notes, however, that the 1673 transcript omits the names of certain miners involved in this transcription. He explains that this, and later printed versions, contain 'some emendations and misreading which one suspects to be simplifications of then unfamiliar terms'.[316] This codification, then, suggests the paradoxical nature of the process whereby 'acts' were 'reduced to writing' and local mentalities met with state influence. In a culture with a high residue of oral communication, custom could be articulated and interpreted in a more malleable fashion. These traditional perspectives were constituted through the continually shifting lens of the local taskscape rather than by attempts to fix these legal codes in writing. While the aim of

---

[316] Hart, *Free Miners*, 35.

the records appears to have been simplification, much complexity was generated through attempts to detach these legal codes from local experience. What had been implicitly understood and articulated metonymically through the broad terms 'open forest' and 'ancient custom' was rendered explicit. The extensive number of clauses implies the complexity of attempts to categorise and document contingent practices.

Standardisation through the written record not only simplified, but also omitted crucial performative aspects of mining custom that could not be captured in the *Laws and Privileges*. As custom became legible to a broader audience, so it changed its meaning as it was pried away from the social context of the taskscape. This was a crucial step in the process whereby outsiders started to gain a foothold in the Forest's mining industry. The miners' *Laws and Privileges* of 1673 illustrate this tension between implicit and explicit statements of customary practice associated with the shift from incorporating to inscribing practices. They identify certain characteristics of the miners' institutional logic, allowing comparison between their organising principles and the competing logics of those institutions that pushed to improve the Forest during the second quarter of the seventeenth century.

The *Laws and Privileges* reveal that mining custom shared many principles with the popular *habitus* of this ancient forest. The first paragraph states that 'the Customes and Franchises ... were granted time out of mind and after in tyme of the Excellent and Redoubted Prince King Edward unto the Miners of the Forrest of Deane and the Castle of St Briavels and the bounds of the said Forrest'.[317] While this document attempted to reify mining custom, the industry was still defined by the physical and mutable rituals that underscored the perambulation of the Forest's bounds. The miners also claimed their occupational custom within a dual timeframe that chimed with the 'timeless' nature of the Forest and the more temporal authority of a royal grant.

The miners were tied into Dean's taskscape through a vision of mutual obligation between themselves and the Crown, a relationship that was defined through the activities of the Deputy Gavellor and the Mine Law Court. The *Laws and Privileges* highlight the crown share of minerals as a physical contract that allowed miners jurisdiction over their industry, referring to this due as 'Lawe Oare'. This system was frustratingly opaque to both Jacobean and Caroline regimes, particularly in the context of mounting fiscal pressure and increasing coal prices during the seventeenth century. The mining community, however, understood the importance of maintaining this opacity as the *Laws and Privileges* specifically refuse access to any 'Stranger' of 'what degree soever', asserting that 'if any other come to travayle and to worke within the place aforesaid hee shall be forbode from the Fellowship of the pitt'. This document was aimed at restricting the scale of mining, decreeing that 'noe Smith holder neither Myner neither any other shall make carriage of the said Myne neither by Cart nor by waine but only by the measure called Belleyes', a local term meaning a workman's hod. Although this document was written from the perspective of the forest community the dual timeframe invoked for the

---

[317] *The Laws & Privileges of the Free Miners of the Forest of Dean* (London, 1673) URL: http://eebo.chadwyck.com/home   Date accessed 21/09/2008.

origins of these rights strongly suggests that the miners were conversant with both national and local institutional logics. The *Laws and Privileges* thus suggest that while these miners recognised the value of the written record, they believed that enforcing the continuity of practice was the most effective way of preserving their occupational custom.

Events in early-seventeenth century Northamptonshire demonstrate a wider popular belief that maintaining the physical integrity of a local 'countrey' would help to preserve its 'certain particular laws' to adopt Manwood's phrase. [318] In 1602, Philip Pettit informs us, Brigstock Parks were granted in feefarm to Sir Robert Cecil. He explains that 'James I confirmed the grant on the understanding that Cecil maintained a competent number of deer for the King's recreation'. The area was divided between the Great Park and the Little Park, and Pettit suggests that 'if all the deer to be retained were driven into the latter, Cecil's agent still expected to get from it an annual rent of £200, and by Whitsun, to have the Great Park fully stored and agisted with cattle'. The commoners of Brigstock evidently realised the impact that this change would have on their own commoning rights and apparently decided to use their combined physical force to literally maintain the integrity of the two parks. Pettit describes how 'as the deer were being driven into the forest, 120 men of Brigstock and Stanion stood upon the pale and kept

---

[318] Manwood, *Laws*, 41.

them back'.[319] The Dean miners' *Laws and Privileges* of 1673 betrays a similar belief in the link between the precedent of spatial continuity and legal authority. The seventh clause states that 'the Myners have such libertyes and Franchises that for cattle to them due for their Myne that they beene Bayliffes to take the Cattle of their debtors and to arrest them without the leave of any man till gree bee made if hee bee within the bounds aforesaid'.[320] While the free miners began to adopt the written record at the beginning of the seventeenth century, it was with the primary aim of enforcing existing physical practices that would maintain the protectionism and legitimacy of their small-scale industry.

The institutional logic of this industry coincided with the more general need for an 'open' and commonable forest which was fundamentally incompatible with the logic of improvers and projectors. The most obvious difference was the preference of the latter for the written record and inscribing practices that rendered embodied rights more vulnerable to appropriation by outsiders. While the written record was being used to unlock Dean's mining industry and open it to capital exploitation, miners were drawing on the same technology to preserve the smaller-scale, opaque and customary nature of their operations. It is argued, however, that this

---

[319] P. A. J. Pettit, *The Royal Forests of Northamptonshire: a Study in Their Economy; 1558-1714* (Gateshead, 1968), 172-3. Victor Skipp discusses similar tensions and popular action in other afforested regions of early seventeenth century England in his study of the Forest of Arden. V. Skipp, *Crisis and Development: an ecological case study of the Forest of Arden, 1570-1674* (Cambridge, London, New York & Melbourne, 1978).

[320] *The Laws & Privileges of the Free Miners of the Forest of Dean* (London, 1673)

ultimately weakened the position of Dean's miners in the late seventeenth and eighteenth centuries.

III Custom and the authority of writing

Early seventeenth-century searchers like Otho Nicholson, private projectors and recipients of royal grants, formed the vanguard of efforts to render the practices of this region legible, redefining customary rights, and giving these novel 'categories the force of law'.[321] Royal commitment to these efforts, aimed at increasing the profitability of this forest, was demonstrated by the scale and detail of the map commissioned by James I in 1608. The detailed representation of most major routes, landmarks, trading points, industrial sites and field layouts in the Forest painstakingly recorded the lords and tenants of each holding. A large body of literature addresses mapping as an act of domination or colonisation in its selective and political representation of space.[322] In the 1608 map, the process reproduced the world-view of cartographers and those parties that commissioned them. Contrasting with flexible memories which underpinned local knowledge of customary and multiple use-rights, this detailed and ossified record implied exclusive tenure and rights of access to

---

[321] Scott, *Seeing Like a State*, 3.

[322] For example, see A. Smith, 'Landscape Representation: Place and Identity in Nineteenth-century Ordnance Survey Maps of Ireland' in Stewart & Strathern (eds.), *Landscape, Memory and History*, 71-88; B. Friel, *Translations* (London, 1981) and B.Friel, *Brian Friel: essays, diaries, interviews, 1964-1999* (London, 1999).

these lands. There is no record of fence month, pannage season, or any other custom through which rights of access changed according to the season or practical contingency. The mapping of the Forest perhaps exerted little immediate effect on the customary practices of the community as these tenancies had always been subject to legal records of occupancy while still accommodating coincident uses of the Forest. The automatic omission of multiple use-rights in the cadastral record, however, suggests an ideology that regarded private property tenure as an inevitable element of the march of progress. Tension between the inherent novelty of projects to improve the Forest and traditional rights embedded in collective understandings of the past thus constituted a significant line of division in seventeenth-century Dean. This line was drawn between those who could satisfy the King that they held formal customary rights attaching to property tenure, and those whose rights were ignored by many documents including the 1608 map and the Exchequer decree of 1628.[323]

Legal wrangling over proposals for disafforestation in 1639 indicates that groups of foresters appreciated the implications of formalising custom for the external privatisation of Dean's resources. A number of commoners protesting the inadequacy of the 4,000 acres set aside in compensation for their loss of rights claimed that these usages were being made extinct by certain individuals attempting to secure their 'unitie of possession'.[324] The

[323] TNA, MR 169.

[324] TNA, E112/182/196.

Crown and other parties, it is suggested, attempted to fix rights in the written record, lending authority to their legal definition of the community. These measures were aimed at providing the security of tenure demanded by any potential capital investor since seasonally variant and multiple rights of access would detract from the investment potential of these lands. A unitary understanding of legal access to forest resources would undoubtedly have benefited the Crown in its drive to increase the profitability of its demesne lands. As the construction of the 1608 map depended on interaction between cartographers and local residents, processes of state formation in the Forest and the increasing documentation of litigation in early modern England were not unidirectional.[325] The reciprocal nature of state formation carries implications for understanding agency in processes of historical change. This dialectic is particularly evident in the relationship between traditional oral legal cultures and the written legal record of central equity courts.

From the late sixteenth century, equity litigation was increasingly sought as an avenue of dispute resolution in the Forest. In many respects, this marked a shift away from the physical nature of testimony in late medieval Dean. As described, these embodied methods of determining local customary rights drew on a mnemonically inscribed landscape, the demonstration of

---

[325] S. Hindle, *The state and social change in early modern England, c. 1550-1640* (Basingstoke, 2000); S. Hindle, *The birthpangs of welfare: poor relief and parish governance in seventeenth-century Warwickshire* (Stratford upon Avon, 2000); S. Hindle, *On the parish?: the micropolitics of poor relief in rural England, c. 1550-1750* (Oxford, 2004); S. Hindle, 'Hierarchy and Community in the Elizabethan Parish: the Swallowfield Articles of 1596', *The Historical Journal*, 42, 3 (1999), 835-851; M.J. Braddick, *The nerves of state: taxation and the financing of the English state, 1558-1714* (Manchester, 1996); M.J. Braddick, *State formation in early modern England, c.1550-1700* (Cambridge, 2000); M.J. Braddick and J. Walter (eds.), *Negotiating power in early modern society: order, hierarchy and subordination in Britain and Ireland* (Cambridge, 2001).

uninterrupted practice and the spoken testimony of older, predominantly male, foresters. Extant documentation of the Elizabethan Exchequer court, however, reveals significant continuities between the central written record and traditional legal practice. Rather than the supercession of oral testimony by more formal documentation, these records reveal the complex interplay of spoken and written evidence. Details of a pannage dispute from 1591 are preserved in the written records of the Exchequer court, but this evidence was entirely dependent on the oral memory of the local community. Providing a resource for local and popular conflict resolution, the court recorded elements of local practice in the testimony of Henry Yeroth, a seventy eight year-old free miner of Coleford and his fellow deponents. This group consisted mainly of miners, yeomen and husbandmen. Out of twenty five male deponents interviewed in this case, only four were under the age of fifty while seven were older than seventy. All of these deponents, including a gentleman of Rodley and a weaver from Minsterworth, one of nine deponents from outside Dean, were asked to state how long they had remembrance and knowledge of the region and its customs. The majority stated that they had known the Forest for fifty or sixty years. Thomas Morse, a sixty eight year-old Tanner, confirmed that he had known the area and its customs for 'all the tyme of his remembrance' as did John Donnynge who was also sixty eight. William Hyett, a seventy four year-old husbandman of Rodley, also claimed that he had known the Forest for 'all the time of his memorie'.[326] This group of foresters and the line of questioning demonstrates that, while the written record of the equity court was increasingly viewed as a resource for popular appropriation, the

---

[326] TNA, E134/34Eliz/Hil23.

200

definition of valid legal testimony in these courts resembled that which underwrote local custom.

A boundary dispute from 1593 shares many similarities with the pannage case. Claiming that their lands were 'parcel of the boundes of the said Forrest of Deane', witnesses described various elements of the landscape and local boundary markers. One deponent made the ubiquitous claim to have known the area 'for all the time of his memorie', adding that 'more than this he hath heard crediblie from his ancestors'. Richard Aguillam, a seventy year-old joiner of Castle Morton, near the Forest of Dean, deposed that 'he knoweth a brooke running under or nere the Towne of Newnham descending into the River Sevearne there, dividing the boundes of the said Forreste from the said Towne'.[327] These, and many other cases initiated to reinforce claims to threatened custom, resulted in the slow accretion of local knowledge within the records of central equity courts. This information was recorded in the language of those who inhabited the Forest and its immediate vicinity. Aguillam's description of the Forest bounds, for instance, is evocative of popular descriptions of local space contained in the fourteenth-century perambulations of Dean.

Local and national legal senses were not mutually exclusive or fixed, but were malleable and dynamic ways of seeing the world which could be invoked by the same person with no apparent sense of contradiction. This polyphasia thrived at all levels of the forest hierarchy. Despite his contempt for the 'pretended custom' of the miners and the wider forest community, for example, Sir Edward Winter was willing to call upon the evidence of

---

[327] TNA, E134/36Eliz/Hil21.

ancient men of the Forest in 1616, defending his title to land against the claims of the Attorney General. John Tanner, a seventy four year-old yeoman of Flaxley, deposed that he had known this defendant 'to be seised' of his tenure since the death of his father, Sir William Winter, and that he had 'known both to be seised all the time of his remembrance'. Thomas Maddock, a sixty six year-old gentleman of Tidenham, recalled that 'by all the tyme of this deponents remembrance [Edward Winter] hath taken ploughbote'.[328] Local industrial gentry also provided this type of testimony in defence of customary and smaller-scale industries of the Forest. In 1624, for instance, Sir William Throckmorton and Bainham Throckmorton were involved in the defence of mining and quarrying custom against the Attorney General. This legal action was also dependent on the testimony of forest inhabitants and knowledge of the region in which they had been born and raised. Several free miners were thus called upon to explain how they had come to understand the regulation of their industry.[329]

At the same time, however, the documentary process stripped evidence of customary rights of its dynamism, fixing it in the dated and written record and forming a major strand of the impulse to quantify this region more scientifically. Again, this was not driven solely by the Crown or other state interests. In the pannage dispute of 1591, Thomas Moorelande claimed 'to have common in the Forrest under collour of the Charter of Rodlieghe and

---

[328] TNA, STAC8/303/7 & TNA, E134/14JasI/Hil18.

[329] TNA, E134/22JasI/East8.

not otherwise'.[330] Just as spoken testimony was central to the documentation of legal process, claims to local custom had long relied on written evidence. Comparatively novel, however, was the increasing use of documents in their own right, not simply to ascertain legitimate tenure, but also to order recollections of the past. Adam Fox notes that 'the records of decisions and agreements made locally could be superseded by the decrees of the central common law and equity courts to which increasing resort was being made in the sixteenth and seventeenth centuries'. Fox thus highlights one way in which the written legal record was influential in augmenting or, indeed, supplanting the remembrance of 'ancient' local witnesses.[331] The speech of deponents was fixed, reified, and diachronically ordered in the records of the central courts.

These documents described forest life, but stored it in a manner that allowed select elements to be recalled through an understanding of the law that, it was claimed, operated according to good conscience in the equity courts. In short, this type of legal record worked to impose diachronic order and permanency on the more synchronic and malleable evidence which had traditionally legitimated custom. Contradictory claims were increasingly difficult to overlook because, in many cases, documentation worked to establish a permanent and more formal record of entitlement to common within the Forest. While formal rights attaching to property tenure were generally recognised, this view of forest life tended to disregard the needs

---

[330] TNA, E134/34Eliz/Hil23.

[331] A. Fox, 'Custom, Memory and the Authority of Writing', in Griffiths, Fox and Hindle, *Experience of Authority*, 108.

of those dependent on less formal access. This group, crucially, included the majority of the free miners. From the perspective of improvers, the contingent and complex negotiations of local custom could be viewed as the stubborn protectionism of a region that remained tied to the dogmas of an opaque and hierarchical past.

A brief survey of Dean's records for the late sixteenth and seventeenth centuries suggests many reasons for seeking redress in these courts. Due to their father's reputation, the Gyes family aimed to escape the censure of their neighbours or the 'jury called the countrey'. When faced with substantial opponents like the Catchmay and Bond families in 1582, John Gyes complained that these deponents had been acting 'contrarie to all equitie' and that their influence dominated local legal processes. Gyes, therefore, sought arbitration through the less personal, and to an extent more indifferent, mechanisms of this court.[332] In 1612, John Sallens complained of the detrimental effects of the Earl of Pembroke's grant, which he claimed would 'soon destroy the forest' and prayed 'that this case may be weighed as well in equitie as in lawe'.[333] As discussed, Christopher Hawkins, a gentleman of Newnham, entered a bill in 1616 complaining that William Brayne, William Meeke and Henry Daniell had managed to take possession of the deeds relating to his lands, leaving him without remedy in attempting to prove his title. Hawkins suggested that these 'indirect dealings' were 'contrary to law and equitie' and requested that he might 'be

---

[332] TNA, E112/15/9.

[333] TNA, E112/82/300.

aided and relieved herein by this honorable court'.[334] Applicants to this court during the seventeenth century sought legal proceedings according to 'equity and good conscience' of the type promoted by Church's fictional Surveyor in *An Olde Thrift*. Many plaintiffs to this court, however, were seeking redress from the obstructive use of equity proceedings themselves. In his tithe case of 1662, Benedict Fox, vicar of Lidney, complained that he had been 'putt and forced by the said confederates to very chargable and expensive suits'.[335]

Equity courts were driven by increasing amounts of business at a local level. While a more reciprocal process than Scott suggests, equity litigation was a central element of the cadastral state, supplementing more overt attempts to chart economy and industry in the Forest. Highlighting the limitations of state mapping, Scott explains that 'the cadastral lens also ignored anything lying outside its sharply defined field of vision'.[336] Surveys and maps recorded only those elements that could be reduced to geometric and numeric definitions, ignoring the intricacies of daily life which sustained traditional senses of the Forest. The records of disputes between foresters provide a more expansive view, generating large amounts of information regarding social relationships in the region. These

---

[334] TNA, E112/82/331.

[335] TNA, E112/403/12.

[336] Scott, *Seeing Like a State*, 47.

proceedings reveal aspects of seigniorial conflict, local ecological knowledge and popular legal mentalities. Much of this detail may appear less relevant to the regulation of industry but was integral to the everyday experience which conditioned perceptions of custom and local identity. Benedict Fox, for example, complained that several members of Lidney parish were guilty of confederating against him to obscure the true amount due in tithe payment arrears following the upheaval of the 1640s and 1650s. As noted, Fox claimed to be seeking equitable judgement from the Exchequer as this particular grievance had 'noe remedie at the Common Law'. While the case focused on an economic dispute, depositions recorded far more information than the payment of tithes. The documentation generated by this complaint revealed:

> what quantities of wooll, Hempe, Flax, Eggs, apples, pears and other fruit each of them had yearly there in those years as aforesaid. And what number of sheep Ewes, pidgeons, Cowes Sowes and Mares and how many dry Cattle Each of them have agisted and fed there yearely in those yeares, And what Nomber of Lambs Colts Piggs Each of them had yearely fallen there in those years.[337]

Thus, the hegemonic apparatus of the Jacobean and Caroline state depended on its capillary action. To regard the growth in equity proceedings as the unidirectional imposition of a centralised legal system is to misunderstand the way the court penetrated the localities in early modern England. This process was driven, in large part, by the internal wrangling of local people in their daily life. This evidence suggests an increasing

---

[337] TNA, E112/403/12.

cultural division within the Forest, related in part to the growing tendency of sections of the community to seek satisfaction in these courts.[338]

Popular use of equity courts, certainly in Dean, was motivated by various factors, most of which aimed at transcending the potential protectionism of the local situation. The quantity of initial bills vastly exceeds the number of cases that reached the stage of deposition. This implies that approaching the court was perceived by certain sections of the community as a coercive measure, rather than a signal of intent to follow through to prosecution. This type of case increased throughout the seventeenth century, with many of them suggesting that the court was being used to pressurise opponents or to open communication with central government in a form of petitioning. Thus the courts received complaints from those concerned about the title of lands for which they had compounded with Otho Nicholson and from those complaining about the level of spoliation caused by increased industrial activity. To certain inhabitants of the Forest, litigation was evidently more palatable and less dangerous than the physical petitioning of riot or the forced opening of enclosed land.

The hegemony of these courts represented an apparently level playing field with predictable rules that would allow for security of capital investment.

---

[338] For further reading regarding a perceived 'division of cultures' in many parts of England during this period see Hindle, 'Swallowfield Articles'; D. Levine and K. Wrightson, *Poverty and piety in an English village: Terling, 1525-1700* (Oxford and New York, 1995); K. Wrightson, *English Society, 1580-1680* (London, 2003); P. Burke, *Popular culture in early modern Europe* (Aldershot, 1994); P. Burke, *Languages and community in early modern Europe* (Cambridge, 2004); P. Burke, *What is cultural history?* (Oxford, 2005); S. Hindle, 'Power, Poor Relief, and Social Relations in Holland Fen, c. 1600-1800', *The Historical Journal*, 41, 1 (1998), 67-96; J. Broad, 'Parish Economies of Welfare, 1650-1834', *The Historical Journal*, 42, 4 (1999), 985-1006; S. Hindle, 'Custom, Festival and Protest in Early Modern England: The Little Budworth Wakes, St Peter's Day, 1596', *Rural History*, 6, 2 (1995), 155-78.

From the second quarter of the seventeenth century, however, the number of actions instigated by, and on behalf of, the mining community rose sharply. Many of these cases sought to protect the customs of their trade from external capital interests. Seventeenth-century disputes in this court were reviewed at a distance from local rivalries, an aspect that contributed to the reputation of equity proceedings for transparency and indifferent judgement. The selective vision that constituted this progressive world-view regarded the 'pretended custom' of local inhabitants as a vestige of the 'irrational' traditions which had contributed to the inefficiency of forest governance during the previous three centuries. While customary law and local courts operated somewhat idiosyncratically, the statute law of central courts was coordinated at a national level. Theoretically, its tenets could be applied in the same fashion throughout the realm, allowing the wider population to consider themselves as equals before the law and free from local antagonisms or protectionist attitudes.

Most plaintiffs in the above examples cited undue influence among the reasons that they sought to escape the apparently backward-looking and prejudicial nature of local justice. Instead of standing before a court that could be dominated by the more substantial inhabitants of the region, those seeking judgement in 'equity and good conscience' looked for their case to be heard according to the 'quality of being equal or fair'.[339] These courts were increasingly regarded as the dispensers of rational and predictable justice by comparison with the irrational and opaque governance that had

---

[339] The Oxford English Dictionary defines 'equity' as 'the quality of being equal or fair; fairness, impartiality; evenhanded dealing' quoting examples which date from the fourteenth century onwards. For literature on the growth of equity court influence from the late sixteenth-century, see the *Introduction*.

apparently allowed royal forests to fall into the hands of the local populace. The proceedings of these courts, though, only seemed fair and open to certain sections of the local community including the freeholders and copyholders of the Forest or agents of the Crown and outside investors seeking to gain a foothold in the industries of the region. The situation looked far less equitable to those among the forest community who were witnessing the erosion of their ancient customary rights, which were becoming less visible to the cadastral gaze of the Jacobean and Caroline state. Increasing recourse to the written legal testimony of these equity courts appears to have been one element of an attempted rationalisation of forest space and the sedentarisation of those who lived within it. Testimony demonstrates, however, that this rationalisation was not as unidirectional as Scott suggests.

The most noticeable aspect of the depositions taken by commissioners for the Court of the Exchequer is the increasing numbers of cases brought to this stage during the late sixteenth and early seventeenth centuries. Only two cases directly relating to the Forest of Dean were brought to deposition during the last two decades of Elizabeth's reign, compared with five during that of James I. Ten cases were addressed by commissions under Charles I and, following the turmoil of the 1640s, this legal avenue was swiftly re-established as depositions were recorded for two cases, one in 1652 and the other in 1653. Six cases were tried between 1660 and 1683. Analysis of these proceedings demonstrates that most of these actions during the late sixteenth and seventeenth centuries were brought by the Attorney General against local industrial gentry or resulted from disputes over competition for concessions to the region's material resources. A survey of deponents supports Wood's suggestion that an increasing recourse to equity also resulted in a narrowing of the common voice of the 'countrey'. In other words, as the legal processes and governing principles for this region gradually became external to the forest community, the poorest inhabitants of this region were no longer given the consideration that they had been.

Among the fifty nine deponents called upon during Elizabeth's reign, forty five were yeomen or husbandmen while four of the remaining fourteen were miners.[340] The group also contained two gentlemen. Those recorded during the reign of James I were drawn from a similar group, the majority of whom were yeomen and husbandmen, with several miners and carpenters listed. By the time Charles I succeeded his father, the increasing business received by this court is evident, as is the greater variety of occupations listed for each deponent. The group was still composed, primarily, of those described as yeomen, husbandmen, and gentlemen, but now included many in artisanal trades, such as blacksmiths, dyers, joiners and carpenters. The mining community was also well represented amongst these deponents and, in fact, constituted four out of the thirteen questioned during the 1650s. Between 1660 and 1680, of the forty deponents traceable from the 1672 hearth tax returns for Gloucestershire, only fourteen were rated on one hearth, while none of those traceable appeared on the lists of exclusions on grounds of poverty.[341] While these deponents were evidently still being chosen for their knowledge of the case, it seems that the commissioners did not seek the testimony of the poorest inhabitants. The

---

[340] TNA, E134.

[341] GRO, D383/1; TNA, E179/247/13; TNA, E179/14 & TNA, E179/16.

most important exception to this narrowing of participation was the mining community which still remained vocal. Their engagement with this central court, however, helped to render their operations and the practices of the wider forest community legible to outsiders.

Many of these Exchequer proceedings illustrate a more subtle aspect of crown attempts to tighten and formalise access to its forest wastes and demesne lands. They suggest that, as scrutiny of custom progressed during the early seventeenth century, a perceived laxity in regulation had prompted officials to call for enforcement of the original spatial limits of these uses. Many deponents in these cases testified to the nature of rights they had previously enjoyed, despite being resident outside the bounds of the Forest of Dean. Much business of this court related to disputed lands on the periphery of the Forest and its bounds. Thus, in 1591, we find Thomas Moorelande and his claims to common in the forest by virtue of the 'Charter of Rodlieghe'. Moorelande was recorded as a resident of Westbury, outside the bounds of the Forest and could not, therefore, lay claim to these rights through his residence. As noted, nine deponents in this case were resident beyond the forest bounds, largely in Rodley or Minsterworth to the north-east of the area marked by official perambulations. There were many similar cases during the following decades. In April 1653, a court session for Minsterworth and Hartpury was evidently still concerned with this question. The session noted 'a paper containing the customs of Minsterworth taken from a court roll' which stated that 'the inhabitants have had time out of mind free common within the Forest of Dean for all manner of beasts and sheep and pannage for their swine'.[342] The reintroduction of the Forest Eyre in 1634, however, suggests that equity litigation was understood to be inadequate in meeting the extreme financial exigencies faced by the government of Charles I.

IV The 1634 Justice Seat in Eyre

In 1634 the Caroline government trumpeted its intention to assert royal authority over the Forest of Dean by reinstating the Justice Seat in Eyre at the city of Gloucester. It had been 300 years since these sessions were held in the Forest, and this was perceived by some to be responsible for a decline of royal authority and the subsequent fall of regional governance into the hands of the local population. Although the riots which constituted the Western risings of 1628-31 were caused by local grievances, Chapter Three demonstrates national anxieties over these disturbances. At a time when royal government was suffering the material consequences of rule without Parliament, these risings, together with suspected industrial abuses of crown wastes, pointed starkly to the need for the stricter regulation of these 'dark corners'. The Forest of Dean was a particularly sensitive area in this respect. Following the grant to Pembroke in 1611, and the steadily rising price of quality timber and coal, this area was one of the few that were actually profitable. The urgent need for crown revenue and a fear of rebellion were two among many factors behind the decision to reintroduce the Eyre in 1634.

---

[342] TNA, E134/34Eliz/Hil23; TNA, E134/36Eliz/Hil21 & GRO, D640/E4.

Anxiety over the commoners of this area was personified in John Williams, alias Skymington, who was to spend the middle years of this decade suffering in Newgate prison. This was compounded by conflict between local industrial gentry attempting to secure rights to increasingly valuable resources. There were obvious concerns over the instability of this region and the possible effect on royal income. There were many overlapping and competing claims to estovers, more industrial types of wood, and coal supply. Complaints emerged from all social levels that various members of this community were undermining the local ecology and jeopardising future resources. Much of the seventeenth-century litigation concerning preservation of wood stocks claimed to be directed at maintaining supplies of quality ship timber for 'furnishing the Royal Navies'. [343] It would appear, however, that the vast majority of spoil within the forest was actually being generated by the voracious appetite of local iron industries. Competition between Sir John Winter, Sir Baynham Throckmorton and Sir Edward Terringham over the raw materials of industry can arguably be regarded as the defining conflict in this respect.

Efforts to tighten regulation of the wastes dominated Exchequer litigation of this period from both local and central perspectives. In 1632, Thomas Hall complained that Harry Dowle and other defendants, residents of Stanton, had unlawfully broken down his encoppicements, thus exposing this woodland to their cattle and the forest, causing great spoil. [344] Hall, a

---

[343] TNA, E112/182/196 & TNA, E112/183/230-240.

[344] TNA, E112/180/57.

gentleman of Heighmeadow, was later accused by Christopher Tucker, acting as Deputy Gavellor, of attempting to influence the operations of the mining industry by offering to pay legal costs for some members of this community.[345] Increasing crown concern over rights of access to surrounded lands (those reclaimed through drainage or damming) resonates in the responses of local residents to a complaint made by Sir Robert Heath, Attorney General, in 1632. They claimed rights to a piece of land on the eastern edge of the Forest known locally as 'Arlingham Wharths'. According to their testimonies, the land was constantly moved and shaped through the silt deposits of the River Severn. The answers of these inhabitants reveal much about the fluid nature of local custom and contrasts, instructively, with efforts to fix rights in the written record. Heath registered governmental concern regarding 'divers messuages Tenements & Mills and cottages' which had:

of late years been made and built upon the said Forest and hath been inclosed by divers and sundry severall persons and by them converted to their owne uses to the great annoyance of the said Forrest.

Arlingham Wharf was a particular cause for concern. Thomas Yate, gentleman, argued that his manorial rights included 'herbage depasturing and feeding thereof', stating that:

the said River had not longe before and within the memory of man worne away swallowed up and gained from the dry land and soyle of

---

[345] TNA, E112/183/220.

the said ground called Arlinghams wharth and in or neare the very same place where the said Fortie acres is now left.

According to Yate, local inhabitants understood that they had always had access to this land, despite its constant shifting, 'according to a certain Rule and course as hath byne by them auncyently used & accustomed'.[346] The fluid and unstable boundaries of this land would have been difficult to document with any sense of permanence. This constantly evolving landscape and the rights that it helped to perpetuate could best be understood through local knowledge of past practice. During the seventeenth century, the improvement of surrounded lands presented an imposing obstacle to attempts at fixing the regulation of commons and wastes.

In the face of this complexity and the confusing nature of claim and counter claim, the decision to reintroduce the Eyre signalled the Crown's intent to reimpose medieval forest law. It thus represented an attempt to halt a perceived decline of the previous three centuries. In preparation for the Justice Seat, Cyril Hart explains that:

> regarders were ordered to make a perambulation of the Forest. Sir John Finch (King's Counsel) later made notes of his actions in the Justice Seat of Eyre of 1634. He used them to set down for Charles I a comprehensive report of the proceedings at the eyre. Following a swanimote court held at Mitcheldean, the Justice Seat in Eyre opened

---

[346] TNA, E112/180/55.

on 10 July 1634 at the same village and was adjourned to Gloucester Castle.[347]

The tone and substance of questioning by King's Counsel during these proceedings emphasises that the main concern was to check abuses of wood stores by local ironmasters. They also aimed to ensure that the Crown was duly compensated for any past spoil which had exceeded the legitimate allowances. This session was also notable for its definitive decision over which set of perambulations were to constitute the royal Forest and associated rights. Questioning whether the perambulation made in 28 Edw I 'ought to stand in force', Finch, the Grand Jury, and the twelve officers of the Forest together with the 'Fayre men and Reeve' agreed to:

> leave out the latter parte of there verdict and let the First parte only stand for there verdict (vizt.) we agree that the meets and bounds of the Forrest of Deane ought to be according to the perambulacions made of H.3 [et] 10.Ed.3.

This ruling was keenly felt in some areas close to the edge of the Forest, holding real material consequences for claims to custom both in the present and the past. Records note that 'by this the king had much enlarged the Forest of deane and all within the 17 Townes were fearefull they should have been questioned for many things done contrary to the Forrest Lawes'. Finch evidently recognised the fierce sense of legitimacy which could be fostered through the memory of long and continuous practical access to

---

[347] Hart, *New History*, 54.

resources. He 'thought it not fitt to proceed with any of [the retrospective abuses] at that Judgment seate' because of their 'Longe usage'.

Once these boundaries had been established and settled, attention turned to those responsible for the industrial scale of spoliation within the Forest and consequent loss of crown revenue. John Gibbons, for example, had been charged at the Swanimote court with 'spoyling certain coppices to the damage of 22000 li and for inclosing nine hundred acres & 40 valued at 113 li 13 s 4 d per annum with a wall'. Gibbons denied any wrongdoing but was convicted for 'cuttinge downe 4000 oakes and 2000 beeches worth 20 s a peece' and manipulating land holdings granted to him by a lease from James I. The court heard that:

> [w]hilst this lease was obteyned and before it was passed Mr Gibbons sett some on worke to Joyne in one inclosure those two parcells severally enclosed and by that meanes drew into the inclosure soe much more not intended him as made the 574 Acres to be between 1000 and 1100 Acres and therein the King was deceived of 500 Acres or thereabouts and the trew value of what hee had is more 200 li per annum at the least and wilbe worth twise as much more within a few years.[348]

These accusations against Gibbons highlight the kinds of obfuscating practices and potential concealments that faced the Caroline government and explain efforts to scrutinise such a peripheral yet profitable region. Not only were many of the profits from crown estates being obscured, but this

---

[348] CUL, LL.4.7. Proceedings of the Justice of Eyre held for the Forest of Dean at Gloucester Castle, 1634. Actually filed under reference CUL, LL.3.10.

loss was compounded by the impact of inflation. Sir John Winter's business associates, Sir Basil Brooke and George Mynne, were prosecuted for grossly exceeding the wood allowances of their lease. The court heard that, as assignees of the Earl of Pembroke, they had 'a graunte from the King for diverse yeares yet to come of 1000 Cords of Complement wood and the windfalls offals and Logge woods for maintenance of the Iron workes in deane Forrest'. King's Counsel, apparently, 'charged them with two things [vizt] the number of cords and the abuses in taking them'. The perceived gravity of these abuses was reflected in the fine that was handed down to these two defendants. Between them, Brooke and Mynne were fined £50, 039 16s 8d. According to the court records, while watching these proceedings, Winter came to the conclusion that his case bore many similarities to that of Brooke and Mynne and confessed to his own abuses, for which he was fined £20, 230.

The most prominent concerns regarded the practices of Brooke and Mynne. They had apparently evaded royal officers in the collection of wood to serve their ironworks. According to 'a Jury of the best in Ranke and qualitie', they had blatantly arranged for the delivery of 'great quantities of Cord wood' without the knowledge of these royal officials. In addition were more subtle techniques which had been developed to evade the regulation of Dean's resources. In every bundle of twenty cords was found concealed an extra five. Not only that, but 'they had invented a way of making half Cord wood instead of whole and by that had soe increased the size that in every two whole cords they gained a Fourth parte'. The more expensive and higher grade of cord wood had regularly been accounted for as 'windfalls and offalls' but, most alarming to King's Counsel, was the accusation that they had:

by cutting glades and distroyeing the shelter of great tymber trees left them open for the wind upon sides of hills and in wett grounds soe as when winter came the wind haveing power upon them blew downe a great number of goodly tymber trees 1000 in one night many of them marked for the king and those they tooke as winde falls.

This session also upheld complaints of excessive spoil caused by Cabiners living off the Forest who had been brought in to cut down wood and make charcoals for Brooke and Mynne's iron-making activities. These two associates of Winter were also charged with exerting the undue influence of their local status in threatening 'officers to have them turned out of there places if they pry too narrowely into there accounts'.[349] In all of these acts the jury concluded that 'the King was deceived'. Essentially, the 1634 Justice Seat demonstrates royal concerns over the inefficiency, opacity and protectionism inherent in the management of this increasingly valuable crown estate.

The records of Exchequer and the Justice Seat suggest that the Crown, and various agents thereof, were demanding that those with 'pretended customs' should 'set these claymes in writing' to 'his majesties satisfaction'.[350] Estovers, pannage, grazing and mining rights were formally defined and reified, certainly by comparison with the ideal of oral, overlapping practices which had traditionally formed the customary

---

[349] CUL, LL.4.7. Proceedings of the Justice of Eyre held for the Forest of Dean at Gloucester Castle, 1634. This document is actually filed under reference CUL, LL.3.10.

[350] TNA, E112/182/196.

taskscape of this forest. These sessions represent an important stage in the rationalisation of forest space and the formalisation of custom. A 1635 warrant granted a 'Commission to Henry, Earl of Holland', also Lord Chief Justice of the 1634 Eyre, and others for disafforesting the forests of Dean and Essex. This suggests that the forest Eyre had set out to impose a rigorous interpretation of medieval forest law upon this region, with the express purpose that the Crown would then court proposals for its disafforestation.[351]

In the upheaval following the massive fines handed down to Winter, Brooke and Mynne for their industrial spoliation, a letter in December 1635 from Sir John Finch to Sir John Bankes, then Attorney General, proclaimed that:

> According to your Lordshippes direccion I have in the presence of Master Sergeant Whitfield conferred with Sir Baynham Throckmorton, Sir Sackville Crowe, and Sir John Winter, and uppon longe debate I find the differences between them may well be reconciled upon these terms.

The essence of the settlement between Winter and his main industrial rivals was that he should 'continue his Iron workes in the old perambulacion of Deane Forrest' and to continue to receive wood for such purposes but 'they shalbe such woods of his owne as lye in Lidney, Newent, Newlande and Awre, and the Abbottes in which he hath some interest by way of lease'. On top of these restrictions, it was agreed that 'Sir John Winter shall not digge for by himself, or by any other, nor buy use or employ aboute his said iron

---

[351] Bodleian Library, MS Bankes 55, fol. 50.

workes any Mynes or Cinders but such as hee shall have from his Majesties Farmors'.[352] This proposal suggests the way that Charles I and his government were increasingly seeking to profit from the appropriation and sale of rights which had 'anciently' been attached to those who were born and raised in the Forest.

The alienation of customary usages, particularly free-mining rights, is clear in the 1636 warrant which granted the lease of Crown ironworks to Sir Baynham Throckmorton, Baronet, Sir Sackville Crowe, Baronet, John Taylor and John Guning, the younger. Under the terms of this lease, Throckmorton and his fellow lessees had gained the rights to:

> all our Cynders Oare & Mynes of Iron, aswell open as covert, within anie part of ye said Forest, with libertie to dig there for ye opening ye covert Cynders Mines of Iron & Quarries of Stone ... late in ye tenure of Sir Basil Brooke George Mynn & Thomas Hackett or theire assigns.

Not only were these rights being traded on paper between various interests profitable to the Crown, but the latest industrial partnership to take a formal hold of the Forest's material resources depended upon finance provided by Taylor and Guning, two merchants from Bristol. The Throckmorton family, themselves, had only been resident in Dean since the beginning of the seventeenth century.

The language of this lease is similar to that adopted by many surveys of Dean during this period. By contrast to the manipulation of wood

---

[352] Bodleian Library, MS Bankes 40, fol. 2 r.

measurements employed by Brooke, Mynne and, presumably, Winter, Throckmorton's twenty one year lease stated adamantly that all wood was to be taken under the strict supervision of the Crown and its officers, and that 'every Cord whereof is to containe 8 foote & 4 inches in lenght, 4 foote & three inches in bredth, & 4 foote & 3 inches in height'.[353] A similar quantifying imperative is evident in the 1638 'Directions for the Commission' of 'Deane Forrest', which related to more advanced proposals for the complete disafforestation of the region. These instructions directed the commissioner to 'certifie the number of the woods and the trees in generall', 'what timber trees there are', and 'How manie of those trees wilbe fit for shipping of all kindes'. The instructions then move to enquire about Dean in its entirety, directing the relevant commissioner to record 'what parte of the said Forest & How much thereof is without wood or timber & where it lyeth whether in the skirtes of the Forest or otherwise' and, crucially it seems, 'to certifie the values of the wood & trees'.[354] A very different picture of the Forest emerges from the more cadastral perspective of central government. Data derived from surveys, maps and litigation all generated a rather abstract notion of the Forest in its entirety. This was a simplified and standardised vision from outside that contrasted starkly with the complexities and contingencies of local perspectives. The subjective experience of the Forest taskscape was far too complex to be recorded in anything other than the most selective and simplified manner.

---

[353] Bodleian Library, MS Bankes, 59/7, fol. 10 r.

[354] Bodleian Library, MS Bankes 32, fol. 16 v.

From the cadastral perspective, it might have appeared self evident that the Forest should be enclosed and encoppiced. Those who were losing rights to common through improvement could simply be compensated through allocation of a portion of the wastes, proportionate to the stake they had enjoyed in the previously 'open' Forest. An anonymous letter addressed to Bankes, although probably relating to 1639 proposals for disafforestation, highlighted the link between royal income, national interest, and the benefits of a widespread campaign of 'improving' crown waste and demesne lands. The author proposed that the King's prerogative was sufficient to 'enter any man's land' if such an act was deemed beneficial to that most malleable of state metaphors, the commonwealth. The author's notion of a national community, particularly a concern for providing aid to the rapidly increasing poor, allowed this potential projector to couch his progressive ideology in terms that recalled the basic tenets of paternalistic duty. The opening section of this letter attempts to reconcile the apparent contradiction between the author's own private interest and its intrusion into public finance and the customary rights of the commonwealth. Worth quoting at length, it begins by explaining:

This kingdom is grown very populous, which is one of the greatest reasons given wherefore corn and all other kinds of provisions are at a very dear rate and are likely to be dearer. To prevent this there is one that by improvement of much lands in many parts of this kingdom, Wales and Ireland (by God's blessing) will very much increase corn, beef, mutton, butter, cheese, and all other provisions, wool, and the best native commodities, and thereby prevent scarcity and relieve the poor by setting them on work and otherwise, who do very much increase and complain of want; so as he may have free liberty without interruption of the owners of the lands to improve what lands he finds meet for improvement. This improvement will be constant and permanent (by God's blessing) to the end of the world with small charge and little looking to when it is finished, and a very great benefit to the commonwealth in general in divers ways and no prejudice to any particular subject.[355]

Towards the end of the 1630s, as royal finances grew even tighter with tensions and the outbreak of war in the north of England, Sir John Winter proposed terms to take responsibility for disafforesting the whole of Dean. This plan was fairly rapidly accepted by the Crown in 1639. Ralph Anstis notes that:

the transaction was virtually a sale of the Forest. Included in the deal was the transfer of the King's Ironworks, the right to take timber (except trees that could be used for making ships for the Navy) and all the coal, iron-ore and stone beneath the surface.[356]

18,000 of the 22,000 forested acres were to be enclosed and encoppiced to protect current wood store, to allow for more efficient farming of certain areas, and to secure future growth of wood to sustain both the royal navy and the local iron industry. The remaining 4,000 acres was to be divided from the improved areas and left as commons and wastes in compensation

---

[355] Bodleian Library, MS Bankes 48, fol. 22.

[356] R. Anstis, *Four Personalities from the Forest of Dean; Sir John Wyntour, Catharina Bovey, Timothy Mountjoy, Sir Charles Dilke* (Coleford, 1996), 26.

to the poor of the Forest and those others who would lose their customary access.

A letter of July 1640 from the Lord Treasurer to Bankes points to the link between local projects and the increased financial fluidity being realised by the Crown. Development and consolidation of wider systems for the circulation of capital allowed individual improvement to be conceived as part of a larger, centralised drive for national economic progress. The letter refers to the 'drayning of the Great Levell in the severall Counties of Huntingdon, Cambridge and elswhere' and suggests that the treasury was experiencing difficulties in financing such a project. The Lord Treasurer referred to 'Sir John Winter knt Fee Farmour of his Majesties Forest or late Forest of Deane and of all his Majesties Landes Iron Workes and other hereditamentes there'. He noted that Winter was set to pay '1500 li at our Lady day next 1641 and 1500 li more at Michaelmas next following', suggesting that these payments, and others, could be used to help finance crown projects for the drainage of the East Anglian fens.[357] From this abstracted perspective, private interest could be shown to operate to the general benefit of the commonwealth. In this world-view the maximisation of productivity in local economies, together with division of land into more discrete and efficient parcels, seemed equitable enough, particularly with the presumption that adequate provision would be made for the compensation of the poor in these regions.

From the other side of the fence, however, the rationalisation of Forest space and the allocation of 4,000 acres of common land was far from

_____
357

adequate compensation for the loss of customary access to an 'open' forest. Exchequer litigation of this period reveals how those who claimed customary rights attaching to property were compelled to make their case to the Crown. The alternative was to be added to the record of those who should be compensated for the loss of access to Dean's resources. Many depositions from 1640 contesting total disafforestation raise the question of which groups the commissioners had consulted in the Forest. These records make it clear that it was not only the poor and propertyless inhabitants who registered opposition. Christopher Worgan, fifty two year-old yeoman of Newland, confirmed that 'his Majestie did intend to disafforest the said Forrest for the ymprovement thereof' while his father, Christopher Worgan, the elder, added that a ratio of two to one copyholders and freeholders of this region had 'not assented to the allotment of Foure thousand acres of Common in the sayd Forrest'. John Lewis, twenty two year-old yeoman, asserted that the 'Freehoulders & copyhoulders of the tything of Newland whereof hee this deponent is one have not consented unto the allotment of four thousand acres of comon in the said Forrest of deane'. Similarly, William Wargeant, forty eight year-old gentleman of St. Briavels parish, assured the court that:

the greatest number of the Freehoulders & thinhabitants of the forrest of deane have not accepted or esteemed the allotment of 4000 acres to be a fitt & proporcinable Comon for soe great a multitude of Comoners inhabiting within the said Forrest of deane And this deponent doth verily believe in his conscience that that yf noe greater Allotment of Comon then the said 4000 acres and ground of noe better nature quality & condicion then the same is which is allowed to the defendants Inhabitants & commoners, it will be a great prejudice &

226

ympoverishment to all the defendants inhabitants & Comoners and in short time produce the ruine & destitution of many an honest poore family inhabiting there'.[358]

While the commissioner Sir Charles Harbord sought advice and approval for these plans from a relatively narrow selection of foresters, consent from within this group was by no means unanimous.

Allowing for the potentially rhetorical aims of his deposition, Wargeant's testimony suggests that, quite apart from the inadequacy of these 4,000 acres, there were also serious misgivings regarding the quality and location of these lands. The answers to a 1668 Exchequer complaint in which the Attorney General requested written notification of those who claimed formal customary rights attaching to property tenure, referred retrospectively to the proposed disafforestation of 1639 and 1640. Claiming the right to graze sixty commonable beasts within the Forest, John Aram, a gentleman of Awre, informed the court that such:

> allotment is very unreasonable Considering the great number of Commoners that have right of Common in the said Forrest and that the said Forrest is of much greater extent then by the bill is sett forth and that such allotment also was of the most barren ground in all the Forrest being most apt to beare just Briers and brambles and ful of stones and pitts and very little grasse or feeding for their Commonable cattle.

---

[358] TNA, E134/16&17Chas1/Hill.

Not only were the 4,000 acres 'the barronest and poorest land in all the said Forrest and beneath for the most parte furze and Briars & Brambles', Aram continued, but it was 'sett out in the very utmost parts of the said forrest'.[359] This rationalised segmentation of forest space restricted customary use of the 'open' Forest's diverse ecological and mineral resources. Despite the ideological platitudes of improvers, rights to common in one particular and distant part of Dean would have been of little use to the majority of commoners who did not live in the immediate vicinity of these lands.

While these implications were problematic for those able to claim formal customary rights through the 'satisfaction of his Majestie', this rationalisation was potentially devastating to those who depended on less formal customary uses. Perhaps most significantly, mining rights were obviously jeopardised by Winter's proposed purchase of the region and its mineral resources. Moreover, as part of the wider community of those who depended on rights to pannage, estovers and grazing, free miners required unrestricted access to different parts of the whole forest at different times of the year, rather than constant access to one particular designated area of land. High levels of resentment were aroused by Winter's proposal to take the whole forest under single undivided management. Explaining his apparent intention to completely dominate the industries of Dean, Hart notes that Winter's Catholicism prohibited him from ordinary public service, thus possibly pushing him towards the less orthodox method of making money through technical innovation. He suggests that '[l]ocal opposition and Parliamentary antagonism to a Roman Catholic official of

---

[359] TNA, E112/403/8.

the Queen's household outweighed Winter's personal popularity and the rational advantages of his scheme'. Winter was therefore compelled to 'relinquish his purchase' of the Forest. Winter calculated that he was still owed £15,000 but, as Hart observes, 'in any event, the disposal of the Forest, the repayment of debts and even the formal surrender of the patent were all swallowed up in the Civil Wars (1642-7)'.[360]

V The Forest of Dean during the English Civil Wars

Although divided by their differing confessional faiths and competing commercial interests, Sir John Winter and Sir Baynham Throckmorton, as High Sheriff of the region, both appear to have attempted to preserve the royal forest during the civil wars of the 1640s. On 13 August 1643, Throckmorton wrote of the 'present necessitie to employ divers workmen & materialls' to lay siege to Gloucester which was 'now in Rebellion against us', specifically suggesting that forty miners were required to 'repair to our Trayne of Artillery before Glocester'.[361] Despite the traditional ideal whereby mining rights within the forest had been derived from royal authority since a 'time out of mind of man', support for the King's cause was proving difficult to muster. Throckmorton had written to Prince Rupert three days earlier, explaining that:

---

[360] Hart, *New History*, 15.

[361] GRO, D115/9.

this morninge Collonell Vavaser desired me to summon in the Countrey againe tomorrow, and desires I will stay to receave their appearance because I have a Little Command over them, And therefore I have now sent humbly to Crave your Highnes pardon that I waite not on you now; I had a very good apperance upon tuesday last of ye Countrey of about two thousand, but few or noe armes, I hope I shall see more Armes tomorrow.[362]

Writing to Prince Rupert on 22 November 1644, Winter also demonstrated the integral role of local knowledge in effectively defending this region from rebel forces. Bemoaning the foul weather that had hindered operations, he suggested that the Prince had:

observed soe well the ill consequences of the rebels havinge footinge in Monmouth sheere that I doubt not but you wil command a stricter care to be had of those partes then formerly was in my poore judgement a good garrison at Monmouth, an indifferent one at Chepstow and some forces at Ross or the pass there over the bridge wil sufficiently secure (at least for this Winter) al the partes both of hereford and Monmouth sheere on that side of Wye which wil not be foordable or but in very few places which may easily be spoyled soe that the leavyes of men monyes, or quartering which your highnes may desseygn in those partes you may more comfortably rely on.[363]

---

[362] B.L., Add. 18980. *Rupert Correspondence.*

[363] B.L., Add. 18981. *Rupert Correspondence.*

Winter was eventually forced to raze Whitecross, his family home at Lydney, to prevent it falling into the hands of Parliamentarian forces before making his escape across the Wye into Wales. This was a spectacular and significant event from the perspective of the forest community as evidenced by its inscription into the local landscape. Discussing popular perceptions of Dean, Chapter One noted 'Wyntour's Leap', a 200 foot ledge which overhangs the Wye Valley and that to this day, according to local lore, records the site from which Winter leapt in making his escape from Parliamentarian soldiers.

The turmoil of the mid-seventeenth century also had a significant legal impact on the mining culture in Dean. Christopher Tucker's complaint in an Exchequer suit of 1656 helps to explain the mid-century change in legal practices of the Dean mining fraternity. It also registers conflicting perceptions of custom and cultural division. This case suggests that one of the most profound changes in the relation of this community to central government had very little to do with the intentionality of the Stuart state. Tucker, 'Gaveller and receiver of the rentes and duties due and answerable to his Majestie from the miners in the Forest of Deane', was concerned by the disarray that had enveloped this industry during the troubles of the 1640s. Tucker claimed a breach of 'ancient' mining custom which dictated that the area for twenty four yards around any gale, or the distance that the said miner could throw scree from his pit, was prohibited to any other member of the 'Company of Miners'. He complained that:

> nowe soe itt is that one William Stone Thomas Morgan John Rocke Richard Nashe Thomas Dawe John Voys als Broadbridge Thomas Rocke Henry Machen & Thomas Hall with divers others ... do

combyne & confederate themselves to disturbe and interrupt your said orator in the quiet holding and enjoying the said worke & profit thereof & doe threaten and give out in speeches that they will dig & sincke pittes within ye said markes and boundes by the laws & customes aforesaid.

Tucker was particularly concerned by Thomas Hall, claiming that he was unable to 'satisfie his majestie such rentes and & duties as are due' because:

the said Hall though noe right in the said coale pitts his family nor himselfe inhabiting within the said Forrest hath sundry times incouraged & sett on the other defendants to disturb interrupt & oppose your said orator in the said Sough or work by telling them that hee the said Hall would beare them out and mainteyne them in such their disturbance.[364]

This gentleman from outside the Forest, claimed Tucker, was attempting to gain a foothold in the mining industry through offering to support these miners in the costs of their Exchequer litigation.

The various defendants clearly understood the situation very differently but agreed that they were arguing this issue in an equity court due to the lapse of the Mine Law Court 'by reason and distraccione of these tymes'. The defendants reaffirmed that there:

was & tyme out of mind hath ben a cort called by the name of the Mine Law Court in which all ... Trespases & differences whatsoever

---

[364] TNA, E112/183/220.

betwixt miners and Quarriers their said mines within the said Forrest ought there to be herd & determined and not elsewhere.

They suggested that Tucker was acting in direct contravention of mining custom by bringing this case to the Court of the Exchequer. Rather than having answered the charges directly, the defendants claimed that Tucker was a man 'much addicted to suits in lawe' and that he had taken this action simply to oppresse his poore neighbours & Miners of the said Fraternitie'. They suggested that his motivation was 'to ingrosse all or moste parte of the Mines within the said Forrest into his hands and possession and soe to inhaunce the rates & prices of coales', by sinking pits in as many parts of this area as possible and claiming that anybody who attempted to mine therein was encroaching upon his '24 yard' gales. The plan was illegitimate, claimed the defendants, as local custom dictated that 'everie such pitt unfinished & nott wrought as for the space of one yeare & one day the same is then intended to be noe pitt'. While claiming the legitimacy of traditional mining custom, they were careful to frame this conflict in a larger political context. Demonstrating their knowledge of the national situation, they claimed that:

since the high Court of Parliament had placed a Garrison in the Cyttie of Gloucester for preservacion of ... the said Cytie & countie hee the said Complainante ... by and with the Consent Combinacion & Confederacion of one Sir John Winter Kt a greate papist & Mallignant to the state did make & cause to bee made within the ... Forrest one quarter mile compasse and boundes in gales & pitts to ... ingrosse all or most parte of the said Cole works into his own hands And to prevent theis defendants and other those Miners there to come within that compass & Circumference being the chief place of hoying [removing] stone Coles within the said Forrest that soe by that meanes the said garrison at glouc was in very great want of forage for two Winters successively.[365]

The cessation of the Mine Law Court had apparently allowed Hall and Winter to assert undue influence over the mining industry and cut off supplies to the Parliamentary garrison at Gloucester. This statement also suggests the complexity of popular allegiance in the Forest of Dean and that those opposed to Tucker were left with little option but to argue for their rights through central courts. Fractures among the usually coherent fraternity of free miners were apparently compounded by the lapse of the Mine Law Court. This seems to have contributed to their increasing engagement with central legal processes and the documentary evidence of the written record.

While this period marked an important shift, miners had been using equity courts more regularly since the early years of the seventeenth century. In 1611, as discussed, the Earl of Pembroke had been granted rights to forest resources and miners had taken defensive action in the Exchequer court.[366] The free miners' rights had been more explicitly embroiled in the interaction of written and spoken record since the 1613 decree ruling that they engaged in their occupation 'by grace and not by right', and the

---

[365] TNA, E112/183/220.

[366] TNA, E112/83/411.

written codification of the miners' *Laws & Privileges* in 1610.[367] In 1625, Sir William Throckmorton and his son, among others, deposed to Exchequer commissioners confirming the custom of the free miners in response to legal action by the Attorney General. Miners' litigation increased sharply during the 1630s. This is unsurprising in the face of crown leases to private individuals and other proposals for disafforestation and enclosure which restricted miners' access to seams of iron and coal within an 'open' forest. Edward Terringham, a royal lessee, told the court in 1636 that the King, by his letters patent, did 'demyse, graunte & to Farme sett unto' him 'All those his Majesties Mynes of coale & Quarries of Grindstone as wel open as coverte scituate & being within the said Forest and in all places within the lymytts & perambulacions of the said Forrest'. Terringham requested that a writ of sub poena be directed at Sir John Winter, among others, for taking and carrying away coal from pits in Norchard near Lydney.[368] The years 1638 and 1639 saw two similar cases in which several deponents recounted local mining custom. This litigation must be seen in the context of Winter's proposal to purchase the Forest during the late 1630s.[369] In addition to Tucker's suit, the Exchequer court

---

[367] TNA, E126/1, fol. 305.

[368] TNA, E112/181/155.

[369] TNA, E134/13&14Chas1/Hil16 & TNA, E134/14Chas1/Mich42.

was also called upon to help resolve physical strife between miners over sinking pits in Dean in 1646.[370]

Walter J. Ong's work on orality and literacy illuminates the shift from embodied to written legal records in Dean towards the end of the seventeenth century. Ong discusses the permanently fluid nature of sound in terms that echo the function of speech and oral testimony in supporting the popular taskscape of the Forest. He notes that:

> [t]here is no way to stop sound and have sound. I can stop a moving picture camera and hold one frame fixed on the screen. If I stop the movement of sound, I have nothing – only silence. All sensation takes place in time, but no other sensory field resists a holding action, stabilisation, in quite this way. Vision can register motion, but it can also register immobility.[371]

It follows that the visual technology of the written record is central to fixing oral interpretations of precedent in a chronological order. Ong also highlights the lack of mnemonic repetition and the redundancy of copious additive formulae generally found in oral memories, suggesting that the written record can influence more purely analytical thought processes. Of visually based, written, descriptions of the world, he notes that:

---

[370] TNA, E134/22&23Chas1/Hill.

[371] Ong, *Orality and Literacy*, 32.

In the absence of elaborate analytical categories that depend on writing to structure knowledge at a distance from lived experience, oral cultures must conceptualize and verbalize all their knowledge with more or less close reference to the human lifeworld, assimilating the alien, objective world to the more immediate, familiar interaction of human beings ... Oral cultures know few statistics or facts divorced from human or quasi-human activity. An oral culture likewise has nothing corresponding to how-to-do-it manuals for the trades.[372]

This suggests the profound influence of the written legal record upon the way that miners perceived their industry and the environment in which they lived and worked. Late medieval Dean was far from a 'primary oral culture' and the Crown had always operated, at least in part, through the customary mechanisms of local governance.[373] This shift towards the written record, however, was integral to a set of processes whereby the regulation of this region was being abstracted from its lived social context. From external perspectives this generated a more narrowly focused and selective, yet diachronically ordered and legible, representation of this region. The

---

[372] Ibid., 42-3.

[373] For further reading on the relation between orality, literacy and collective memory see Tonkin, *Narrating our pasts*; J. Goody, *The Domestication of the Savage Mind* (Cambridge, 1977); J. Goody, *The Interface between the Written and the Oral* (Cambridge, 1987); J. Goody, *The Logic of Writing and the Organization of Society* (Cambridge, 1986); Ong, *Orality and Literacy*; Fentress and Wickham, *Social Memory*; J. C. Miller, *The African Past Speaks: Essays on Oral Tradition as History* (Folkestone and Hamden, 1980); Clanchy, *From Memory to Written Record*; M. McLuhan, *The Gutenberg Galaxy: The Making of Typographic Man* (Toronto, 1962); R. H. Canary and H. Kozicki (eds.), *The Writing of History: Literary Form and Historical Understanding* (Madison, 1978); W. L. Chafe, 'Integration and involvement in speaking, writing, and oral literature', in D. Tannen (ed.), *Spoken and Written Language: Exploring Orality and Literacy* (Norwood, 1982).

mining community of the Forest of Dean developed a modified collective sense of themselves and their region through increasingly documentary 'habits of mind' during the seventeenth century.[374] This self-perception was influenced, but not determined, by the way that they were understood and viewed by the English state.

This shift was reflected in the changing strategies adopted by the mining community in resisting encroachment upon 'open' forest and the customary rights that attached to this ideal. Resistance had traditionally consisted of communally inclusive rituals of protest such as those adopted in the Skimmington riots. The symbolism of these protests at once grew out of, and articulated, the daily experience of life in a community that shared a common understanding of popular legal cultures. Increasing engagement with central equity courts appears to have engendered a divergence of legal senses in seventeenth-century Dean. The increasing abstraction of legal practices is visible in the 1636 grant to Sir Baynham Throckmorton et al. The lease, drawn up in June of that year, directed that the delivery, felling or collection of wood should be reported to royal officers, if not in person, then 'in writeing at their houses', and that all such transactions were to be:

> entred att the time of the delivery in three Bookes, The one to be kept by some or one of the Verderers, who is to returne it yearlie into our Exchequer, and another Booke to be kept by our Surveyor generall of our landes, and the other by the lessees which are to containe the daies of deliverie, the quantities & qualities of the Wood: which Bookes are

---

[374] Fox, *Custom*, 111.

to be interchangeably signed by our Officers predicte & at the delivery
of the Wood & by the lessees or one of them.[375]

The majority of deponents and complainants to the Court of the Exchequer
during this period were recorded either as gentlemen, yeomen or
husbandmen. One section of the forest commonalty that kept pace with
these changes was the fraternity of free miners. This was despite the fact
that this was strictly prohibited by the *Laws and Privileges* threatening, as it
did, the monopoly of jurisdiction enjoyed by the Mine Law Court. As
suggested by Tucker's action of 1646, this legal option became the only
non-physical channel of recourse following the interruption of this court
during the chaos of civil war.

In this climate, it is easy to understand how the legitimation of custom
might have become abstracted through the process that Thompson referred
to as the 'commodification of use rights'. The case of Dean's mining
industry demonstrates just how reciprocal this process could be. Through
the actions, at least in part, of this mining community in defence of their
occupational custom, these rights were no longer strictly embodied in or
attached to the person of those born into the Dean mining industry. The
year 1652 saw the first recorded sale of a pit to an 'outsider'. John Brayne's
purchase was, unsurprisingly, hotly contested in the Exchequer court but
seems to have been allowed to stand. Prior to this, as mentioned, Guning
and Taylor, merchants of Bristol, emerged as business partners to Crowe
and Throckmorton with a 'legal' interest in the region's mineral resources.
Brayne's purchase of a gale, however, seems to have been particularly

---

[375] Bodleian Library, MS Bankes 59/7, fol. 10 r.

significant, coming as it did at a time when legitimation of mining custom was in a state of flux following the discontinuance of the Mine Law Court. Even though the court was reconstituted at the end of the 1660s, the order that marked this suggests that, by this point, the detailed written record seems to have been the most reliable way of maintaining their traditional industry. Their practices thus became more legible and the protracted engagement with central courts would have implied acceptance that their occupation was now subject to forms of regulation beyond the local monopoly of the Mine Law Court.

This chapter opened with a discussion of DiMaggio's appraisal of institutional logics and the relation between cultural perceptions, social life, and particular methods of production. According to DiMaggio, these logics are, in no sense, fixed, immutable or discrete. Different people or communities are able to adopt many, often contradictory, elements from a continuum of divergent world views according to their particular situation. During the late medieval period, however, the Mine Law Court had drawn its coherence from a set of principles that were largely coterminous with those that informed popular perceptions of the region. During the course of the seventeenth century, it appears that a combination of material conflicts over their 'ancient' and occupationally-defining rights, coupled with an increasing recourse to equity courts, resulted in a move towards the institutional logic of the Stuart state and improvers. This was not an intended outcome of either the mining community or the state but, rather, the unintentional consequences of miners' increasing engagement with equity courts in defence of their customary industry. This shift was related to a division within the, albeit idealised, traditionally shared culture of the Forest. The division was closely tied to the formalisation of custom, and the migration of meaning attached to the language of use-rights. As the century progressed it seems that official notions of custom were being emptied of their social content, relating only to those rights which were recognised by the cadastral mechanisms of the Stuart state. From this perspective, custom thus came to denote a more exclusive and official interpretation of rights to forest resources than the socially inclusive ideal outlined in Chapter One. As Steinberg notes, language is first and foremost a process of physical and social interaction. Like the reciprocal dynamic of Bourdieu's *habitus* or Giddens' structures of social reproduction, it is a medium that shapes the ideological forms that in turn influence the social formations responsible for its production.

The case of Dean demonstrates the fundamental incompatibility of world-views or institutional logics that either perpetuated customary perceptions of the region or characterised the perspective of forward-looking improvers. This polarising conflict, however, did not lead inevitably to the vanquishing of the Forest's popular communalism and traditional lifestyles, nor did it herald the victory of the large investor or a new definition of exclusive property rights. It seems to have encouraged, rather, a re-alignment of principles and logics as this Forest community and its inhabitants reoriented themselves according to the circumstances of the later seventeenth century.

Chapter Five

Space, text and popular memory: 1660-1777

When these court cases were brought up the constable of St. Briavels
had to attend and whoever was proved to be in the wrong had to
compensate the other miner. It was never in money, I know because
I've seen some of these old write ups it was always in weight of coal
and back in those days the weight then ... it wasn't like weights we've
got today, it was bushels, quarts and pecks it was then ... I can
remember my father telling me to go to the shop he used to say go to
get a peck of potatoes and as a kid I could carry that, you know, a bag
about that tall ... of seed potatoes to plant in the garden.

72 year old free miner of the Forest of Dean. Interviewed in
September, 2007.

I 'Settling' the forest

Following the restoration of the Stuart monarchy in 1660, efforts to 'settle'
the forest were taken up with renewed vigour. Both the quality and quantity
of the Forest's timber stocks had declined and this was largely blamed on
the lack of consistency in forest management during the upheavals of the
previous twenty years. Chapter Four examined the impact of the war on the
Mine Law Court and political division between certain sections of the
mining community. Following the cessation of hostilities the military
regime of the 1650s caused yet more damage to Dean's wood stocks in
appropriating the local iron industry unhindered by local gentry who, the

Earl of Northampton had suggested earlier in the century, were essential to the effective governance of this region. The influence of this group was heavily restricted by sanctions placed upon them as a result of their Royalist allegiances during the previous decades.

Despite damage sustained by Dean's ecological system under Major John Wade during the Protectorate, the 1650s did witness attempts to reinstate the local court system. In 1656 a Swanimote court was held, gathering information to be heard and ratified at the Justice Seat in Eyre of that summer. The Dean Eyre in 1656 represented an attempt to take stock of, and rectify, abuses committed on the demesne lands during the turmoil of the previous decade. These sessions recorded a detailed list of encroachments, illegally erected cottages, perprestures, unlicensed coppices and a variety of other presentments together with the names and abodes of those responsible.[376] In addition to this Eyre, 1656 also saw the first session of the reconstituted Mine Law Court.[377] Herbert concurs that:

> Under the Protectorate the Forest was more efficiently administered, and after the Restoration Charles II's government, committing itself to a policy of preservation to raise ship timber, inclosed over half the demesne under an Act of 1668, removed the ironworks and illegal

---

[376] GRO, D2026/X14.

[377] Hart, *Free Miners*, 77-80.

squatters, and added more effective elements to the cumbersome administrative apparatus.[378]

The Act of 1668 was to assume huge significance for the Forest but the Mine Law Court session in 1656 reveals much about industrial culture in post-war Dean. In contrast to previous records of this court and its meetings, these proceedings were thoroughly documented. The nature of each plaintiff's grievance was recorded in full and the documents note the defendant's answer and verdict. While this provided a more reliable record for legal defence, it also marked a significant shift towards the legibility of the industry. Certain aspects did not change. The proceedings still stipulated that the jury was to consist of twelve, twenty-four or forty-eight free miners which ensured that the majority of those responsible for delivering verdicts in disputes and ratifying the orders of this court were from the community of poor, propertyless foresters.[379] From the later seventeenth century until the dissolution of the Mine Law Court in 1777,

---

[378] Herbert, *VCH, Vol. V*, 292.

[379] The 1668, 1674 and 1678 'Orders' of this court provide three lists of this jury in its fullest sitting of forty-eight free miners. Of these 144 names, thirty-three are of men who served more than once, leaving 111 eleven individual miners whose presence and authorization had been required to ratify orders that attempted to protect the local mining industry from external interests, to whom, it was becoming increasingly attractive. In correlating this list with the Hearth Tax returns for 1671-2, I have only been able to trace just over a third of those who served on these juries. Of these forty-three miners, however, twenty-eight were registered as having one hearth, twelve with two, and three with three hearths. Whilst this is not necessarily a representative sample of jury members, the very high proportion of single hearth households, together with the possibility that some of those unrecorded were living and working in the extra parochial demesne lands of Dean suggests that this influential regulatory body consisted, at least in part, of jurors from amongst the poorer sections of the Forest community. GRO, D383/1.

larger capital investors and local gentry were increasingly able to insinuate themselves in this lucrative industry by one means or another.

Despite the popular constituency of its jury, these later seventeenth-century court records bore many similarities to the documentation of the equity courts. Chapter Two discussed Crehan's view of hegemonic negotiation as the struggle to determine the legal structures within which the exercise of power is framed and contested. From the very material nature of physical petitioning, consensus over legitimate forms of legal process had undergone a profound shift by the late seventeenth century. This was related to, or influenced by, the aforementioned migration of customary meaning in Dean. In short, these records suggest that the embodied nature of traditional legal memory was superseded by an increasing faith in written evidence. Those who had depended upon the local court system, the free mining community in particular, were keen to emulate the processes of central courts.

Controversy still raged in Dean following the Restoration in 1660. Sir John Winter attempted to resume operations as they had been before the 'late distracciones', apparently encouraged by the fact that he had not technically surrendered his original grant as the entire situation had been thrown into chaos by the outbreak of domestic hostilities. This drew stiff opposition from many within the forest commonalty. The majority of these complaints, relating to the amount of spoil which had been caused by Winter's pre-war ironworks, were argued through the Court of Exchequer as were many disputed tithe cases provoked by a similar air of confusion and contention.

---

[380] TNA, E134/18&19Chas2/Hil10; TNA, E134/19Chas2/Mich31; TNA, E112/403/40; TNA, E112/403/12; TNA, E112/403/26; TNA, E112/403/27& TNA, E112/403/8.

Equity litigation from the early 1670s also demonstrates that members of the mining community were very concerned by the implications of Winter's attempts to gain these concessions and the continued involvement of the Terringham family in the iron and coal industries.[381]

An Exchequer case discussed previously demonstrates the relation between this increasing engagement with equity courts, the formalisation of custom, and the changing nature of collective legal memory. In 1668, Attorney General Sir Geoffrey Palmer entered a bill which effectively sought to identify those who claimed formal rights of common within the Forest attaching to property tenure. Palmer particularly sought to clarify the situation as it had been before proposals for the region's total disafforestation were interrupted by the outbreak of war. Effectively, this case represented an integral strand of attempts to settle the forest. The four gentlemen defendants, Anthony Arnold, John Aram, Jeremy Dyett and Richard Henry were engaged in a formalised legal contest over the meaning of events during the 1630s, and the implications of these events for the assertion of customary rights in the late 1660s. The case debated the question of whether or not pre-war commissioners had allowed the commoners of Dean to present their claims and, particularly, the proportion of those who agreed to make improvements on the proviso that 4,000 acres were to be left in common. Of these 4,000 acres, the 'fourth parte whereof was to be subdivided to the use of the poore within the said Forrest'. Arnold and his fellow gentlemen protested that 'they nor either of them is

---

[381] TNA, E134/27Chas2/Mich28; TNA, E134/27&28Chas2/Hil21 & TNA, E134/35Chas2/Mich40.

partie or privie to any suche agreement'. They hoped 'to prove that ... it was not above a tenth parte' of all the commoners who acquiesed, the 'maior parte who claimd common in the said Forrest by prescripcion' withheld their consent. These defendants were adamant that they could 'not by that meanes be preiudiced or barred from enjoying their Antient and undoubted Rights of Common in the said Forrest of Deane'. Their testimony recalls forced enclosure by the late 'usurping powers' and they unanimously referred to the happy restoration, 'since which time the waste grounds of the said Forrest have continued open as they heretofore were'. Arnold and the other defendants were ultimately concerned with their:

> liberties belonging to the said severall & respective auntient messuadge lands and tenementes & hereditaments for all the time whereof the memory of man is not to the contrary ... that is to say Common of pasture and herbadge in all the open & cominable places of & within the said Forrest.

The group bluntly rebuffed Palmer's suggestion that they were claiming these rights out of the simple desire for opposition, stating that they hoped to prove their rights 'legal by the law of the Realme'. They claimed that their rights had been confirmed at the Justice Eyre of 1634 but it is significant that they chose to affirm legitimacy through national law rather than local precedent. Furthermore, they promised not to encourage those who did not have 'lawfull rights'.[382]

---

[382] TNA, E112/403/8.

The manner in which the past was recalled in this case, illuminates the nature of official remembrances of the situation in Dean as it had been before the war. The most striking aspect is the myopic memory of these defendants which chimes with the restricted vision of the cadastral state. Dwelling on the nature of commissions, court documentation, proposals for disafforestation, and legitimating parliamentary acts, there is no mention of the more physical negotiations of the 1630s. The Skimmington riots and other socially inclusive acts of physical resistance to enclosure were, quite simply, ignored as were the implications of these acts, pointing to the ascension of the written record over traditional collective legal memories in the seventeenth-century Forest of Dean. Earlier in the century the physical protests led by John Williams were certainly considered a significant influence as they drew on traditional modes of remembering that were tied to the memories of living and working in the region. These recollections were certainly very influential in the popular uprisings of the early nineteenth century as explored in Chapter Six. Post-restoration attempts to settle the Forest concentrated on the depositions of a particular group of property holders which completely overlooked the claims to resources that were being made by the propertyless during the 1630s. As the Barons of the Exchequer attempted to apportion rights in accordance with the situation before the 'distracciones', the accounts of these deponents, while disagreeing over the exact terms of settlement, presented a very hollow picture of the 1630s. This picture completely overlooked the claims of those who had enjoyed less formal access to pasture and other resources. Effectively, a dispute which involved the physical action of the wider forest community had become a quarrel between landholders with access to central courts. While these deponents claimed to speak on behalf of more humble foresters, the fiercely contested and physical negotiation of the late 1620s and 1630s was now a legal debate over which of Dean's copyholders and freeholders had consented to proposals for disafforestation of the region.

This was not the end of physical protest over access to the Forest. Further anti-enclosure riots occurred in 1669/70, 1688 and 1690 while, in May 1696, Philip Ryley, deputy surveyor of the Forest, was 'connected with the proceedings against ten people convicted and outlawed for 'a pound breach and riot".[383] It seems, rather, that physical protest was far more limited in its extent than it had been in the early seventeenth century. As suggested in Chapter Two, the satisfaction of miners' claims probably contributed to a reduction in the scale of protest in the 1620s. Their leadership was undoubtedly central to effective organisation of resistance in the Forest. By the later seventeenth century, it is argued, a changed legal context which had ensued following the civil wars and Protectorate encouraged the mining community to reconstitute their court along similar lines to the equity courts. The institutional logic of this occupational group was substantially different to the principles which had guided it until the 1640s. Earlier chapters have described similarities between the material practices and symbolic constructions through which the miners organised themselves and those which informed the activities of the wider forest community. Evidence suggests that, by the 1660s, these similarities were less obvious.[384]

---

[383] Hart, *New History*, 160-203.

[384] Friedland and Alford, 'Bringing society back in', 223-62.

In short, the mechanisms of the Mine Law Court were no longer as aligned with the world-view which had underpinned more traditional customary perceptions of the region and had been instrumental in forging such an effective alliance within the forest commonalty. DiMaggio's work implies that this dissonance is likely to have impacted negatively on the capacity for popular collective agency in Dean.

Popular complaint was evidently a factor in the decision taken to halt Winter's third grant to the Forest in 1667. It is evident, however, that by this point, many aspects of local industrial life were being contested in equity courts. This type of negotiation was primarily the preserve of crown agents, minor industrial gentry and more middling inhabitants with the obvious exception of some artisanal foresters and the free-mining community. Due to difficulties in reaching agreement over access rights to Dean's resources, the matter was referred to Parliament in 1668. It is clear that the voice of poor, propertyless foresters was largely ignored in this debate over settlement of the Forest. The resulting Act was to define such usages for the next 150 years and a breach of these terms was, in fact, the primary cause of Warren James' actions in 1832. Herbert notes that:

> The main provision of the Act was that 11,000 acres of the demesne should be inclosed, to be progressively laid open and replaced by other inclosures as the new growth of timber reached sufficient size to be safe from browsing animals. Rights to common of pasture, defined as those lawfully used in 1634, and mining rights were to continue in the unenclosed land, but the commoners agreed to give up estovers in

response to the Crown's offer to lift the forest law from the manorial lands and end ironworking on the demesne.[385]

The tendency of Charles II's government to promote a management style that attempted to preserve Dean's timber stocks and balance the interests of the more visible elements of the forest community, therefore, was clearly reflected in the terms of the Dean Forest (Reafforestation) Act of 1668.

II Dean's Mine Law Court: innovation and change

The nature of the Dean Mine Law Court records illustrates the foregoing discussion of the increasing legibility of the region's industrial operations. By comparison with the paucity of information from previous centuries, increasing documentation gives the impression that this mining community steps into the light during the later seventeenth century. This was also the period during which Mine Law Court sessions became fixed permanently in one location. Until 1680, the Mine Law Court had no settled meeting place and had been held in different parts of St. Briavels Hundred. In 1625, Anthony Callowe had deposed that 'this court has been usually kept in some open place of the forest, for that there is no house or certain place appointed for the same', suggesting the court's more fluid engagement with the mining industry and the spatial relations which governed its operation.

---

[385] Herbert, *VCH Vol. V*, 366.

[386] TNA, E134/22Jas1/East8.

While Townley has suggested that many sessions had been held at Hill Pytt near Lydney, in 1656 the court was held at Littledean and it later convened at Clearwell, Coleford, Mitcheldean and Ruardean. In 1680 the court was held at the Speech House which became the fixed location until its discontinuance in 1777.

In his analysis of *Ancient Law*, Henry Maine observed that 'When primitive law has once been embodied in a Code, there is an end to what may be called its spontaneous development. Henceforward the changes effected in it, if effected at all, are effected deliberately and from without'.[387] From Maine's comments, Jack Goody concludes that 'after the code comes into existence, 'legal modification' can be attributed to the 'conscious desire for improvement'.[388] These observations are pertinent to perceptions of mining custom following the civil wars of the 1640s and the Protectorate of the 1650s. Records of the Mine Law Court from February 1676 reflect this process of conscious adaptation. It is recorded that:

> Att this Court 12 out of the 48 Jurymen whose names are undernamed
> have been elected and chosen to consider of such Orders as have
> heretofore been made for the better ordering and management of the
> concerns of the Myners, and to consider which of them are fit to be

---

[387] H. S. Maine, *Ancient Law: Its Connection With Early Ideas Of Society, And Its Relation To Modern Ideas* (London, 1870), 21.

[388] Goody, *Logic of Writing*, 138.

made void and revoked and what Orders are fit to be continued and remain.[389]

The paucity of Mine Law Courts records from before 1656 makes it impossible to be certain regarding many changes or continuities in operations other than the court's increasing tendency towards documentation and its fixed location. It does seem, however, that the impact of writing would have been deeper than the mere recording of information. This change in documentation would surely have been qualitative as well as quantitative. The 'conscious desire for improvement' outlined by Goody implies an analogy between the rationalisation of land management and the codification of legal practices current in the Forest. This was particularly true of those governing extractive industries. Both impulses imply a shift from legitimation grounded in the material past to a more abstracted and self-reflexive world-view that oriented itself towards future progress, suggesting a change in the way that the free miners understood themselves. This change can be attributed, not only to external pressure but also to an increasing engagement with the written record. The following discussion suggests that the influence of the documentary record inculcated a particular understanding of the relation between geographical space and historical time which privileged private property ownership. There were, thus, links between the improvement of land and the improvement of law centred on increased codification. Both tended towards the legitimation of exclusive property tenure or ownership and both were related to the increased prevalence of the written record. As has been suggested, the

---

[389] GRO, D23/X1.

miners appear to have adopted the written record in an attempt to preserve the traditional protectionism of their small-scale industry.

An order of 18 March 1668 prohibited any 'Foreigner living out of this hundred' from transporting or carrying coal 'contrary to our custom'. It also placed a check on the potential manipulation of iron-ore prices by making all bargaining the responsibility of 'six men (being free myners) chosen by the Company of Myners'. The same order stipulated that:

> No one of the said six men shall hereafter make any bargaine for any Iron myne without it be with the consent of the said six Bargainers or the major parte of them notwithstanding the Company of Miners (if they find just cause) with mutuall consent may alter or change the said Bargainers at their wills and pleasures.

This document also restricted the amount of coal that could be transported by each free miner to that which could be carried by 'four Horses Mares or Mare foals'.[390]

This documentation, generated in an attempt to protect customary mining rights, rendered the operations of the industry more legible to outside parties. It was not only the central equity courts and the written record that increased the vulnerability of the trade. In the eyes of some, external investment was deemed necessary to finance expensive machinery which could reach coal seams previously beyond traditional small-scale customary mining operations. Increasingly sophisticated drainage equipment was brought into use within the Forest during the later seventeenth century and,

---

[390] GRO, D5947.

notes Jurica, 'much mining was on a larger scale than had been permitted by ancient custom'.[391] Mine Law Court orders were evidently aimed at restricting the scale of these operations and preventing the apparent inward flow of those seeking to earn a living from this region's increasingly lucrative industries. These orders reveal various pressures on the miners to account for local needs while attempting to maintain the smaller scale of their traditional trade. An order of 1668 confirmed their exclusive privilege of supplying iron ore and coal outside of St. Briavels Hundred. This, however, was rescinded in 1674 as it was imposing on the interests of several powerful parties, including the constable of the hundred in front of whom, of course, the Mine Law Court was held. By 1687 the situation had again reached crisis point as it was noted that the increased demand for coal was depriving local residents of adequate supplies.[392]

Even while the local mining industry reacted, as a whole, to the potential for profit through an increased demand, the court was still concerned not to alienate other residents who constituted the wider Forest community of which they were a part. In 1687 the court ordered:

That all ordinances and orders made since the happy Restoration of his late Majesty King Charles the second of ever blessed memory that doe anyway relate unto the settling of rates and prizes of Oare and Lime coal to any the furnace or other place whatsoever or that doe nominate

---

[391] Herbert, *VCH Vol. V*, 329. See the *Introduction* for a discussion of changes in the Dean coal mining industry during the early modern period.

[392] Ibid., 329.

and appoint Bargainers for the same be from henceforth totally repealed and made void and of none effect to all intents and purposes as if the same had never been made and that all miners be left at liberty to sell carry and deliver their Oare and coale to whom where and at what reates and prizes they can best agree for without incurring any penalty or forfeiture for so doing.

In rescinding its previous ordinances the court also ordered that the residents of the Forest were to be loaded before colliers as:

> complaint hath been made that the Inhabitants of the Hundred of Saint Briavells cannot have their Horses and other Carriages laden with fire Coale for their owne private uses at the several Cole Pitts within the same Hundred until the Collyers belonging to the said Pitts have first laden their owne horses with Coal to transport and carry the same out of the said Hundred whereby the Horses and other Carriages of the said Inhabitants are many times forced to stay at the said Pitts all day and sometimes to come home again unladen to the great prejudice of the said Inhabitants.

The mining community thus demonstrated their concern to compensate for the loss of local protectionism. The court was keen to adopt innovatory practices, keeping pace with commercial opportunities offered by the national market for coal, but was also careful to minimise impact on the local community. As sessions and orders become more thoroughly documented, a clear picture emerges of the Mine Law Court's pivotal position in negotiating the conflicting pressures of the local and national coal trades.

As it attempted to retrench its hold on the regulation of its industry, the court explicitly recorded and implicitly legitimated many instances which appeared to contradict the customary ideal of this small-scale operation. While primarily intended to secure the miners' own capacity for self-definition, these acknowledgements could substantially undermine perceptions of rights as the prerogative of those born into the occupation within the Forest. At the same time as the order of 1668 declared that 'noe younge man shall or may hereafter worke att myne or Coale (although he be borne within this hundred) if he hath not worked lawfully twelve months and one day', it also conceded that exception could be made if 'he be bound apprentize unto a Free Myner and lawfully serve him as an apprentize for the tearme of five years'. A penalty for breach of this condition was set at the rate of 'one hundred dozen of good sufficient oare or coale the one halfe to be forfeited to the Kings Maiestie and the other halfe to the myner who shall sue for the same'.[393]

Tightening the definition of those who were eligible to mine, the court evidently needed to allow additional workers required by the growth of this industry. This, once again, weakened the literal interpretation that this occupation was open only to those born within St. Briavels Hundred as the son of a free miner. In a somewhat radical departure from traditional mining custom, migrants who had been the source of so much concern or those who had simply not been born into the trade were allowed access provided that they fulfilled certain criteria. At this session in 1668, the court decreed that:

---

[393] GRO, D5947.

noe person whatever that was borne upon the waste soile of the Forest as a Cabenner shall work at Myne or Coale or shall or may transport or carry the same with any manner of carriage except he hath lawfully worked for the space of seaven yeares already under the penallty as aforesaid.

This stipulation was evidently insufficient as further Mine Law Court orders went further in defining and formalising this process of apprenticeship. In April 1680 it was explained that this court:

for the better reforming and preventing of the inconveniences hapning amongst the said Myners by the many young men and boys that contrary to former usage have of late tymes set up for themselves to worke at and carry Myne and Cole not renting Land and keeping house as by the custome they ought Doe now order and ordayne That noe person shal bee reputed or taken to be a free Myner within the precincts thereof or shall keep horses for carrying any Oare or cole untill every such person shall have lawfully served in the art or mistery of Myning by the space of five years as an Apprentice to bee bound by Indenture to his father (being a free Myner) or to some other person that is a free Myner and shall attain to and bee of the full age of one and twenty years.[394]

Restricting encroachment, the Mine Law Court simultaneously opened a legitimate channel through which those not born in to the trade could attain the right to sink pits in the Forest.

---

[394] GRO, D5947.

While miners accepted that outsiders were necessary in this context of expansion, they also understood the importance of maintaining control of those entering the trade. Increased regulation and written prescription helped to restrict entry, but the 'ancient' and quasi-familial structure of this group helped to perpetuate inner coherence during a time of considerable change. Entry was to be gained only under the extensive supervision of existing miners while seventeenth- and eighteenth-century Mine Law Court proceedings demonstrate that grievances were often argued, not between individual miners, but between a miner '& his verns'. This term had long been used to connote the sense of brotherhood or fraternity from which this community derived its fiercely resistant collective identity. This self-reflexive process of assimilation and the construction of a popular corporate identity was crucial to the 'butty system' which predominated in the face of large externally-funded mining operations of the eighteenth century.[395] Despite a tendency towards the reification and abstraction of regulatory codes, this system remained integral to the capacity for self-organisation through which Dean's miners were able to resist proletarianisation to a greater degree than workers in other industries during this period. This resistance was clearly aided by the idiosyncrasy of

---

[395] Chris Fisher explains that 'In the Forest of Dean, when the relatively large pits began to work in the 1820s, the master introduced the 'Little butty' method of work organisation. In this scheme the miners worked in gangs led by skilled adult hewers. The hewer and his partner, the butties, worked on contract rates and employed the other members of the gang on day rates. The little butty was an entrepreneur and an employer in his own right, as interested in the condition of the product market and its fluctuations as the master with whom he bargained for the contract ... thus the dispossession of the free miners and the new organisation of the mining industry did not create an homogenous, solidary mass of wage labourers who brooded on their loss. The new generation of miners grew into the altered order, accepted its essential characteristics and struggled to define a place for themselves in it'. Fisher, *Custom, Work and Market Capitalism*, xiii.

this environment and the nuanced sense of place that was central to successful mining operations.

Mine Law Court records also suggest that the reification of occupational identity generated tension between traditional practices and the more formal nature of this trade as it developed during the eighteenth century. Increased documentation and written recollections of past activity apparently expunged many ambivalences and ambiguities which had been a characteristic functional element of the industry since the twelfth or thirteenth centuries. In February 1676, William Adams complained to this court that George Lodge had been 'following two professions and callings, a Myner and Collyer and a quarryman contrary to our Law and Custom'. Lodge answered that he had followed 'sometimes one Calling and sometimes the other calling as other men do and is not contrary to the Custome'.[396] By 1719 it was evidently deemed necessary, not simply to be known as a miner by others within the community, but for this status to be recorded in official court proceedings. This was the case with John Goding of English Bicknor who, it was recorded at the session held in 1719, prayed:

> leve to prove himself a free Miner which was graunted him and upon the oath of one Witnese and his owne who both swore that he had Lawfully wrought a Yeare and a day at Cole. And thereupon he was adjudged a Free Miner as any other in the Forest of Deane.

---

[396] GRO, D23/X1.

George Churcham of Stanton was similarly confirmed as a free miner of Dean during this session. The list of those fined two shillings for etiquette or procedural breaches during the court session in 1719 highlights the relatively formal nature of legal proceedings by the early part of the eighteenth century. Three people were fined for 'talking in Court', six for otherwise 'disturbing ye Court' while Richard Goding and Edmund Symons were fined for not appearing to 'serve on ye Jury'.

The 1719 proceedings were significant in another, more profound, sense that seems to be linked to the efforts of central government to make its presence more keenly felt in this region. The early eighteenth century witnessed attempts to apply the national poor law in the Forest of Dean, as elsewhere. The session in 1719 occurred during a period in which Gloucestershire Quarter Sessions were involved with a 1716 'enquiry into poor relief' in Dean. The payment of relief, in 1729, to poor pensioners of St. Briavels Hundred was sustained out of the county stock as there had been no local provision for them. At this point then, the poor in this region were becoming a national concern. In this context of state enlargement, the Mine Law Court was similarly brought under the scrutiny of central government in 1719, as it was placed in the charge of the Lord Chief Steward of the Court of Pleas.[397] As early as 1694, the jury of the Mine Law Court had agreed that they should give their verdicts according to the method and usage of other courts of law. The 1719 sessions, therefore, marked increasing central influence over the proceedings of this once fiercely autonomous occupational court.

---

[397] GRO, Q/50/4; Q/FAc1 & D5947/10/1.

In 1754 the jury took the apparently unprecedented step of admitting more than twenty free miners into their trade in one session. Many of these newly constituted free miners were from outside Gloucestershire and did not fit the traditional profile of those entering the trade. Among them were members of the industrialising gentry, including 'The Right Honorable George Augustus Lord Dursley Charles Wyndham of Clowerwall Esquire The Reverend Reynor Jones of Monmouth', 'Kedgwin Hoskins the elder of Clowerwall Gentleman William Probyn of Newland Gentleman' and 'Kedgwyn Webley of London Gentleman'.[398] Christopher Bond, a prominent member of a local gentry family, had already been confirmed as a miner in 1737.[399] During the course of the eighteenth century, the institutional logic of mining operations in the Forest was becoming more closely aligned with both the elite culture of the local industrial gentry and the equity courts of central government. The world-view which supported traditional ideals of 'open' forest and that which informed the ideology of improvement and enclosure were each underwritten by different perceptions of historical time and geographical space. As Christopher Bond confirmed his interest in the free-mining industry, the history of his family offers an illuminating study of the intersection between elite and popular spatial senses which were briefly discussed in Chapter One.

---

[398] GRO, D5947.

[399] GRO, D2026/F/18.

III Elite and popular perceptions of time and space

In 1736 Christopher Bond junior succeeded his father, Christopher Bond senior, as a regarder of the Forest. His grandfather, George, had been one of twelve forest regarders during the later seventeenth century. This family history suggests that Christopher Bond junior was well placed to manage his estates in the Newland area towards the west of Dean's central demesne lands. The Bond family had held substantial amounts of land in this area since the fifteenth century. During the seventeenth century this branch of the family resided at Upper Redbrook farm in the Newland valley. They had accumulated various parcels of adjoining land and farms between Newland and Clearwell, building what was, by the beginning of the eighteenth century, a considerable estate in the west of the Forest.[400] According to the records of the Justice Seat in Eyre of 1656, part of this estate had been appropriated by Throckmorton and Hall, both gentlemen with large-scale industrial interests in the Forest. The records of this court note that:

> there are divers mines of Iron in the lands of Baynham Throckmorton, Esq., Benedict Hall Esq., the lands late of Sir John Wintour, John Gonning, gent., Christopher Bond, Henery Hooper, Edward Worgan, [and] Mr William Sternill.[401]

---

[400] Hart, *New History*, 122.

[401] Ibid., 122.

That this region of the Forest was named after the reddened, ore-laden river which flowed through the Newland valley suggests that these lands were very well situated for iron mining.

By the beginning of the eighteenth century, family papers suggest that these lands were once again in the hands of the Bonds and that both Christopher senior and his father, George, were keen to regulate the management of woodlands on their estate. These papers coincide chronologically with extant Mine Law Court documentation from the second half of the seventeenth century, allowing a comparison of elite and popular perceptions of forest space in this period. This section explores the continuum which connected these perceptions, considering implications for the broader argument of this study. These were not, however, discrete or mutually exclusive frameworks, but could be held simultaneously in fluid and contingent combinations by commoners, miners and gentry alike.

The extensive records of the Bond estate during this period reflect many aspects of Scott's cadastral vision. This part of the Forest was recorded as a series of managed encoppicements, with their growth recorded and the various lands represented collectively in a tabular and simultaneous overview. The format of these records would have been familiar to Church's apocryphal surveyor earlier in the century.

These written records suggest an objectifying perspective, somewhat divorced from the popular experience of those who dwelled and worked within Dean.[402] Despite the increasing abstraction of its records and

---

[402] GRO, D2026/A1-3.

proceedings, the documentation of the Mine Law Court still referred, primarily, to the embodied spatial experience of its members. Broadly speaking, the Bond papers reveal an abstracted vision of forest space in its entirety, while the Mine Law Court offers a perception that was more rooted in the practical experience of the mining community. The latter records describe this forested region in accordance with the human scale of its operations. Previous chapters have argued that miners needed to be attuned to the complex social, industrial and economic activity which constituted Dean's taskscape. The records of their court also reflect these embodied senses of the local material environment.

Typical of complaints brought during a session of this court held in April 1719 was that of William Lewis against William Morgan. Lewis was complaining against Morgan for '32s that he ows ... for 4 Tuns of fire Cole delivered at the box bush in the Hundred of Saint Briavells'. Nine of the twelve cases heard before this session related to unsatisfied debts for coal delivered to the 'Box Bush' which was evidently a central collection and delivery point for distribution throughout St. Briavels Hundred. During the same session, Thomas Moning complained against Anthony Roberts '& his verns' for 'forbiding me out of my pitt which I had a part in belonging to my Levall upon the Lowry Delph nere unto Birchwood in the Forest of Deane'. Giles Lokier 'and his verns', meanwhile, were complaining against the same Thomas Moning for 'mineing up to our Colepitt as we was takeing up in the Lowry Delph in our Gavell place of Oakepitt'. The margins of this document have been annotated thus:

It is Ordered by this Court that this Cause depending between Giles Lokier Plt. & Thomas Moning Dft. is referred to George James [*name illegible*] Brayne & Rob. Wood or any two of them to Determine ye Some and that they make a Report thereof at ye next Court ... This was referred in the presence of ye 48 free miners.

The nature of the cases brought before this court demonstrate the central role that local knowledge played in this jurisdiction and in the capacity of its jury to reach satisfactory verdicts.

The 'Order to sett the Boundaries above & beneath the wood' in 1741 outlined the bounds of the Forest in active terms that bore greater resemblance to a physical progression through space than to the fixed and visible representation of the cadastral map. Under the terms of this order, for instance, no coal was 'to be sent lower then the Island in Wye at Lidbrook'. The order explained that Dean's mining jurisdiction had, 'time out of mind', been divided into two regions. The areas that were 'above' to the south west of the woods and those 'below' towards the north east, were described in the following terms:

> Beginning at the River Wye at Lydbrook where the Brooke there leadeth from the Forges falls into the said River and so up the said Brooke or Stream into a place in the said Forest called Moyery Stock and from there along a Wayne Way at the bottom of a place called the Salley Vellett and so along the same way between the two old enclosures that did belong to Ruardean and Little Dean Walks unto Cannops Brooke and down the said Brooke to Cannops Bridge And from thence along the road or Highway to the Speech House And from

thence along the said Highway to Joses Bridge and from thence down Blackfaced Brooke to Blakeney.[403]

The forest bounds as decreed by these court jurors reflected the fluid and active spatial senses that had traditionally defined customary perceptions of Dean.

Symbolising its performance of authority, the mining court clearly demonstrated its close ties with the Forest and those who lived within it. The ninth clause of the printed *Laws and Privileges* from 1687 stated that:

> the debtor before the Constable and his Clerk the Gaveler and the Miners and none other Folke to plead the right, onely the Miners shall be there and hold a stick of Holly, and then the said Miner demanding the Debt shall put his hand upon the said Stick and none other with him, and he shall swear by his faith that the said debt is due to him.[404]

Discussing the 'holly and ivy' carols of the fifteenth and sixteenth centuries, Arthur Moore suggested that holly 'perfectly symbolizes the division of the sexes'. He noted that these carols do not necessarily reflect ancient custom in this respect as the role of holly in medieval tradition was more ambivalent in its potentially feminine fruit-bearing role. Despite this, Moore was confident that in these carols, 'Holly with "hys merry men" symbolizes the masculine element dominating the feminine "Ivy and hur

---

[403] GRO, D5947.

[404] *The laws and customs of the miners in the Forrest of Dean, in the county of Gloucester* (London, 1687)

267

maydenys"'.[405] It is not difficult to imagine analogies between a perennial, prickly and impenetrable plant and the self-perceptions of this protectionist male-dominated mining community. Just as local mining custom had depended on its continued practice since 'time out of mind of man', holly did not grow and fade with the annual cycles as many other less permanent elements of forest flora. In 1600, Robert Albott was contrasting the 'funerall Cypresse' with the 'Holly ever green'.[406] In his analysis of the Celtic influence on English folklore and legend, Arthur Cook also suggests the eternal and mystical powers long associated with 'greenwood' and the holly sprig. Cook explains that in the ballad of *Syr Gawayn and the Grene Knight*:

> On a New Years Day, while Arthur is keeping his Christmas feast at Camelot, a gigantic knight, clad in green, mounted on a green horse, and carrying in one hand a holly bough, and in the other a "Danish" axe, enters the hall and challenges one of Arthur's knights to stand him "one stroke for another".[407]

The use of the holly sprig in the theatre of the Mine Law Court would likely have signified a permanence and legitimacy that had grown from, and was

---

[405] A. K. Moore, 'Mixed tradition in the Carols of Holly and Ivy', *Modern Language Notes*, 62, 8 (1947), 554.

[406] R. Albott, *England's Parnassus: or the choysest flowers of our modern poets* (London, 1600) URL: http://eebo.chadwyck.com/home Date accessed: 21/05/2009.

[407] A. B. Cook, 'The European Sky-God. VI. The Celts (Continued)', *Folklore*, 17, 3 (30, 1906), 308-348.

firmly embodied within, the Forest. The seventeenth clause of the *Laws and Privileges* stated that if, upon the arrival of the Gavellor to collect 'Law Oare' from each pit, 'the debtor will not at that time pay, then the Gaveller shall forbid so much of the mine there as it is due to the King by Witness of the Miners, and underneath he shall put a stick of holly'. The sprig of holly perhaps symbolised, or was taken to represent, associations between the legitimacy of the Mine Law Court and the authority of an ancient royal forest. During the eighteenth century, Sir Robert Atkins observed that 'Every miner is to be sworn touching the bible with a holly stick that they may not defile holy writ with unclean hands'.[408] This represents a profound misinterpretation of the forest and mining custom from a more elite perspective. Despite its prevailing tendency towards documentation, the Mine Law Court continued to be enmeshed, both physically and symbolically, in the vernacular traditions of the forest community.

Through the office of regarder, members of the Bond family were familiar with popular perspectives of the Forest, coming into regular contact with commoners over uses and abuses of the central wastes. The three volumes that recorded the management of their estate between 1653 and 1750, however, demonstrate an increasing tendency towards documentary 'habits of mind'. Annual accounts from 1653 onwards contain detailed records of rent collected from various parcels of land. In 1668 we find detailed records of the cost, yields and amounts of 'Corne Sowne', 'Suger pease', 'pige pease' and many other types of agricultural operations in the 'Schoolhouse ground' on the Bond estate. There are also increasingly

---

[408] Hart, *Free Miners*, 75.

intricate accounts of 'moneys' paid for 'making fagotes' and other types of woodcutting in the area. From the beginning of the eighteenth century appear detailed records of coppice management towards the western edge of the Forest in the region of Redbrook and Newland parish. These allow comparisons between representations of Dean's material environment in the Bonds' papers, and how this space was described by the Mine Law Court in the same period.[409]

During the opening decades of the eighteenth century, the Bond records documented the maintenance of twenty two groves, areas of managed wood growth. The most prominent of these bore names such as Daffall Grove, Longland Grove, Hornbridge Grove, Creeping Hill Grove, Courts Grove, Hobs Grove, Forsters Grove, Davids Grove, New Wear Grove, Upper Birchin Grove and Lower Birchin Grove. As well as recording the cycles of growth, cutting, and regrowth, the family papers also detail the processes involved in managing their area of the forest more generally. In Hornbridge Grove, for instance, in 1720 the family spent £2 16s 6d on cutting '6 ½ cord of wood', £3 15s on 'Grinding', 8s 6d on cutting 'Band Hoops' and 10s had been spent on the 'Carriage of White Rods to Redbrooke' which sold for £1 10s. The fact that £2 2s 9d was spent on 'Carriage to Bristoll' for this single grove suggests the scale of this operation and that only a proportion of the wood, so cultivated, was destined to remain within the Forest.

According to these papers, Hornbridge Grove was cut in 1709 at eleven years growth, while the Lower Moity of Courts Grove was cut in 1710 at thirteen years growth, Church Grove in 1710 at eleven years, Forsters Grove

---

[409] TNA, MR 179.

in 1712/13 at twelve years, Hobs Grove in 1712/13 at twelve years and Upper Birchin Grove next to Redbrook was cut in 1712/13 at twelve years growth. This pattern is repeated for the duration of these records, as certain segmented areas of the Forest were cut, while others were allowed time to replenish themselves in time to take their place in the cycle of managed wood production. In addition to these accounts, Christopher Bond also recorded occasional detail regarding the condition of these groves during his observations. Hornbridge Grove was 'much abused by cattle', while Creeping Hill was 'a very clean well wooded Grove & was sold cheap'.[410] While the encoppicement and managed growth of woodland was certainly not a novel development, this chronological order does suggest the potential of the written record as a technology capable of objectifying the time and space that it represents. The multi-sensory popular moving tour and the cadastral bird's eye view constitute very different understandings of the environment. These two types of spatial sense and their respective modes of operation are not fixed or discrete, but are fluid and contingent ways of seeing the world.

Despite the embodied nature of Dean's customary mining rights, the court that governed this industry was becoming more dependent on the written record and increasingly engaged with trading and investment networks external to the Forest. The grounding of its regulations in human action had been an integral element in attempts to restrict the scale of this industry through maintaining the illegibility of regionally variant and idiosyncratic practices. The later seventeenth century, however, saw moves to quantify

---

[410] GRO, D2026/A1-3.

ordinances of the industry in abstracted, mathematical measurements. Between 1676 and 1697 the space to be maintained between individual workings, customarily determined by the distance a miner could cast scree from his pit, was raised from 100 to 300 yards. By 1754, innovations such as the 'water wheel Ingeon att the Oiling Green near Broadmore' had evidently influenced the order that 'no Freeminer or miners shall or may sink any water Pit and get Coal out of it above and beneath the wood within the Limitts or Bounds of One thousand yards of any Freeminers level to prejudice that level'. Several orders of this period also contested or confirmed the standardisation of weights, measurements and prices within the industry.[411]

Just as an increasingly cadastral perception of this region was essential to Dean's mining industry, the records of the Bond family's estate management were dependent upon, and embroiled in, popular perceptions of the Forest. An analysis of names such as Longland Grove, Creeping Hill Grove, Moon Grove and Church Grove reveals the family's engagement with the popular mnemonics of Dean's memory palace. Little Ruffet grove, whose name apparently derived from the word 'Roughit', commonly used to denote an area of uncultivated ground set aside for winter pasture, would surely have evoked memories of the land's previous incarnation, while the name of Fence Grove reflected enclosure within the Forest.

The Bond papers thus also reflect Dean and its woodlands as these places were experienced in popular senses. Interspersed with documents recording the management of groves were recipes and directions for medical

---

[411] GRO, D5947.

treatments which used ingredients to be found in the Forest. Immediately below a list of rents collected from various parcels of land in 1668, the same hand continues to record 'The maner how to make the green water soe excellent for the curing of all maner of sores & ulcers in a horse'. This recipe involved the use of local honey and 'a branch of Rosemary bayle'. According to other annotations, 'reesage' was an integral part of a 'good receipt to cure a stitch in the side', while eating sage was 'good against abortion' and therefore recommended for 'Child bearing women'. 'Rue ... being eaten or chued ... purgeth the sight', as did 'distilled water of Rue ... vervine Fennell & Celandine'. These records also contained recipes 'to helpe & prevent Great & Flaggie Breasts' and 'to stop bleeding of the nose', both of which involved herbs and plants that were to be found growing within the Forest.[412] While the Bonds charted growth and profit from this area of woodland, the presence of these recipes in the family papers suggests their concern with treating ailments, several of which related to women's reproductive health. These could reflect the interests of women in the Bond family, but the focus on generation could equally represent male concerns over the production of an heir, particularly in a family of this status.   Whichever interpretation is more likely, these papers demonstrate that forest resources were valued not only for their industrial uses. Once again, the Forest sustained porous boundaries between domestic and industrial life.

The increased reach of equity courts and the more thoroughly documented Mine Law Court, together with managed wood growth, all contributed to

---

[412] GRO, D2026/A1-3.

273

the legibility of the region and its industries. This process, however, was far more complex and contingent than the unidirectional gaze of cadastral mapping. In many cases, the national incorporation of peripheral areas was the outcome of operations implemented by industrialising gentry and other private men involved with local business and trade. The divergent elite and popular senses of space outlined by Rollison are, thus, in no way discrete, opposable or fixed. The evidence from two distinct yet related industries suggests that, in practice, both forms of spatial perception were intrinsically intertwined.

Evidence suggests that by the beginning of the eighteenth century the industrial and economic spheres of the gentry and the free miners were becoming less distinct. This shift, perhaps, contributed to a context in which the mining industry became less impermeable to strangers and in which, of course, the Mine Law Court was to be discontinued in 1777.

A study of these perceptions, their relation to collective memory, and the interpretation and defence of use rights has thus far considered time, only implicitly, as the corollary of space. There is a large body of work which suggests the cultural relativity of temporal experience, and the way that perceptions of the world and the subject's place in it are shaped by this experience.[413] Nancy Munn outlines the complexities and 'inescapable convolutions' inherent in the analysis of time. No conceptual discourse, she argues, can ever be anything other than temporal in form, adding:

> a further complication appears in the fact that, as in the infinite book of sand, time and space are integral to each other. Although Western theory frequently treats space as time's antithetical 'Other', time's Other turns out somewhat embarrassingly to be its Other Self. In a lived world, spatial and temporal dimensions cannot be disentangled, and the two commingle in various ways.[414]

Any action or event is inextricably and continuously embedded in both spatial and temporal dimensions. What is acted in space is, simultaneously, acted in time. Outside of theoretical or idealised conceptualisations, therefore, time and space are not discrete elements that can be reified. These are differing aspects of the way that people interpret their world. Chapter One analysed the forest *habitus*, for example, outlining a timeless ideal that underpinned customary perceptions of the region. This ideal, it is

---

[413] N. D. Munn, 'The Cultural Anthropology of Time: A Critical Essay', *Annual Review of Anthropology*, 21, (1992); O. Ivinskaya, *A Captive of Time: My Years with Pasternak* (London, 1978); E. P. Thompson, 'Time, Work-Discipline and Industrial Capitalism' in Thompson, *Custom*; A. Gingrich, E. Ochs and A. Swedlund, 'Repertoires of Timekeeping in Anthropology', *Current Anthropology*, 43, Supplement: Repertoires of Timekeeping in Anthropology (2002), S3-S4; J. Fabian, *Time and the Other: How Anthropology Makes its Object* (New York, 1983); W. J. Orlikowski and J. Yates, 'It's about Time: Temporal Structuring in Organizations', *Organization Science*, 13, 6 (2002), 684-700; K. Pickering, 'Decolonizing Time Regime's: Lakota Conceptions of Work, Economy and Society', *American Anthropologist*, New Series, 106, 1 (2004), 85-97; N. Boivin, 'Life Rhythms and Floor Sequences: Excavating Time in Rural Rajasthan and Neolithic Catalhoyuk', *World Archaeology*, 31, 3, Human Lifecycles (2000), 367-388.

[414] Munn, 'Time', 94

argued, represented a pragmatic fiction, its spatialisation of history and the synchronic legal record of the landscape forming an important mechanism in accommodating overlapping use-rights. This is not to suggest that the commonalty of the Forest were unaware of chronological time. More likely, inhabitants may have perceived their world through reference to their local spatial senses rather than the clock and the fixed historical record. Similarly, it would be absurd to suggest that the modern factory worker was incapable of functioning outside routines imposed by the mechanised clock. It is more sensible to consider the relation between time and space as a continuum, one end of which would be dominated by spatial referents, the other by a strict adherence to linear time. At one extreme might be found, for example, the timeless customary ideal of Chapter One and, at the other, regimes that attempt to impose the rigid time discipline of the modern factory system.

It is important to recognise that any individual or group would be capable of adopting different positions on this perceptual continuum. From the evidence of Dean, for example, the arboricultural management recorded in the Bond papers might be placed near the centre of this continuum. These records tended towards diachronic regulation of large areas but still demonstrated a strong awareness of local and customary senses of this part of the Forest. Christopher Tucker, Deputy Gavellor during the mid to late seventeenth century, adopted a combination of these positions in mediating relations between the local mining culture and equity courts. Extant documentation suggests that the Mine Law Court, in its institutional practices, shifted significantly along this continuum during the seventeenth century.

Those perceptions of the world that tend toward spatial ordering apparently dominated local communities in England during the late medieval and early modern period. From the sense of social continuity offered by perambulation rituals to customary notions of work and community (the timeless ideal *par excellence*), life cycles were embedded in spatially referent calendrical timeframes. The ritual calendar of this period was attuned to the cyclical and seasonally variable activities of the community and this, in turn, was overlaid with Christian significance through the festivals and holy days of the church calendar. Edward Muir explains that:

> The ritual commemoration of the life of Christ in the liturgy kept time with the passing of the seasons, creating a festive counterpoint to work, making the mission of Christ, relived each year in the church's feasts, as much a part of the universal order as the waning or waxing of the moon or the apparent movements of the planets.[415]

Related to spatially-dominated temporal senses, Munn suggests an anthropological distinction between qualitative and abstract time. 'These categorical distinctions (days, seasons etc)', she suggests, 'form a meaningful, qualitatively varied rather than an abstract, homogeneous temporality'.[416] She quotes much work on this type of calendrical timeframe, concluding that the calendar 'segments time but does so

---

[415] E. Muir, *Ritual in Early Modern Europe* (Cambridge, 2nd edition, 2005), 65.

[416] Munn, 'Time', 95.

qualitatively: periods are defined by specific social activities or 'facts'. Calendars do not so much measure time as give it rhythmic form'.[417]

The opposite extreme, it seems, lies in Benedict Anderson's much-challenged notion of emptied and homogeneous time which invokes the simultaneity of experience that characterises the readership of the novel. He draws an analogy between this historically advanced readership and the way in which a modern nation collectively imagines itself.[418] The implied link between state centralisation and increasing attempts to discipline, commodify and empty the time of the working classes of eighteenth- and nineteenth-century England is essential to understanding differences between the Skimmington riots of 1631 and the Warren James' protests of 1831. Munn notes the Durkheimian distinction between subjective inner consciousness of time, 'the undifferentiated flow of duration which I feel passing within me', and social time's morphology of cognizable units that imposes itself in 'all minds'.[419] Where spatial referents dominate over diachronic order, a higher correlation exists between the personal time of an individual and the rhythms of the material environment in which that individual lived and worked. This would accord strikingly with Thompson's

---

[417] Ibid., 95.

[418] B. Anderson, *Imagined Communities: Reflections on the Origin and Spread of Nationalism* (London and New York, 2006), 26.

[419] Ibid., 95.

interpretation of *habitus* in an early modern agrarian context. Thompson also quotes Edward Evans-Pritchard's study of the time-sense of the Nuer in East Africa. Evans Pritchard explained that:

> The daily timepiece is the cattle clock, the round of pastoral tasks, and the time of day and the passage of time through a day are to a Nuer primarily the succession of these tasks and their relation to one another.[420]

The commodification or necessity of selling one's time held a profoundly alienating significance in the protracted and uneven process of proletarianisation which increasingly characterised labour forces across pre-modern Europe. Thompson notes the influence of the clock and progressive utilitarian ideologies on the poor of England suggesting that:

> enclosure and agricultural improvement were both, in some sense, concerned with the efficient husbandry of the time of the labour force. Enclosure and the growing labour-surplus at the end of the eighteenth century tightened the screw for those who were in regular employment;

---

[420] E. E. Evans-Pritchard, *The Nuer* (Oxford, 1940), 100-4, quoted in E. P. Thompson, *Customs in Common: Studies in Traditional Popular Culture* (New York, 1993), 355.

they were faced with the with the alternatives of partial employment and the poor law, or submission to a more exacting labour discipline.[421]

The free-mining community of Dean tenaciously resisted this imposition, maintaining the capacity to organise their own labour through the butty system in spite of large-scale investment in the Forest's mining industry during this period.

The influence of time and space on the constitution of collective memories shaped experiences of the mining trade, fostering a level of communal feeling which made it more resistant to increased time-discipline. Fentress and Wickham explain their understanding of the relations between class and memory. They make an instructive distinction between the memory patterns they attribute to peasant communities and those which they suggest characterise working-class communities. In doing so, they point to the significant number of peasant communities that:

> have appeared to commemorate the past exclusively through personal memories, and these personal memories often seem to be focused less on 'historically relevant' events than on the recurrent processes of the life cycle of the family, going back at the most to grandparents: daily

---

[421] Thompson, 'Time discipline', 380. For proletarianisation and the rise of capitalist economies see L. Shaw-Taylor, 'Parliamentary Enclosure and the Emergence of an English Agricultural Proletariat', *The Journal of Economic History*, 61, 3 (2001), 640-662; L. Shaw-Taylor, 'Proletarianisation, Parliamentary Enclosure and the Household Economy of the Labouring Poor: 1750-1850', *The Journal of Economic History*, 60, 2 (Jun., 2000), 508-511; P. Kriedte, *Peasants, Landlords and Merchant Capitalists, Europe and the world economy, 1500-1800* (Providence, 1983); J. De Vries, *The economy of Europe in an age of crisis* (Cambridge, 1976); Dennis Potter records resistance and resentment to externally imposed time amongst Dean miners as late as the 1960s as those who were made redundant were offered factory employment in Gloucester and other nearby urban centres. D. Potter, *The changing forest: life in the Forest of Dean today* (London, 1962).

life, the seasons, festivals, and the world of nature (often expressed in supernatural or folk lore terms), with life histories superimposed onto and structured by these sorts of memory alone.

While it is difficult to sustain this distinction in practice, Fentress and Wickham outline a synchronic sense of relations between time and space in which both are more attuned to the cycles of nature and human activity. They offer a particularly useful contrast in their analysis of working-class memory patterns, specifically those engendered through the time-discipline of the modern factory system. They do, however, emphasise that this is only one of a number of potential mnemonic frameworks that informed members of this labour force.

The experience of factory discipline, then, was only one aspect of life but, as Fentress and Wickham suggest, 'it does at least guarantee a certain linearity of recollection that can make more concrete the perception of historical change and development'.[422] Under factory conditions the relation between time, space and collective memory are more susceptible to external influence or control, certainly by comparison with the structures of the classic peasant memory. Fentress and Wickham crucially highlight a distinctive characteristic of the latter, noting that it is 'structured outwards: first, doubtless, from the individual to the family and its life cycle; but then, through the social relationships between families, both amicable and hostile, from the family to the community'.[423] Collective memory

---

[422] Fentress and Wickham, *Social Memory*, 120-1.

[423] Ibid., 113.

structures, in a peasant community, are built from within rather than imposed from without. Earlier chapters discussed the tendency of the Dean mining community towards less distinction between home and work life. This, in combination with a necessity for technical skill and sensitivity to environment, produced a tenacious resistance against external domination over the rhythms of their lives and collective memory. The interviewee who introduced this book, for instance, invoked constitutional history, but strictly through reference to the needs of his life and occupation. Resistance to time-discipline was emblematised in the butty system, which remained operative when the interviewee began his mining career in the early twentieth century.

These distinctive perceptual schemes exerted a profound influence, not only upon the strength of community feeling, but also upon the way that the free miners understood their place beyond their immediate geographical surroundings. Fentress and Wickham explain that the 'most powerful element we have met [in the peasant community] is the memory of the community in opposition to the outside world', an observation pertinent to the disposition of the Dean miners and the wider forest commonalty in this period.[424] Locally specific opposition to outsiders, according to Fentress and Wickham, contrasts with the memory structures that supported the burgeoning national consciousness of England's working classes during the late eighteenth and early nineteenth centuries. Following their notion of the linearity of recollection within this labour force, the increasing experience

---

[424] Ibid., 114.

of work discipline managed through abstracted units of empty time contributed to the generation of national working-class consciousness. As discussed in Chapter Six, the eighteenth century witnessed a shift of this kind in the culture of England's labouring poor, while the Forest of Dean retained a high degree of local solidarity and enmity towards radical ideals of national working-class enfranchisement. The homogenous quality of national time and its recall of a causal historical past complemented increasing levels of communication between erstwhile isolated local communities. In short, while the imposition of a precise and nationally co-ordinated linear timeframe increased the productivity levels of industrialists, it also fostered a national consciousness of common interest between working people in eighteenth- and nineteenth-century England.

In the context of this study, it is significant that the written record follows this pattern, privileging linear time in its representation of the past. Deeds, charters, statute laws and equity decrees all work to construct a definitive and diachronic record of the ownership and use of space. In contrast to the spatialisation of history which allows for contradictions of collective and seasonal uses, the written cadastral record implies and helps to construct an ideology of exclusive property ownership.

Thus we have two potential lines of conflict related to class interest during this period. On one hand were those conservative and ostensibly deferential protests in defence of local custom. On the other were the more radical protests of those involved in the progressive fight for the rights of the labouring poor in recognition of national class interests. These were related, in complex ways, to the intersection of memory structures, the written record, and the naturalisation of class distinctions and private property. It is argued, however, that this reductive distinction is unsustainable, at least in the pre-modern Forest of Dean. Popular political consciousness in the Forest, while focused primarily on the miners and their court, had long been manifested in the negotiation of customary governance and the hegemonic mechanisms of the English state. The position of Warren James as the son of a free miner, for example, suggests that he was well-placed, both culturally and geographically, to organise sustained unrest in June 1831, straddling older, traditional methods of popular protest and the more radical, national struggle for class emancipation. Just as the Dean mining community operated at the nexus of local and national senses of time and space, Warren James, in many respects, appears at the conjunction of the old and the new in terms of popular political protest. That, more properly, is the subject of Chapter Six. The remainder of this chapter considers the context in which the legal regulation of miners and their trade, previously the exclusive prerogative of the Mine Law Court, became subject to the hegemony of national statute law.

IV Common law, assizes and the end of the Mine Law Court

To this day, the reasons behind the discontinuance of the Mine Law Court in 1777 remain obscure. Hart quotes several conflicting recollections cited in the records of a commission conducted in 1832 in the wake of the Warren James' riots. Among these was the statement of James Machen, aged ninety, who believed:

that the Mine Law Courts dropped because the miners behaved badly, and there was always so much confusion that the gentlemen would not attend; the miners quarrelled amongst themselves and created disturbances.

Thomas Davis of Five Acres, an eighty year-old free miner, on the other hand, stated that he had:

been at Mine Law Courts; while they lasted no foreigner ever thought of having refuge in the Forest. The court was given up because of a dispute between free miners and foreigners whom we did not consider fit to carry on the works.[425]

Whichever of these two versions is more likely, the monopoly of jurisdiction enjoyed by the Mine Law Court was perceived as a powerful obstacle to external investment in the Forest of Dean. The Commission of 1832, in fact, suggests that the court collapsed following the disappearance of the 'Book of Denis', a carefully preserved collection of 'ancient' decrees and court rulings which miners would regularly produce in defence of their legal interests. This, itself, is compelling evidence of increasingly close relations between the written record and the perceived validity of legal claims during the eighteenth century. While the closure of the Mine Law Court was keenly felt by many foresters as a moment of profound change and loss, this was but one element in a wider process of national transformation which contributed to the vulnerability of traditional industries and culture in the Forest of Dean.

Much ink has been spilled over the nature and impact of criminal justice reform in eighteenth-century England, even more over the motivations of

---

[425] Hart, *Free Miners*, 145-6.

reformers. Christopher Hill posited what he understood as a bourgeois revolution, during the civil war period of 1640 to 1660. By the 1660s, he argued, British property laws and the court systems that upheld them were directed towards the circulation of capital and the preservation of private property ownership.[426] The preceding chapters have demonstrated that this view holds much credence, even in a marginal area like the Forest of Dean. It could be argued that the next British revolution constitutionally enshrined many of these tenets in the *Bill of Rights* of 1689. Bringing what was seen an arbitrary royal prerogative under the rule of 'the known laws and statutes and freedoms of this realm' which had been made for the 'liberty of the subjects', the Act declared that 'jurors which pass upon men in trials for high treason ought to be freeholders'.[427] The Glorious Revolution, then, consolidated the rule of law at a national level while assuring the interests of a property-holding class through the ascendancy of Parliament.

Thompson agreed that, by the early eighteenth century, the British legal system was far more inclined towards the protection of private property. He observed that 'The British state, all eighteenth-century legislators agreed, existed to preserve the property and, incidentally, the lives and liberties, of the propertied'. [428] Significantly, the later seventeenth century witnessed an

---

[426] C. Hill, 'A Bourgeois Revolution?', in J G A Pocock (ed), *Three British Revolutions: 1641, 1688, 1776* (Princeton, 1980), 124.

[427] *Bill of Rights* (1689) URL: http://avalon.law.yale.edu/17th_century/england.asp Date Accessed 4 July 2013.

[428] E. P. Thompson, *Whigs and Hunters: the origin of the Black Act* (Norwich, 1977), 21.

increased state involvement in the prosecution of property crime with the introduction of rewards for the apprehension of those guilty of specific offences. 1692 saw rewards of £40 paid for the successful prosecution of highway robbers and, in 1695, the same amount was paid for the apprehension and conviction of counterfeiters. Burglary was added to the list in 1699 and, between 1741 and 1742, smaller rewards of £10 were introduced to address the problem of sheep stealing. Specific rewards were also offered by royal proclamation in reaction to particular anxieties.[429] The accession of the Hanoverian royal family in 1714 did little to impede the process of legal reform. Primarily passed to deal with potential rebels in the Scottish border region during the early eighteenth century, the Riot Act of that year had a significant impact on the way that authorities were able to deal with problems of disorderly crowd action. The Black Act of 1723 famously added fifty capital offences, most of which were aimed directly at curtailing a perceived rise in property crime in the wake of the celebrated case of the Waltham Blacks. Thompson suggests that 'although a tendency to attach the death penalty to new descriptions of offence can be noted in previous decades, the Black Act of 1723, which coincided with the year of

---

[429] For further reading on the introduction of the reward system and development of the thief-taker, see J. M. Beattie, *Policing and Punishment in London, 1660-1750: Urban Crime and the Limits of Terror* (Oxford, 2001); G. Howson, *Thief-Taker General: The Rise and Fall of Jonathan Wild* (London, 1970); L. Moore, *The Thieves' Opera: The Remarkable Lives and Deaths of Jonathan Wild, Thief-Taker, and Jack Sheppard, House-Breaker* (London, 1997); R. Paley, *Thief-takers in London in the Age of the McDaniel Gang, c. 1745-1754* in D. Hay, and F. Snyder (eds.), *Policing and Prosecution in Britain 1750-1850* (Oxford, 1989), 301-42; T. Wales, 'Thief-takers and their clients in later Stuart London', in P. Griffiths and M. S. R. Jenner (eds.), *Londonopolis: essays in the cultural and social history of early modern London* (Manchester, 2000), 67-84.

Walpole's final political ascendency, signalled the onset of the flood-tide of eighteenth-century retributive justice'.[430]

The nature of these offences has caused many historians to speak of a criminalisation of custom during the eighteenth century. Gleaning, the gathering of estovers, traditional rights of commoning, and other allowances which had been essential to the household economy of poor families in Britain, were now subject to increasingly harsh penal codes, in some cases punishment by death. There is a healthy body of literature which examines the increasing disparity between popular and official senses of justice in the eighteenth-century provinces. George Rudé identified the idea of social crime as 'Offences defined by law as crimes but not regarded as such by the vast majority of the community' while Sharpe discusses 'Those forms of offence that are best interpreted as rational and coherent actions arising from, or justified by, a commonly held set of attitudes different from those of officialdom'.[431]

The impact of Britain's 'Bloody Code' has generated intense debate in recent years. Did the severity of these laws send many more destitute thieves to the gallows? Alternatively, did this severity encourage more

---

[430] Thompson, Whigs and Hunters, 23.

[431] J. Sharpe, 'Social Crime and Legitimizing Notions', in *Crime in Early Modern England 1550-1750* (London, 1984), Chapter 6; P. King, 'Gleaners, Farmers and the Failure of Legal Sanctions in England 1750-1850', *Past and Present*, 125 (1989) reprinted in P. King, *Crime and Law in England 1750-1840, Remaking Justice from the Margins* (Oxford, 2006); J. Styles, 'From an Offence between Men to an Offence against Property: Industrial Pilfering and the Law in the Eighteenth Century', in M. Berg, P. Hudson and M. Sonenscher (eds.), *Manufacture in Town and Country Before the Factory* (Cambridge, 1983).

leniency and sympathy in cases where Justices of the Peace understood that they would be sending desperate and relatively minor offenders to their deaths? One facet of this transformation is clear. By the end of the eighteenth century, the figure of the Assize judge came to dominate local prosecutions through the application of a unitary and national common law. Previous chapters have examined the rise of 'civil' litigation and the interests of private property in the Forest of Dean, but this represented only one aspect of legal change in this region. This chapter closes by examining the ways that a national criminal legal code came to implicate itself more thoroughly in the regulation of this geographically peripheral yet important royal forest.

Presentments to the Oxford assize circuit are revealing here and, aside from some mould-damaged volumes, survive in a reasonably complete run from 1660. From this period, the courts undoubtedly received much business and a substantial proportion of this was from St. Briavels Hundred. Between 1667 and 1682, 425 presentments were made and forty of these were from parishes within the hundred. 1,392 presentments were made between 1724 and 1741, thirty three of which were from Dean, while 832 were recorded between 1741 and 1771, with forty one from the region. Proportionally, only a slight fluctuation occurred between the number of local presentments from the seventeenth-century selection and those dating from the later eighteenth century. Qualitatively, however, these records suggest a change in the type of business arising from the Forest of Dean. In the earlier records, defendants were being presented for assault, murder, breaking and entering, sexual assault, keeping disorderly alehouses, 'stopping up an antient footway', perjury, theft and fraud, while isolated presentments accused defendants of 'buggering a black mare' and 'poisoning a setting dog'.[432]

In the later seventeenth century, Assize prosecutions in Dean reflect this general picture but, as the records move into the eighteenth century, presentments reflect more prosecution for offences involving the appropriation of forest resources. From early in this century, there is a marked increase in presentments for stealing timber from the King or timber and grain from the estates of local gentlemen in the Forest of Dean. [433] While there appears to be an increase in what was possibly regarded as social crime, records also suggest conflict and antagonism over these prosecutions. A sharp rise in attacks on forest officials reflects widespread animosity to this intrusion of national criminal law. In 1727, several defendants were presented in a case surrounding the keepers of the Forest and John Walding, yeoman of Ruardean. They stood accused of:

assaulting beating & wounding George Falnes, William Jelfe Richard Jelfe and John Reynolds keepers of the Forest of Deane in execution of their office & Rescuing the said John Walding out of their Custody whom they had taken to carry before a Justice of the Peace for carrying a gun in the said Forest.[434]

[432] TNA, ASSI 4/15

[433] TNA, ASSI 4/19; TNA, ASSI 4/20.

[434] TNA, ASSI 4/19.

In 1736, Giles Lockyer of Newland and Henry Smith of Mitcheldean were called before the court for beating and wounding Josiah Williams, keeper of the Forest.[435] In 1742, these records tell of the presentment of John Badden, tailor of Newland, for beating and wounding George Morgan and George James, keeper and underkeeper of the Forest, in the execution of their duties. Records also suggest some sympathy shown by Dean's authorities towards those arrested for offences against the venison and vert of the Forest. William Morgan, High Constable of St. Briavels Hundred, was presented in 1733 for negligently allowing William Jones to escape from his custody for stealing a fallow deer out of Lord Gage's paddock at Newland.[436] Six years previously, Jonathan Martin, 'Constable of the parish of Blazedon' had been presented 'for not bringing in his return to this assizes.[437]

In some of these Assize presentments, it is also possible to detect the influence of the Riot Act and the availability of formal mechanisms for controlling crowd action over disputed customary rights. 1738, for instance, saw the prosecution of 38 miners and other labourers for riot at Bilton in Knightlow hundred, Warwickshire, a county which lay outside the jurisdiction of the Oxford circuit. The defendants stood accused of common

---

[435] TNA, ASSI 4/19.

[436] Ibid.

[437] Ibid.

riot at Bilton coal works, destroying carts and ropes, throwing down a stone wall, and mixing earth with the pits.[438] It may be significant that coalminers in other areas were prosecuted at common law, while Dean's free miners are conspicuous by their relative absence from these records until the end of the eighteenth century, at least as far as their customary privileges were concerned. It seems as though most conflict over the industry was either precluded or constrained by the monopoly of jurisdiction enjoyed by the Mine Law Court. The prosecution of miners from the Forest of Dean before the Assizes appears to have been problematic. In 1749, John Taylor and Francis Meeke, both coal miners of Ruardean, were presented for stealing timber in the Forest of Dean, but these cases stand out for their verdicts of 'not guilty'.[439] Francis Meeke had previously been presented in 1729 for disturbing the peace and assaulting John Simes, constable, 'in the execution of his office'.[440] When miners were presented before the later eighteenth century, it was for violence and disorder associated with disputed rights rather than direct prosecution for the exercise of these contested claims. In 1733, William Collins, collier of Newland, faced charges for pulling down the gate and stone wall of King's Pond at night time and 'rescuing twenty sheep thereon impounded by Richard Worgan'. He had also, apparently, destroyed Worgan's trees, beans and cabbages while breaking his pails and

---

[438] Ibid.

[439] TNA, ASSI 4/20.

[440] TNA, ASSI 4/19.

windows'.[441] Thomas Keare, also a collier of Newland, was presented for beating and wounding Josiah Williams, keeper of the Forest, and 'rescuing' six cows from him.[442]

This was all to change following the discontinuance of the Mine Law Court. Directly after this in 1777, free miners of the Forest of Dean were prosecuted in the Quarter Sessions for cutting timber.[443] The Mine Law Court was discontinued in the same year that its business was first prosecuted through the Quarter Sessions or the Assizes. Due to the growth of this industry, the changing nature of its regulation, and the increasing legibility of the trade, more powerful industrial interests in Dean apparently decided to dispense with this vestige of the protectionist past. In 1780, Richard Glassonberg of Littledean 'Labourer' and James Trigg 'the younger of the same place Coalminer' were prosecuted:

in Pursuance of an Act of Parliament passed in the Ninth Year of his present Majesty King George the third, for cutting downe an Oake Timber tree in the said Forest Contrary to the statute in that case made and provided.[444]

---

[441] TNA, ASSI 4/19.

[442] TNA, ASSI 4/19.

[443] GRO, Q/SIa/1775/Epiphany.

[444] GRO, Q/SR/1780/A.

The miners' customary right to wood from within the wastes and demesne lands of Dean, long derived from local precedent, was now prosecuted according to national statute law.

Bob Bushaway quotes a report of a doling custom of St. Briavels that was still in practice during the second half of the eighteenth century. The author of this contemporary account noted that:

> One of the most strange customs that time has handed down to us prevails at St. Briavels, Gloucestershire. On Whit-sunday, several baskets full of bread and cheese, cut into small squares of about an inch each, are brought into the Church; and immediately after divine service is ended, the church-wardens, or some other persons, take them into the galleries, from whence their contents are thrown among the congregation, who have a grand scramble for it in the body of the church, which occasions as great a tumult and uproar as the amusement of a village wake; the inhabitants being always extremely anxious in their attendance at worship on this day. The custom is held for the purpose of preserving to the poor of St. Briavels at Hewelsfield the right of cutting and carrying away wood from 3,000 acres of coppice land in Hudknolls and the Meend; and for which every householder is assessed 2d, to buy the bread and cheese given away.[445]

---

[445] B. Bushaway, *By Rite: custom, ceremony and community in England, 1700-1800* (London, 1982), 16-17.

Judging by this account, customary practices were still essential to many aspects of life in the Forest of Dean. This tradition, in its provision for the poor, was presumably increasingly essential in the face of the loss of common rights through improvement and enclosure. Through the formalisation of custom, practices relating to commoning had been emptied of their social content. Those relating to the mediation of community interaction, this contemporary observer implies, reinforced a division of cultures, distinguishing between families who sought practical relief and neighbours who saw these customs as a seasonal amusement. In this respect, the discontinuance of the Mine Law Court, as a bastion of local custom, profoundly influenced the process whereby this region was inscribed in the bourgeois hegemony consolidated in the 1832 reforms. The 1834 'MEMORIAL BY THE FREE MINERS AND THEIR CASE AGAINST THE 'FOREIGNERS"' reflects this sentiment. The miners explained that, in defence against the claims of 'foreigners' to 'have found a proof of their usage in working the mines as well as free miners', they had 'now traced the history of the Mine Law Courts, and of the practice of the free miners, from the reign of King Edward 3, through the reigns of James 1, and Charles 1, to the reign of Charles 2'. They evidently sought to legitimise the monopoly of the Mine Law Court in terms of a chronologically ordered constitutional history. Regarding the discontinuance of the court, the miners claimed:

That the foreigners finding the Mine Law Courts an insuperable obstacle to their success, and more particularly that by the orders last quoted of 1775, there was no chance for their being permitted to work in the mines, found that the only means by which they could hope for success was to destroy the Mine Law Courts.

That the documents of this court were always kept in the Speech House in the Forest of Dean, but that after the conclusion of the last court in 1775 some person or persons broke open the chest in which they were contained and removed them.

That the free miners from that period to the present have made repeated applications to the wardens and the gavellers respecting these orders and documents, but that the wardens and gavellers, while they declared that they could not hold the Mine Law Courts as usual without these documents, at the same time denied all knowledge of their existence.[446]

It seems sensible to concur with many of those questioned in the 1832 commission. These miners suggested that the loss of the Mine Law Court, forty seven years previously, had rendered the forest and its resources increasingly vulnerable to the encroachments of 'foreigners' and private interest. During the sixteenth and early seventeenth centuries, local practices were closely associated with the oral testimony of miners and other foresters, which often drew on local knowledge of the material environment. This rendered these processes obscure to external parties and the aims of 'foreigners'. The seventeenth century witnessed an assault on local custom as Dean's material resources became increasingly prized by the Crown and individual projectors.

This book argues that the period not only witnessed more conflict over resources, but also competition over the terms through which these claims

---

[446] Hart, *Free Miners*, 299-303.

could legitimately be made. From the middle years of the seventeenth century, and related in no small way to the upheaval of the civil wars, Dean's legal processes became far more heavily influenced by the written record of central equity courts. This promoted the interests of private property holders and rendered these practices more legible to outside parties, while weakening the protectionism of the mining industry and, by extension, more general rights to common. Additionally, in a national context of criminal justice reform, Assize prosecutions in Dean related increasingly to the appropriation of resources long regarded, at least popularly, as the collective property of those who lived and dwelled within St. Briavels Hundred. Even while this was being fiercely contested, this process culminated in the closure of the Mine Law Court which left the claims of local residents vulnerable to larger capital investors.

Chapter Six examines the extent to which shifting legal cultures of the seventeenth and eighteenth centuries, and the miners' complicity in this process, sealed the breach that Chapter Three explored in terms of Turner's model of social drama. The Mine Law Court had been discontinued, miners and foresters were more legally constrained by national criminal law, larger investors were more prevalent and the mining community was increasingly dependent on paid work in deeper pits. This breach, though, was to become exposed at least once more in 1831 when attempts to disregard the Act of 1668 provoked widespread action under the leadership of Warren James, son of a free miner.

Chapter Six

The Forest of Dean commonalty in early nineteenth-century England

> These hedge-rows, hardly hedge-rows,
> little lines
>   Of sportive wood run wild; these
> pastoral farms
>   Green to the very door; and wreathes
> of smoke
>   Sent up, in silence, from among the
> trees,
>   With some uncertain notice, as might
> seem,
>   Of vagrant dwellers in the houseless
> woods

William Wordsworth, 'Lines composed a few miles above Tintern Abbey'
[447]

I Representing the poor in eighteenth-century England

William Wordsworth's famous description of Dean from above Tintern Abbey on the Welsh side of the Wye Valley demonstrates the contrasting local and national perceptions of the Forest at the end of the eighteenth century. The vibrant and energetic culture of the forest commonalty is rendered silent and passive by the poem's distanced and elevated gaze. The common voice of this region which had lent so much force to resisting encroachment is reduced to the silent 'wreathes of smoke' emanating from 'houseless woods' in a picturesque and idealised pastoral idyll.

---

[447] W. Wordsworth, 'Lines composed a few miles above Tintern Abbey, on revisiting the banks of the Wye during a tour. July 13, 1798' in, S. T. Coleridge and W. Wordsworth, *Lyrical Ballads* (London, 1999), 110.

Wordsworth's description suggests ways in which fiercely contested struggles over changing interpretations of property and use rights in these remote corners of the land may have entered the sitting rooms and consciousness of the English reading public towards the end of the eighteenth century.[448] This was a period of profound ideological turbulence following widespread disenchantment with French revolutionary ideals as Jacobin optimism for an egalitarian republic had largely descended into revulsion at the 'Terror' that had manifested itself in the streets of Paris.[449]

Tintern Abbey was written in the summer of 1798 and indicates a retreat from the more radical sentiments that had informed Wordsworth's political stance in the years leading up to the revolutionary period, during which he had spent much time in Paris. In 1793, however, he had claimed disapproval:

> of monarchical and aristocratical governments, however modified. Hereditary distinctions, and privileged order of every species ... must necessarily counteract the progress of human improvement. Hence it follows that I am not among the admirers of the British Constitution.[450]

---

[448] For a useful collection on literacy and reading in this period, see I. Rivers (ed.), *Books and their Readers in Eighteenth-Century England: New Essays* (London and New York, 2001, reprinted 2003).

[449] See a number of essays in M. Philp (ed.), *The French Revolution and British Popular Politics* (Cambridge, 1991).

[450] E. Selincourt (ed.), *The Letters of William and Dorothy Wordsworth: The Early Years 1787-1805,* revised by Chester L. Shaver (Oxford, 2nd edition, 1967), 123-24.

These ideological leanings were undoubtedly reflected in his artistic concern with the marginal and dispossessed victims of agrarian and industrial improvement. Yet his earlier representations of these characters appropriated, rather than articulated, the voice of the poor in the cause of wider ideological considerations that informed his contributions to the Romantic opposition to utilitarianism. The title of the co-authored volume in which most of these descriptions appeared alludes to the appropriation of the popular ballad form.[451] From the middle of the sixteenth century, the ascendency of a trade in cheap printed material increased the circulation of the ballad which, in its oral incarnation was synonymous with popular cultures, local senses of the past, mythologies, and folklore.[452] Wordsworth and his collaborator, Samuel Taylor Coleridge, adopted the title *Lyrical Ballads* in a self-conscious appropriation of the voice of the rural poor.

Wordsworth reduced Dean's rich and deep-rooted popular communalism to a few enigmatically menacing yet endangered furls of smoke. Thus, he represented the sanitised and symbolic representation of a community which, while living at the cultural and physical margins of late eighteenth- and early nineteenth-century England, was central to the self-definition of a burgeoning and nationally-imagined liberal middle class. In his classic, and much-challenged, definition of the modern nation as a particular type of

---

[451] Coleridge and Wordsworth, *Lyrical Ballads*.

[452] M. Spufford, *Small Books and Pleasant Histories: Popular Fiction and its Readership in Seventeenth-Century England* (Cambridge, 1981), 9-12; R. S. Thomson, 'The Development of the Broadside Ballad Trade and its Influence upon the Transmission of English Folksong', (Unpublished PhD diss., Cambridge University, 1974).

'imagined community', Anderson points to the simultaneity of experience engendered by a conjunction of capitalism and print technology and to the community of readership marked by his notion of 'empty time'. He suggests that:

> The idea of a sociological organism moving calendrically through homogenous, empty time is a precise analogue of the idea of the nation, which also is conceived as a solid community moving steadily down (or up) history. An American will never meet, or even know the names of more than a handful of his 240,000,000-odd fellow-Americans. He has no idea of what they are up to at any one time. But he has complete confidence in their steady, anonymous, simultaneous activity.[453]

In this vein, the Romanticism of Wordsworth and other poets would have had a profound effect on the collective consciousness of their large, national readership. This influence is evident in the journals of Mrs Susan Elwes, a Norfolk gentlewoman, who seems to have taken great pleasure in touring remote parts of the kingdom during the opening years of the nineteenth century, an experience that was central to her sense of the social group to which she belonged. In 1826, she took a trip to the Forest of Dean, noting how, during August, they had driven in their cart:

> to Flaxly Abbey & walked thro a part of the Forest of Dean called the Baily, the next day the 17th we went thro the tunnel (which pases under

---

[453] B. Anderson, *Imagined Communities: Reflections on the Origin and Spread of Nationalism* (London and New York, 2006), 26.

Mr Jones' Garden) to the Coal Pits & had a most beautiful drive seeing a great part of the Forest.

As in Wordsworth's poetry, the heavy industrial activity of Dean is rendered picturesque by a wealthy tourist from the other side of the country as she mused on her surroundings. Elwes' journal continues thus, explaining that they managed to see the town of Coleford, the 'Speech House which stands in a beautiful part of the Forest', and Newland, a 'most beautiful village'. Elwes and her husband regretted stopping at Rayland, however, which she described as 'a small town but nothing worth seeing'. [454]

Noting that the lines of class distinction were to be drawn, very carefully, in the 'franchise qualifications of 1832', Thompson explains that:

> it had been the peculiar feature of English development that, where we would expect to find a growing middle-class reform movement, with a working-class tail, only later succeeded by an independent agitation of the working class, in fact this process was reversed.[455]

Wordsworth's appropriation of the popular voice suggests a similar dynamic of middle-class emulation. These examples suggest an ideological and cultural process of self-definition which resembled a political process whereby middle-class reformers drew coherence from the activities and consciousness of working-class reform movements. Marginal and

---

[454] NRO, HMN 5/34, 737x9.

[455] Thompson, *Making of the English Working Class*, 888.

supposedly backward areas such as the Forest of Dean appear to have figured prominently in this idealisation of a picturesque labouring class. This, however, was a complex relationship which reflected the often contradictory interactions of the middle and working classes amid polarised reactions to events in France during the 1790s.

The very notion of the poor became an ideological battleground in the years following the French Revolution. It is difficult to resist the idea that this unfortunate, and regionally variable, group came to represent a bargaining tool in justifying the calls of some middle class advocates of constitutional reform during the opening decades of the nineteenth century. As mentioned, these groups drew much of their energy from the capacity for self-organisation of the emergent and increasingly self-conscious national working class, while in areas such as the Forest of Dean the poor themselves were more likely to take a conservative view of both encroachment upon their way of life and the organisation of resistance. While more radical elements were pushing for the rights of the poor and the marginal in their stand against hereditary privilege, in the context of Dean certainly, the mobilisation of popular action would appear to have been more in line with Edmund Burke's calls to the defence of the local 'platoon' and the deep rooted justifications of antiquity, despite his famous attack on the poor as the 'swinish multitude'.[456] Thus we can sense the complexity of debate surrounding the nature of constitutional reorganisation within the British polity and, indeed, over the lengths to which such reforms should be taken.

---

[456] E. Burke, *Reflections on the Revolution in France* (Harmondsworth, 1982), 335.

This debate was exemplified in William Hazlitt's question *What is the people?*, as his essay, published in 1818, emulated the very form of this relatively novel sense of public dialogue. Self-consciously engaging the intersubjectivity of his readership, he asked rhetorcially, 'And who are you that ask that question?', answering 'One of the people. And yet you would be something! Then you would not have the people nothing'. Hazlitt thus appropriated the notion of 'the people', who he described as 'Millions of men, like you', in his impassioned attack on 'the drivelling prejudices' of superstition, tyranny and 'Legitimacy – that detestable fiction'.[457] Ellis Wasson alludes to the myriad levels of debate over who should be enfranchised in what eventually became the Reform Act, noting that 'it is often forgotten that 1832 was in its own way a leap in the dark', and explaining that:

The Whigs intended to give the middle class a voice in the political system and believed that the elite had to be made more responsive to public opinion. Even the Marquess of Lansdowne, who felt most comfortable with one foot in both camps, spoke of giving 'persons of small property a decidedly larger share of power'. Grey had long believed, as he wrote to his wife, that 'conciliation' and 'leniency and reasonable concession to the wants and wishes of the people' was necessary and salutary.[458]

---

[457] W. Hazlitt, *Selected Writings with an introduction by Jon Cook*, (Oxford, 1991), 3.

[458] E. A. Wasson, 'The Spirit of Reform, 1832 and 1867', *Albion: A Quarterly Journal Concerned with British Studies*, 12, 2 (1980), 164-74.

The reorganisation of the British polity and the debate over enfranchisement, encapsulated in many respects by Hazlitt's question, bore similarities to the question of who retained customary use rights following the disafforestation of large parts of the Forest of Dean during the seventeenth century. The answer to both questions was very much related to private property rights.

Thompson quotes a hand-loom weaver who was brought before a parliamentary committee in 1835 and asked to state the opinions of his co-workers on the Reform Bill. He suggested that they were not satisfied, viewing:

> the Reform Bill as a measure calculated to join the middle and upper
> classes to Government, and leave them in the hands of Government as
> a sort of machine to work according to the pleasure of Government.[459]

There is no doubt that several projects, both governmental and industrial, were underway during this period. These incentives were aimed at incorporating the Forest population and resources within the bourgeois hegemony that was apparently consolidated in the 1832 reforms. This book examines in particular the increasing recourse to central equity courts, and its long-term effects in rendering the forest and its industries more legible to external interests. This process appears to have been, at least partly, an unintended consequence of the miners' attempts to preserve their occupational rights from 'foreign' interests. The extended reach of equity litigation, the discontinuance of the Mine Law Court, and the closer

---

[459] Thompson, *Making of the English Working Class*, 915.

alignment of criminal law with the defence of private property in the Forest, combined with specific measures to tackle concerns over poor propertyless foresters who were regarded as an increasing problem during the eighteenth century.

In 1785, a committee under the direction of Sir George Onesiphorus Paul 'secured an act of parliament for building a new gaol at Gloucester and four houses of correction in other parts of the county', one of which being at Littledean.[460] The beginning of the nineteenth century also witnessed heavy investment in establishing a profitable and efficient rail network to service the Forest's increasingly large-scale mining operations, while lengthy discussion ensued regarding the potential local application of the new poor law.[461] In addition to these debates, the records of Quarter Sessions from the early nineteenth century contain entries relating to several Acts of Parliament that had been passed to bring the extra-parochial Forest of Dean under normal jurisdiction.[462]

Many contemporary texts reveal elite anxieties over a perceived politicisation of the poor. Reactionary projects of the 1790s suggest a profound fear of working-class radicalism. Linda Peterson, for instance,

---

[460] ONDB: http://www.oxforddnb.com/view/articleHL/21597?anchor=match (Dec., 2008).

[461] GRO, Q/FAC 1; GRO, D2091/X6 containing 'Legal opinion on application of the New Poor Law to extra-parochial areas of the Forest of Dean, 1834; letter about poor and church rates, 1837; 6 printed orders of Poor Law Commissioners'; GRO, D421/X5.

[462] GRO, Q/RI.

suggests that Harriet Martineau's 'little books' represented a set of moralising tales and didactic poems which were intended as a complement to the work of Hannah More in an 'attempt to stifle the revolutionary impulses of the working classes and divert them into religious channels'.[463] The varied nature of protest during the eighteenth century, however, questions the radical nature of some popular political action. Protests aimed at defending 'ancient' and local custom, by definition, drew on a conservative world-view which stood poles apart from the radical views of writers such as Thomas Paine. In 1831, the breach between proponents of 'open' and 'closed' forest once again manifested itself in large-scale popular action, this time led by Warren James, resident of Parkend and the son of a free miner. The strategy adopted by Warren James and his followers was, in many respects, emblematic of both old and new traditions of resistance which characterised the emergence of national class consciousness in many parts of England during the late eighteenth and early nineteenth centuries. Before analysing these disturbances, it is necessary to outline the changing contexts of popular protest within which James was operating.

Some eighteenth-century radical writers, like Paine, saw the emancipation of the poor in terms of progressive change at a constitutional level. The sense of loss and hardship experienced in some local communities during this period, however, was attributed to encroachments upon 'ancient' customary rights. That these rights looked to history for precedent and legitimacy implies that protests in their defence would be less likely to

---

[463] L. H. Peterson, 'From French Revolution to English Reform: Hannah More, Harriet Martineau, and the 'Little Book", *Nineteenth-Century Literature*, 60, 4 (2006), 409-450.

define themselves in terms of the radical rejection of the shackles of the past. Paine's radical thinking, while aimed at helping to enfranchise the labouring poor was, in principle, opposed to the protectionism of local custom. His vision, in fact, shared many characteristics with the rationalising common sense, and supposedly transparent, ideology which underpinned moves to improve the Forest of Dean in the name of private and exclusive property ownership.

James Epstein underlines the ideological impact of Paine's work in popularising the notions of openness and reason which underwrote a rational drive towards the inclusion of 'the people' in the British polity. He explains that:

> Paine's concept of legitimate constitution making is inseparable from Enlightenment notions of language derived principally from Locke - it links transparency of rational expression to democratic politics and the encoding of democratic principles within a constitution...the commitment to linguistic transparency was typically linked to allegiances that were decidedly presentist and cosmopolitan. History and custom were polluting agents: enemies of reason and philosophy - the appeal to precedent was an invitation to chaos.[464]

This is not to reify Paine as an emblem of progressive libertarianism. His work was, in many respects, the consequence of the turbulent ideological dialogue that had ensued in late eighteenth-century England against a

---

[464] J. Epstein, "'Our Real Constitution': Trial Defence and Radical Memory in the Age of Revolution' in J. Vernon (ed.), *Re-reading the constitution: New narratives in the political history of England's long nineteenth century* (Cambridge, 1996), 22-51, 24-25.

backdrop of the loss of the American colonies and the French Revolution. Paine's work is pertinent, however, if only for his widely acknowledged ability to communicate his ideology of common sense in the idiom of ordinary working people, a talent evidenced by the huge sales and widespread diffusion of his writing. Gary Kates quotes John Adams who, in 1805, wrote 'I know not whether any man in the world has had more influence on its inhabitants or affairs for the last thirty years than Tom Paine'.[465]

The notion of social justice proposed by Paine was particularly influential in this period, but his concept of a rational legal system - derived from the universal principles of reason, liberty and human fellowship - was fundamentally opposed to understandings of customary law which constituted the mining rights. Opposition to this kind of local protectionism had provided such advocates of political reform with a series of freedoms won over the unjust constraints of the past. James Vernon observes that 'the concept of narrative shifts the focus from politics as a reflection of 'the real' to how politics imagined 'the real'".[466] This narrative could be assumed to justify both the enfranchisement of the property-holding classes but also, in more radical interpretations, the extension of these rights to all that contributed to the burgeoning wealth of the nation. Just as the benefits of improvement were beneficial to some, others wrote to emphasize the

---

[465] G. Kates, 'From Liberation to Radicalism: Tom Paine's Rights of Man', *Journal of the History of Ideas*, 50, 4 (1989), 569-87, 569.

[466] Vernon, 'Notes Towards an Introduction', in Vernon (ed.), *Re-reading the constitution*, 1-21, 14.

common sense of a meritocratic system and universal enfranchisement. As argued in Chapter Two, however, the way that people and communities imagined the world is rooted in their experience of material reality. Representing the reality of local, particularly rural, experience, this ideology was often in conflict with the interests of the poor for whom it claimed to speak.

It is unlikely, for example, that any free miners of Dean would have sympathised with Wordsworth's pre-revolutionary condemnation of monarchical systems of government as their 'ancient' rights were derived from, or had at least been guaranteed by, the authority of the Crown. Calls for the restitution of the Mine Law Court as a defence against the encroachments of outsiders dominate the records of commissions instigated following the Warren James disturbances of 1831.[467] The ideals of transparency and rationality pursued by Paine and other progressive ideologues would have seemed more in line with the ideology that informed attempts to improve and enclose the Forest than with the protectionism, opacity and intense localism symbolised by the miners' court. While we have volume upon volume of reforming literature which reflects the middle-class view of shifts towards a more inclusive, national polity, there is far less to suggest the opinions of the labouring poor themselves. While there are biographies, pamphlets, and other forms of popular literature, it is possible to glean a broader cross-section of opinion from changes and

---

[467] Cyril Hart quotes a local periodical *The Forester* which, in August 1831, reported that the Duke of Beaufort (as constable of St. Briavels castle) had been 'for nearly three years past trifling with the patience and miseries of the free miners by denying their just demands of opening their Free Miners' Courts'. The same article also notes another complaint of the mining community, namely, 'that 'foreigners' had been favoured 'who have crept in to rob us of our rights'', in Hart, *Free Miners*, 254.

continuities in the nature of protest across the eighteenth and nineteenth centuries.

II Riot and popular protest in the long eighteenth century

The years between the Glorious Revolution in 1688 and the 1832 Reform Act brought tumultuous change which met with popular resistance of varying scales and intensities.[468] Elements of change and continuity in popular protest during the long eighteenth century have allowed historians to explore the social changes and mentalities that helped to make the English working class.[469] A number of central themes have dominated debate over the nature of popular resistance in the eighteenth century, particularly the language used to describe this action. Much attention has focused on distinctions between 'riot' and 'popular protest' as a reflection of different social perspectives in this period, while class affiliations have similarly been analysed for the emergence of a national working-class consciousness.[470] Distinctions between rural and urban protest across the

---

[468] E. P. Thompson, 'Custom, Law and Common Right', in *Customs in Common: Studies in Traditional Popular Culture* (New York, 1993), 97-184; A. Wood, 'Fear, Hatred and the Hidden Injuries of Class in Early Modern England', *Journal of Social History*, 39, 1, 803-26; D. Rollison, 'Marxism', in G. Walker (ed.), *Writing Early Modern History* (London, 2005), 3-25;

[469] E. P. Thompson, *The Making of the English Working Class* (London, 2005).

[470] For a summary of the terms employed in describing social protests, see J. E. Archer, *Social Unrest and Popular Protest in England, 1780-1840* (Cambridge, 2000), 2-4; A. Wood, 'The place of custom in plebeian political culture: England 1500-1800', *Social History*, 22, 1 (1997), 46-60; E. P. Thompson, 'Patrician Society, Plebeian Culture', *Journal of Social History*, 7, 4 (1974), 382-405.

century suggest a very broadly defined division between what might be termed traditional, or conservative, protest and more radical, or 'progressive', politics of crowd action. Rural protest was generally motivated by local, agrarian, grievances over enclosure or disputed rights to gleaning and other customary perquisites.[471] These protesters usually called for the restoration of an idealised economic and political order of the past. Tradition and custom were clearly very significant in forging popular solidarities and informing the 'moral economy' at the heart of these crowd actions.[472]

The eighteenth century witnessed the emergence of urban food riots which protested against fluctuating grain prices as a result of market tariffs, middle-men and engrossers.[473] These were often accompanied, in towns and cities, by political and religious protests. In short, traditional agrarian protests against local grievances still constituted a constant and, in some areas, increasing backdrop of unrest during this century, but more

---

[471] J. M. Neeson, 'The Opponents of Enclosure in Eighteenth Century Northampton', *Past & Present*, 105 (1984), 114-39.

[472] E. P. Thompson, 'The Moral Economy of the English Crowd in the Eighteenth Century', *Past & Present*, 50 (1971), 76-136.

[473] A. Randall and A. Charlesworth, *Markets, market culture and popular protest in eighteenth-century Britain and Ireland* (Chicago, 1996); J. Bohstedt, "We'd Rather be Hanged than Starved!': The Politics of Provisions', in *The Politics of Provisions, 1550-1850* (London, 2010); J. Bohstedt, 'Gender, Household and Community Politics: Women in English Riots, 1790-1810', *Past & Present*, 120 (1988), 88-122.

widespread actions began to develop which were national in scale and the nature of their participation. Various causes began to be perceived at a popular level, on a national rather than purely local scale. In many respects this reflected the shift from local political cultures to a national class consciousness that was outlined in the previous section of this chapter.

Among the first of these were the festivities and protests which accompanied William III's accession to the crown of England in what has become known as the Glorious Revolution of 1689.[474] Political alliances were apparently tied to support for either the Protestantism of Whig constitutionalism or the feared Catholicism of James II and his regime. These divisions were exacerbated during the Sacheverell riots of 1710.[475] In March that year a serious protest against Protestant dissenters and their Whig allies accompanied the trial of Dr Henry Sacheverell, a high Anglican clergyman. Sensing the opportunity to discredit Anglican extremists, the Whig ministry had impeached Sacheverell for preaching against the revolution of 1689. This tactic backfired as Tory politicians were able to manage his defence and present him as an Anglican martyr. His case garnered support through uniting several causes: the state of religion, high wartime taxation and the perceived growth of monied interest amongst government debt-holders. These disturbances suggest the context of growing party political alliances and it seems certain that these allegiances

---

[474] G. S. De Krey, 'Political Radicalism in London after the Glorious Revolution', *The Journal of Modern History*, 55, 4 (1983), 585-617.

[475] G. Holmes, 'The Sacheverell Riots: The Crowd and the Church in Early Eighteenth-Century London,' *Past & Present*, 72, 1 (1976), 55-85.

circulated among ordinary people through the medium of print culture and debate in the convivial environs of the coffee house and the alehouse or tavern.

Further into the century, the Hexham riots offer further evidence of popular communication on a national scale.[476] In 1761, a large and diverse crowd gathered in the centre of Hexham in Northumberland to protest against the imposition of the Militia Act which enforced military service.[477] For disputed reasons, troops from the North Yorkshire Militia opened fire on the crowd, killing dozens of protesters and injuring many more in an event which became remembered both locally and nationally as 'Bloody Monday'. This incident evidently heightened national fears over the British state's use of force against its own population, a debate which was reinvigorated in the wake of the Peterloo Massacre of 1819. The most serious of the eighteenth-century riots were inflamed by Lord George Gordon, president of the Protestant Association in 1780.[478] The protagonists of the Gordon Riots appear to have been incited by anti-Catholic rhetoric in

---

[476] The historiography on the Hexham incident is scant, but a number of antiquarian descriptions of the event survive; see, for example, A. B. Wright, *An Essay Towards the History of Hexham in Three Parts, Illustrating its Ancient and its Present State, Civil and Ecclesiastical Economy, Antiquities and Statistics, with Descriptive Sketches of the Scenery and Natural History of the Neighbourhood* (Alnwick, 1823), 202-203.

[477] N. Rogers, 'Popular Protest in Early Hanoverian London', *Past & Present,* 79, 1 (1978), 70-100.

[478] G. Rudé, 'The Gordon Riots: a Study of the Rioters and their Victims', *Transactions of the Royal Historical Society*, 5th series, 6 (1956), 93-114.

the context of debates over Catholic emancipation. Significantly, these disturbances highlight the relation between religion, more specifically a fervent anti-Catholicism, and a burgeoning popular national identity in later eighteenth-century England.[479]

The context of collective consciousness on the part of many at the lower echelons of British society reflected a national awareness that embodied many elite anxieties over the politicisation of the 'swinish multitude' in the wake of the French Revolution. Many events contributed to these fears from the 1790s onwards but matters only developed into a national issue at St. Peter's Fields, Manchester, in 1819. A crowd of between 60-80,000 had gathered to protest at working conditions, the cost of living, urban squalor among a labouring population and, importantly, many speakers at the meeting were calling for the suffrage of working men and women in industrial towns and cities.[480] This was action in the vein of Painite radicalism which was supported on a larger regional, if not national, scale. There are obvious differences between this action and the localism of reactionary protectionist protests in local agrarian or pastoral communities such as the Forest of Dean. Eventually the cavalry charged the protesters, including many women and children, who had little chance of escape. Fifteen people were killed and a further 400-700 injured. This outrage became emblematic of armed state aggression against the labouring classes

---

[479] Archer, *Social Unrest*, p. 58.

[480] R. Poole, 'The March to Peterloo: Politics and Festivity in late-Georgian England', *Past & Present*, 192, 1 (2006), 109-153; R. Reid, *The Peterloo Massacre* (London, 1989).

as it was broadcast in newspapers and other popular printed material, particularly as it involved the use of military force against many who were suffering in the wake of the recent Napoleonic Wars.

Other forms of popular protest during the early-nineteenth century shared certain characteristics with more traditional forms of crowd action. The machine-breaking Luddite disturbances, for example, sought to impede the march of progress which, they suggested, was responsible for rising unemployment levels through the introduction of labour-saving technology. [481] Similar grievances motivated the Swing rioters, rural counterparts of the Luddites, although historians have recently argued that these widespread disturbances subsumed many other disparate grievances against Benthamite Whig legislation of the 1830s.[482] Both of these episodes were notable for their adoption of the mythical folk leaders Captain Ludd and Captain Swing although, unlike regional leaders such as John Skymington in the 1630s, these drew support on a national scale.[483] In 1831, therefore, Warren James emerged as a leader on the cusp of old and new idioms of protest.

---

[481] K. Navickas, 'The Search for "General Ludd": the Mythology of Luddism', *Social History*, 30, 3 (2005), 281-95.

[482] E. Hobsbawm and G. Rudé, *Captain Swing: a Social History of the Great English Agricultural Uprising of 1830* (London, 1969); R. Dunwiddy, *From Luddism to the first Reform Bill: reform in England, 1810-1832* (Oxford and New York, 1986); P. A. Pickering, "The hearts of the millions": Chartism and popular monarchism in the 1840s', *History*, 88 (2003), 227-248.

III Warren James: old and new idioms of protest

The work of Ralph Anstis on the Warren James' disturbances illuminates the reception of national working-class politics in the Forest, particularly the way that these ideas conflicted with local customary senses of the region. In addition to the tenacious sense of custom that had always characterised the free-mining industry, Anstis explains that:

there were new ideas abroad, political ideas about radicalism and Reform. As yet the concept of workers banding together to form trade unions had not begun to take root in the Forest as it had in other parts of England. It is doubtful whether, even if it had, the free miners would have regarded it as applicable to themselves, for to do so would imply acceptance of their change of status from independent self employed men to employed labourers ... Politics, on the other hand, were a live issue in parts of the Forest. In the late 1820s and early 1830s people in Dean were enthusiastic supporters of the Whig party's proposals to reform Parliament by extending the franchise and abolishing the rotten and pocket boroughs.

[483] T. Harris, 'The Bawdy House Riots Of 1688', *The Historical Journal*, 29, 3 (1986), 537-555; R. Shoemaker, *London Mob: violence and disorder in Eighteenth-century London* (London, 2004); N. Rogers, 'Crowds and Political Festival in Georgian England', T. Harris (ed.), *The Politics of the Excluded, c.1500-1850* (Basingstoke and New York, 2001), 233-64; I. Gilmour, *Riot, Risings and Revolution, Governance and Violence in Eighteenth-Century England* (London, 1993); E. D. Ives, 'Folklore, History and Heroes', in *George Magoon and the Down East Game War: History, Folklore, and the Law* (Urbana, 1993), 3-32; K. Navickas, *Loyalism and Radicalism in Lancashire 1798-1815* (Oxford, 2009); R. Poole, 'French Revolution or peasant's revolt? Rebels and petitioners from the Blanketeers to the Chartists', *Labour History Review*, 74, 1 (2009), 6-26; D.J.V. Jones, *Rebecca's children: a study of rural society, crime and protest* (Oxford, 1989); I. Hayward, *The Revolution in popular literature: print, politics, and the people, 1790-1860* (Cambridge, 2004); I. Dyck, *William Cobbett and Rural Popular Culture* (Cambridge, 1992); E. Robinson (ed.), *John Clare's Autobiographical Writings* (Oxford, 1983).

Anstis outlines the largely hostile reception of William Cobbett's ideals as he worked to raise awareness of the shared conditions of England's labouring poor. While conceding that the anti-Cobbett stance might well be due to partisan reporting, he quotes the *Monmouthshire Merlin's* account of a meeting at Bream in 1830 during which 'the poor miners in the Forest were gulled by inflammatory speeches misrepresenting the causes of their present distress'.[484]

In the absence of union activity, it seems as though the organisation of popular political action was still seen as the preserve of the free miners. As the son of a free miner, Warren James was ideally suited to this role. Warren James grew up in the Parkend area of the Forest, a mining district towards the south of Dean's central demesne lands in close proximity to the more politically active parish of Coleford, and near to Bream, the site of many radical meetings. While his leadership of protest in 1831 drew on local traditions of protest that would have been familiar to foresters in the seventeenth century, he understood more radical strategies current in the early nineteenth century. In many respects, Warren James' organisational role in the riots of 1831 seems to have grown out of local and customary traditions of protest whilst embracing a more modern or national awareness of the rights of England's poor.[485]

---

[484] R. Anstis, *Warren James and the Dean Forest Riots: being the story of the leader of the riots in the Forest of Dean in 1831, with an account of the riots and of their causes* (Coalway, 1986), 83-84.

[485] In this section I refer to Warren James by his full name to avoid confusion with one of the key witnesses, James James.

On 12 August 1831, Warren James appeared before the Assize sessions at the Shire Hall in Gloucester. The first of the two indictments, relating to a charge of felony grounded in the Riot Act of 1715, declared that 'Warren James, together with divers other unknown evil disposed persons to the number of 100 or more, with force of arms did unlawfully, riotously, routously and tumultuously assemble together to the disturbance of the public peace'.[486] The dispute related to a perceived breach of the terms under which the forest had been 'settled' in 1668. This seventeenth-century act stated that half of the 22,000 acres of Dean's central demesne lands could be enclosed to allow for the re-growth of trees planted, replacing those depleted by industrial practices and other uses. In 1831, the area that had been enclosed for the previous twenty years was due to be laid open in accordance with the Act of 1668 and Warren James was confident that it would occur. He explained, Anstis notes, that:

> the enclosures had been set up for 20 years, that the period would expire on 8 June and that the enclosures would then be thrown open. He added that if the authorities did not open them up, the foresters would.[487]

When it became apparent that this would not happen Warren James wrote to Edward Machen, Deputy Surveyor of the Forest, informing him that the

---

[486] TNA, (CL) Assizes 5/151 pt. 1.

[487] Anstis, *Warren James*, 104.

controversial hedges, banks and fences would be removed. By this point, the banks and hedges were well established in the surrounding landscape.

When no further action was proposed on the matter, James decided to publicise his plans for the commonalty of Dean to 'open the Forest' of their own accord. At the beginning of June in 1831, Warren James distributed notices to be pinned to trees throughout the area, which were followed almost immediately by Machen's printed response. Local printer Thomas Stinson recalled that a poster design had been delivered to him by Warren James who gave him 'instructions to print fifty copies of the said paper' and he 'did print fifty copies of the said paper ... and Warren James paid him three shillings for the said copies'.[488] Two copies of Stinson's testimony survive from the Assize court, the second of which has additional comments noted in pencil. These indicate that James arrived at Stinson's shop at 7pm on Friday 3rd June and insisted on waiting until the notices were printed at around 11pm. He also suggested that Warren James was part of a larger group of instigators as five men 'appeared to be waiting for him'. Stinson described the incident in terms that emphasized his disinterested neutrality to avoid implication, but this is belied by his reported conversation with Warren James. Stinson claimed to have asked him, apparently, 'when he intended to begin' and was told that there 'would be five parties at different places and if one was stopp'd the others could be going on', thus illuminating the rioters' strategy.[489] Thomas Hatton, a

---

[488] TNA, (CL) Assizes 6/2 pt. 29.

[489] Ibid.

grocer whose business was located near Stinson's print shop, admitted that he had been on the premises while Warren James was waiting for the posters to be printed.[490] Hatton claimed that he had 'asked him what he was having done, who replied…that it was to give notice to the foresters to meet on the 7th to open the enclosures'. Another penciled note adjacent to these words states 'that he had given notice to Mr Machen of such intention that he certainly intended to carry it into effect – witness advised him not to do it but cannot recollect that he made any answer'.[491] The annotation presumably refers to Warren James' decision to inform Machen of his plans. The response posted by Machen attempted to outline the reasons for the legitimacy of recent enclosures, making clear to residents of the forest, his interpretation of this activity. His notice explained that 'if three or more persons shall assemble for such purpose, all that are present will be guilty of a riot'.[492]

These posters illustrate the ideologies which underpinned, on one hand, both the old customary traditions of local order and, on the other, more 'progressive' ideas of the British polity. Machen assured the inhabitants of the Forest 'that the Enclosures were made under an Act of 48th Geo III. cap.

---

[490] Ibid. Rather tellingly, here, the word 'Shop' has twice been crossed out and replaced with the words 'Print Office'.

[491] Ibid.

[492] Anstis, *Warren James*, 104.

72, the provisions of which are the same as 20th Charles II. cap. 3'. Warren James, by contrast, merely had to announce a meeting of the free miners of the locality 'for the purpose of opening the forest, and their right of common to the same'.[493] Despite the rudimentary nature of his call to action, Warren James received overwhelming support for removing enclosures which had transformed the local landscape.

Although estimates of the numbers involved may be hyperbolic, fears expressed in a letter from concerned magistrates to the Home Office state that up to three thousand people were eventually recruited to Warren James' project.[494] Shortly after the disturbances, in 1838, Dean's free miners were required to register their occupational status in the written records of the Deputy Gavellor. By the end of November 1839, 827 miners had been recorded suggesting that Warren James' call to action had exercised influence beyond those directly employed in the industry.[495] Chris Fisher, quoting the *Gloucester Journal* and the *Monmouthshire Merlin*, notes that in addition to 'Warren James and one or two others who may be identified as the working proprietors of small mines, there were workmen from the larger mines, women and children and men who had land and cottages in

---

[493] TNA, (CL) Assizes 6/2 pt. 29.

[494] *Magistrates to Home Office*, 11 June 1831, TNA, HO 52/12.

[495] *Roll of Honour: Mining & Quarrie Fatalities in The Forest of Dean With Index of Freeminers* (Forest of Dean Local History Society, 2006) *URL:* www.forestofdeanhistory.org.uk Date accessed: 17/2/2013.

the Forest but who did not work as miners'.[496] Contemporary estimates of the figures therefore suggest that support was drawn from a wider section of the forest community than the immediate fraternity of free miners on whose behalf Warren James was claiming to act.

Contemporary reports suggest a more disciplined operation than that implied by the charge of riotous and tumultuous assembly. During a four day period, and apparently at the instigation of Warren James, up to three thousand inhabitants of the forest had mustered at various locations to begin the arduous task of breaking up enclosures which had become the focus of much local antagonism.[497] In form and purpose, the crowds that gathered resembled an organized work-crew that met to remove the enclosures in accordance with a parliamentary act. The *Monmouthshire Merlin* reported that the crowds set about the fences 'in the same way as they would have *worked on anything else*'.[498] Even the deposition of John Langham, Machen's assistant, described the disciplined manner in which, after Warren James had 'struck the first blow with a Mattock or hoe and

---

[496] Fisher, *Custom, Work and Market Capitalism*, 38. Fisher notes that 'no more precise account than this may be offered of the composition of the crowd. The reports of the riot which appeared in newspapers used only such general terms as 'workmen' or 'cottagers".

[497] Estimated numbers are taken from a letter from *Magistrates to Home Office*, 11 June 1831, TNA, HO 52/12.

[498] *Monmouthshire Merlin*, 9 July 1831. Quoted in Fisher, *Custom, Work and Market Capitalism*, 43. My emphasis.

some of the earth fell, the rest of the party immediately commenced working and pulling down the bank'.[499]

The testimony of Langham and James James, another inhabitant of St. Briavels Hundred offer a glimpse of Warren James' leadership role during the second week of June 1831. Both witnesses suggest parallels and contrasts between this episode and John Skymington's leadership of the early seventeenth-century resistance. Goffman's dramaturgical interpretation of social action suggests the importance of Warren James' 'personal front' and the spatial location of his actions in motivating those who followed him. The 'setting' was crucial as the five selected areas were aimed at literally opening the offending 11,000 acres of Dean which, according to the settlement of 1668, was the legitimate course of action. Protesters claimed legitimacy, in one respect, from a ruling made in the distant chambers of Parliament. The physical action of restoring the material environment of Dean to open forest, however, drew upon deeper cultural traditions of protest, and memories of living and laboring in a landscape which had sustained the livelihoods of ancestors since 'time out of mind of man'.

In this respect, Warren James' claim to represent Dean's free-mining community was essential to the manner and appearance of his action. Physically destroying the marks of exclusive ownership in the presence of a free miner's son, coupled with the notion of an open forest, produced a theatrical and generalized interpretation of reality which powerfully reinforced the conviction of the crowds. In terms of the dramaturgical

---

[499] TNA, (CL) Assizes 6/2 pt. 29.

324

purpose of the gathering, their action was thus not only desirable, but just and essential. James James recalled that, 'about 8 OClock on the morning of Wednesday the 8th June', he had seen 'Warren James with more than 100 persons assembled in parties at the Park Hill, Shutt Castle and Bromley Inclosures in his Majesty's Forest of Dean'. Like Langham, he also describes the theatrical nature of Warren James' initial blow with the 'Mattock' or 'Pick Axe' at which stage the rest of the crowd fell to work. He continued to watch them for 'two hours or more during which time they continued to pull down the fences'. Warren James was evidently aware of his presence as a source of motivation, inspiration, and legitimacy as James James described the way that he circulated between these selected sites, leading the task of digging at each point. He describes how he 'saw Warren James with the party at each Inclosure and he was at work at the fence with some tool'. He saw him at 'about ½ past 9 OClock or quite as late as that – at that time he was at Bromley Inclosure and every now and then the party shouted'.[500] Langham also suggested the effect Warren James' presence had in buoying the crowd. He had been at the Park Hill Inclosure at 'about ½ past 7 oclock' when 'the riot act was read by Edward Machen Esquire one of his Majesty's Justices of the Peace'. 'All persons', he recalled, 'were commanded to depart to their habitations'. Apparently inspired by Warren James who 'headed the party', delivering inspirational speeches about the history of the enclosed lands, 'the party still continued throwing down the fence of the Park Hill Inclosure and frequently cheered each other'.[501]

---

[500] TNA, ASSI 6/2 pt. 29.

[501] Ibid.

These reports emphasise Machen's comparative lack of authority against the considerable influence of Warren James within a broad base of the forest community. While Machen listed abstracted parliamentary statutes and ultimately depended on the Riot Act to contain crowds of angry foresters, Warren James was able to draw his authority from deep-seated cultural memories, drawing on the locally metonymic phrase 'open the Forest' and dramatizing his position as a representative of the free-mining community. This type of customary shorthand contrasted starkly with the verbose and bureaucratic list of statutes to which Machen was forced to resort.

As noted in earlier chapters, memories of the loss of the Mine Law Court evidently evoked feelings of vulnerability to outside interests and the forces of a market economy. The cultural and occupational orientation of Warren James and the community of free miners made them particularly suitable agents for the organisation and articulation of collective grievances of propertyless inhabitants, many of whom were previously dependent on rights to common in the forest. In a letter dated 1 June 1831, local magistrates, including Machen, wrote to the Home Office explaining that when informed that the ground might always be enclosed, Warren James had gained credit amongst the people, entering 'thus at length into the history of the Enclosures'.[502] The letter also records that:

---

[502] TNA, HO/52/12. f. 193.

Warren James a miner who had taken great trouble about their rights and has obtained considerable influence amongst them by representations such as these and also by stating that he was countenanced by persons high in authority and by the Severn trust itself at length induced them to join in this desperate undertaking and we fully believe that a great majority have joined under an idea that they were asserting a just right.[503]

Certainly, in the view of events related to the Home Office, James was both aware of the history of the locality and was conscious of the need to demonstrate connections with authority beyond the local magistracy.

In 1831, Warren James rallied the foresters of Dean in a manner that would have been recognizable to protesters in the early-seventeenth century. He undoubtedly deployed the traditional motifs of preserving an open forest and the associated 'ancient' customs, but significant differences distinguished the organization and performance of these protests from those that occurred in the sixteenth and seventeenth centuries. Earlier free miners, for instance, claimed rights deriving from a charter of Edward I but the details of this were obscure; they also adopted a dual time frame, stating that they had enjoyed these rights from 'time out of mind of man'. Warren James' posters and communication with other foresters drew on the idea of 'timeless' custom that was associated with open forest. Yet he was careful to engage with the details of the 1668 Dean Forest (Reafforestation) Act as this lent formal legitimacy to the cause in a legal sense.

---

[503] Ibid.

The 'social drama' that marked the nineteenth-century protests manifested itself in the same breach of custom that had motivated protesters two centuries earlier. Yet a number of distinctions differentiated the ways that the chief protagonists in each event dramatized their actions. It has been argued that the 'Skymington' figures of the seventeenth-century Western rebellion drew upon a tradition of allegorical leadership which both advertised the cause of the protest and offered an alias to protect these folk leaders from the hand of authority. Warren James seems to have performed a similar function but, rather than using an alias, preferred to make his identity known publicly, attempting to formally legitimize the activity of his followers in a national legal context. Not only was he familiar with the terms of the 1668 Act and publicized its bearing on the situation in 1831, but he also claimed family connections with important political figures in London, possibly Lord Lowther, Chief Commissioner of Woods.[504] In addition, he sought guidance and backing from those in authority beyond local Justices of the Peace, particularly the Severn Trust. Despite the miners' antipathy to wider political ideals which threatened to undermine their prized industrial autonomy, these protests were conceived under the influence of non-conformist preachers and radical speakers who had become so prevalent in the vicinity of Parkend. In this respect, it is significant that the second copy of the poster attached to Stinson's testimony has the words 'Old English' inserted in pencil before the phrase 'Free Miners', conjuring the somewhat oxymoronic idea of a national, but simultaneously ancient and local, tradition of entitlement and protest. The symbolism of this protest accommodated discourses that drew on both

---

[504] Anstis, *Warren James*, 77-78.

328

conservative and radical ideas of popular enfranchisement in English political culture.

The posters included in the Assize case suggest the influence of a national popular political culture. During the sixteenth and seventeenth centuries there were various means of popular communication for 'raising the commons' in protest. Rebels in Lavenham, Suffolk, protesting against Henry VIII's Amicable Grant in 1525, had intended to use church bells to communicate the moment of their rising.[505] In 1537, conspirators in Walsingham, Norfolk, described a system of beacons which was to signify their uprising against the planned dissolution of the local abbey.[506] A number of planned risings were spread by word of mouth as demonstrated in the oral communication between militia groups in the Western rising and Skimmington riots of 1628-31. Yet the dissemination of rebels' aims through posting written bills was recorded on several occasions in late medieval England, by Lollard groups in 1414 and against Bishop Beaufort in 1425.[507] The difference between fifteenth-century bill casting and the later publication of rebellious posters, for example, in Dean related to the latter's scale, which involved professional mass production. By the later eighteenth century, radical groups were exploiting the flourishing trade in

---

[505] A. Wood, *The 1549 Rebellions and the Making of Early Modern England* (Cambridge, 2007), 242-43.

[506] TNA, SP1/119, fol. 30r; TNA, SP1/119, fol. 36r.

[507] S. Cohn, *Popular Protest in Late Medieval English Towns* (Cambridge, 2012), 37, 307.

cheap print and urban environments were replete with posters advertising the aims of these groups.[508] Warren James evidently recognized the benefits of this type of publicity which presumed higher rates of literacy than might have been expected in sixteenth- and seventeenth-century local communities.

The events of 1831 also distinguished themselves from their earlier counterparts in their relative lack of violence. The Skimmington riots were notable for the amount of weaponry accompanying the quasi-military operations, culminating in the ritual violence against Sir Giles Mompesson and the disputed pits, as well as the physical violence inflicted on workers employed by Robert Bridges. Warren James' supporters arrived at the scene of their protests armed only with the tools necessary to dismantle the landscape of exclusive ownership. Instead of pikes, swords, longbows and halberds, records speak only of mattocks, hoes, spades and pick axes. Perhaps there was less of a sense of bearing arms as a form of political expression than seems to have characterized Dean during the sixteenth and seventeenth centuries.

Despite these differences, however, Warren James was still essentially calling upon local inhabitants to open the Forest in the name of the free miners, in terms that resonated clearly with the protests of the seventeenth century. As the son of a free miner his actions evidently held powerful symbolic currency, articulating collective memories of this community's

---

[508] C. Parolin, *Radical Spaces: Venues of Popular Politics in London, 1790-1845* (Canberra, 2010), 116-17; for studies on radical print in Leicester, see J. Hinks, 'Networks of Print in 'Radical Leicester'', *The Leicestershire Historian*, 46 (2010), 21-26; J. Hinks, 'Richard Phillips: Pioneer of Radical Print', *The Leicestershire Historian,* 47 (2011), 22-26.

longstanding role in defending 'open' forest and the rights associated with this ideal. The organization of this counter-hegemonic workforce, then clearly drew upon oral traditions which depended upon direct physical action in the setting of the disputed lands. The Mine Law Court had been discontinued more than fifty years earlier but the customary social and industrial networks which had lent the free miners authority had outlived their formal institutional presence. The autonomy of these miners had been severely undermined but traces of their influence survived in the material environment, culture, and taskscape of the Forest of Dean.

Warren James was able to build a broad popular alliance in support of his call to restore the 'customary' landscape which was both symbolically and physically central to the shared local habitus. In responding to Warren James' call, Edward Machen relied on rational parliamentary statute, the hegemonic apparatus of the burgeoning class of property owner. While James and the free miners received the support of between 2,000 and 3,000 people, Machen's attempt to organise the foresters' consent was ultimately replaced by the use of coercive force. A further letter from Machen, P.J. Ducarel and George Crawley to the Home Office dated 23 June 1831 read:

We beg that you will inform Lord Melbourne that since our last communication with his Majesty's Government circumstances have induced us to change our opinion with regard to the removal of the military altogether. The party of the 11th Foot have already left the neighbourhood; and we would suggest that the Dragoons now with us should remain for some time as many prisoners are daily brought before us, and there still appears to be such excitement in the Forest.[509]

This letter makes clear the extent to which Machen and his fellow magistrates felt that the consensual basis of their authority had been undermined following the challenge of James and the free miners. This study has explored the role of the free miners in the negotiation of hegemony in the Forest of Dean between the sixteenth and nineteenth centuries. At the beginning of the seventeenth century, the encroachments of outsiders generated a cleavage in the world-view which had been central to a shared, if idealized, common culture in the Forest. These divergent world-views were tied to senses of legitimate legal activity as projectors adopted formal legal process to not only undermine access to resources but also to challenge the very terms in which access could be claimed. This generated a cultural breach as claims to private ownership overlooked informal access to an 'open' forest that many depended on. It is argued that the changing legal habits of the mining community unintentially contributed to a shift in mentalities which helped to avoid permanent division within the Forest. The compromise over legitimate forms of authority was, however, less than seamless as the hegemony of Macen, Ducarrel and Crawley ultimately depended on the coercive force of the army. For his efforts, Warren James was initially sentenced to death but this was commuted to transportation for life. He was transported to Van Dieman's Land where he died in 1841.

---

[509] TNA, HO/52/12. f. 195.

Conclusion

By the 1840s it was compulsory, by act of Parliament, for free miners of the Forest of Dean to register new coal mines with forest authorities. The *Grant of Gales* marked a significant shift in the regulation of Dean's free-mining industry.[510] During the seventeenth and eighteenth century, gales had been granted, transferred and regulated by a jury of free miners in the Mine Law Court. An *Outline of Proposed Rules and Regulations for the mode of Working the Coal Mines in the Forest of Dean* stated that:

> Every person or persons holding one or more Gales of any Mine or Mines of Coal within the Hundred of St. Briavels as allotted by the Award of the Dean Forest Mining Commissioners or granted by the Gaveller or Deputy Gaveller in conformity with the provisions of the Dean Forest Mining Act Ist and IInd. VICTORIA, Cap. 43, shall be entitled to the free and unrestricted use and enjoyment of all Levels, drifts, drains, cuts out, water courses Pits and shafts, together with all easements, privileges and appurtenances belonging or appertaining to the Gale or Gales so holden ... nevertheless so that the above easements and privileges be exercised in conformity with the

---

[510] TNA, F20/36.

provisions of the Dean Forest Mining Act and with these Regulations. [511]

The systematic registration of the *Grant of Gales* in the nineteenth century was a far cry from the customary claim that a miner could sink a pit wherever he could throw his mattock with the exception of churches and orchards. Ten years after the Warren James' disturbances, in the same decade that saw most of the Forest incorporated into the parish system, this tenaciously autonomous mining culture was firmly enmeshed with Victorian government bureaucracy.

After centuries of dispute over the regulation of this industry, frustrations over its obscurity, and the legitimacy of those who should be allowed entry, the *Grant of Gales* brought the free miners of Dean squarely into the view of central government and investors. The register lists grantees of mines which are easily correlated with the alphabetised index of collieries in accordance with Act 1 & 2 Vict. c. 43, s. 57.[512] Ostensibly, this industry was as legible as any other in nineteenth-century England. Despite the butty system which allowed miners to hire themselves as self-regulating work teams to the larger collieries, this industry was constituted and regulated according to national parliamentary acts while changing patterns of ownership announced themselves in the names of collieries. The Dean Forest Mining Act still defined a free mining community as 'all Male

---

[511] *Outline of Proposed Rules and Regulations for the mode of Working the Coal Mines in the Forest of Dean, as submitted to a Meeting of Free Miners and others at the Angel Inn, Coleford* (Coleford, 1840).

[512] TNA, F20/36.

Persons born or hereafter to be born and abiding within the said Hundred of Saint Briavels, of the Age of Twenty-one Years and upwards, who shall have worked a Year and a Day in a Coal or Iron Mine' but a glance at the register reveals the influence of external investors.[513] Mines named Victoria, Albert, Prince of Wales, Princess Royal, Regulator No. 4, Eton Delight and Harrow Hill, among others, contrast instructively with Greenes Pitt, Pryors Pitt, Newlyned Mine, Pukeputteswey, Monmouth Hill Pitt or Cross Knave from the seventeenth and early eighteenth centuries. Into the nineteenth century, these evocatively describe the shift from small-scale operations embedded in the popular culture of the Forest of Dean, to a trade dominated by larger investors with an eye to national and international industrial affiliations.

In some respects, the Forest of Dean presents a familiar story to historians of eighteenth- and nineteenth-century industrial intensification. By the nineteenth century a small-scale customary trade, governed by local custom and claiming the origin of these rights in timeless antiquity, had been opened up to the wider interests of large-scale investors. An industry which had been firmly under the jurisdiction of local miners through the Mine Law Court was now regulated by parliamentary acts and mining commissioners in a national legal context. The *Grant of Gales* reflects many features of what Scott refers to as the modern cadastral state. The supremacy of bureaucratic administration, the standardisation of local practices, and the sedentarisation of a workforce that could be observed, regulated and administered through these channels. Shifts in this industry

---

[513] Dean Forest Mining Act URL: http://www.legislation.gov.uk/ukpga/Vict/1-2/43/enacted Date Accessed: 10/1/2013.

and the wider forest culture appear to confirm many teleologies of modernity such as the rise of capitalism and private property, industrialisation, the growth of waged labour, the ascendency of literate mentalities, and the development of national class politics. In the context of this region's longer term development, many aspects of the modern state are represented in the impact of the *Grant of Gales.*

The value of the local or regional study lies in the ability to qualify, question or modify the general assumptions of larger historical narratives and the Forest of Dean is no exception. This book has suggested that state enlargement, as experienced in this area, was a reciprocal process. Regarding the rise of literate culture, the development of the rule of law, and the growth of national class consciousness as three aspects of state formation, the example of the Forest of Dean forces a reconsideration of these cornerstones of modern culture. Literate culture has usually been associated with urban elites and the rise of bourgeois hegemony while it has also been credited with a formative role in the division of cultures that historians suggest emerged in certain regions in early modern England. The free miners of the Forest of Dean challenge these assumptions as they swiftly adopted the written record in regulating their industry. As early as 1610, these 'subterranean creatures' of the 'dark corners of the land' had collated their *Laws and Privileges* in written form, and were assiduous in adapting to new procedures of evidence in defence of their customs.[514] While rising literacy levels have usually been associated with novel

---

[514] Daniel Defoe famously characterised a lead miner of the Peak country in Derbyshire as a 'subterranean creature' who he could not understand without the aid of a translator. D. Defoe, *A Tour through the Whole Island of Great Britain* (Aylesbury, 1971), 466.

practices and new cultural forms, it has been argued that Dean's free-mining community drew on the written record in an attempt, primarily, to preserve older forms of industrial organisation.

The development of a unitary code of law and a central legal system which operated to protect the interests of private property has also been identified as a crucial aspect of the modern state. Evidence suggests that this was very much a two-way process in the Forest of Dean. Rather than the imposition of a central legal system, the extension of these courts was driven by popular use. Certain groups within the Forest saw this as an effective way to settle grievances with other residents or, as was increasingly common during the seventeenth century, government officials. The miners were also prominent here as they began to use equity courts to defend their occupational custom against the pressures of large capital investors seeking a foothold in this profitable industry. This influenced forest culture in several ways. This litigation not only had a direct impact in specific cases but also, it seems, worked to inculcate documentary habits of mind and different approaches to the legal defence of local custom. This study has argued that the miners' use of novel legal documentation also had the effect of rendering this industry and region legible to outside interest. It is suggested that the extension of central authority emphasises the agency of this group, demonstrating that state enlargement and capital investment, within this region, depended on the unintended consequences of the miners' innovative legal practices.

The protests led by Warren James in 1831 offer an important opportunity to complicate narratives that imply sharp distinctions between conservative and radical idioms of protest in eighteenth- and nineteenth-century

England. This is significant because it challenges teleologies of class formation and forces recognition that particular forms of popular consciousness evolve and persist in different circumstances despite the influence of national political discourses and novel forms of communication. Radical working-class activism pervaded urban environments characterised by large numbers of labourers working in close proximity and connected to other regions by newspapers and preachers. This was less obviously the case in more scattered settlements of pastoral upland and highland communities. Warren James demonstrated that labouring people of this period were capable of adopting political perspectives appropriate to their situation rather than simply following national trends. He certainly understood this national political environment but also appreciated the social and economic needs of his fellow foresters. Like the Mine Law Court of the seventeenth century, he appears to have adopted novel methods but with the aim of preserving traditional ways of life.

Comparing popular protest of the seventeenth and nineteenth centuries illustrates the development of both hegemonic and counter-hegemonic ideologies and emphasises that, contrary to post-Cartesian Western distinctions, these are grounded in the material experience of daily life. It is here that landscape and the material environment emerge as active agents in the patterns of change and continuity described in this book. It has been argued that the material environment of the Forest of Dean influenced the social structures, world-views and forms of industrial organisation which characterised this region from the seventeenth century onwards. The mineral resources that the Forest holds in abundance have attracted settlement to this peripheral area since before the Roman conquest. From the beginning of the seventeenth century, an increased demand for coal attracted in-migration from those seeking to escape the hardship of other regions with more tightly regulated commons and wastes. The remote and less accessible topography of the region encouraged certain types of settlement and social structures that set the region apart from many other areas of southern England during the seventeenth, eighteenth, and nineteenth centuries. This book has suggested that this engendered certain types of solidarity and political consciousness characteristic of remote areas dominated by mining industries. This bestowed very strong and particular traditions of protest on the region. That these traditions of protest drew on local custom, and the evidence of the material environment as a repository of collective legal memory, allowed them to persist well into the nineteenth century.

Overall, this book has charted the influence of the written record on popular collective memory in this royal forest and examined the economic, social, cultural, and political implications of this shifting context. The local study of the Forest of Dean challenges many preconceptions of the early modern community and qualifies teleologies of the literate mentality, state growth, private property, capital industrial development and the leadership of resistance between the sixteenth and nineteenth centuries in England.

Bibliography

MANUSCRIPT SOURCES

Bodleian Library

Bankes Manuscripts; *The Papers of Sir John Bankes, Attorney General, 1634-40.*

British Library

Add. 18980. *Rupert Correspondence.*
Add. 18981. *Rupert Correspondence.*

Gloucester Record Office.

D5947/10/1 – schedule of orders, copy mine law orders and mine court proceedings: 1668-1777.

D149 – Probate Inventories.

D383/1 – Hearth Tax returns for St. Briavels Hundred, 1671-2.

D2026/X14 – Bond family papers.

Q/50/4

Q/FAc1

Q/SIa/1775/Epiphany.

Q/SR/1780/A.– Records of the Gloucestershire Quarter Sessions.

The National Archives

ASSI – Assize records.

E112 – class of bills and answers to the court of the Exchequer.

E134 – class of depositions to the court of the Exchequer.

E32 – Records of the Justice.

E179/247/13 – Hearth Tax returns for St. Briavels Hundred.

E146/3/29 – records of Speech Court: 1637.

E146/1/44 & E146/3/41 – rolls relating to the Verderer's Court.

STAC 8

SP14 – State Papers of James I.

SP16 – State Papers of Charles I.

(CL) Assizes 5/151.

HO/52/12.

MR 179 – 1608 'King James' map of the Forest of Dean.

Norfolk Record Office

HMN 5/34, 737x9 – Journals of Mrs Susan Elwes.

EDITIONS OF MANUSCRIPTS AND CONTEMPORARY PRINTED WORKS, AND CALENDARS

Alberti, L. B., *The Albertis of Florence: Leon Battista Alberti's Della Famiglia* (Eng. Trans., Lewisburg, 1971)

Albott, R., *England's Parnassus: or the choysest flowers of our modern poets* (London, 1600).

Burke, E., *Reflections on the Revolution in France* (Harmondsworth, 1982).

Carter, S., *Lex Custumaria: or, a Treatise of Copy-hold Estates* (London, 1696)

Church, R., *An Olde Thrift Newly Revived* (London, 1612).

Coleridge, S.T. & Wordsworth, W., *Lyrical Ballads* (London, 1999).

Everett Green, M.A. (ed.), *Calendar of State Papers series, of the reign of James I*, 5 vols. (London, 1857-9).

Hamilton, W.D. (ed.), *Calendar of State Papers series, of the reign of Charles I*, 23 vols. (London, 1858-97).

Hazlitt, W., *Selected Writings with an introduction by Jon Cook*, (Oxford, 1991).

Hoyle, R.W. (ed.), *The Military Survey of Gloucestershire 1522*, (Stroud, 1993).

Manwood, J., *A treatise and discourse of the lawes of the forrest* (London, 1598).

Norden, J., *A Store-house of varieties briefly discoursing the change and alteration of things in this world* (London, 1601).

Norden, J., *The surueyors dialogue very profitable for all men to peruse* (Lomdon, 1612).

Rothwell, H. (ed.), *English Historical Documents, Vol. 3, 1189-1372* (London, 1975).

Smith, J., *Men & Armour for Gloucestershire in 1608* (Gloucester, 1902).

Wilbraham, R., *The Journal of Sir Roger Wilbraham, Solicitor-General in Ireland and Lord of Requests, for the years 1593-1616.*

The Laws & Privileges of the Free Miners of the Forest of Dean (London, 1673).

BOOKS AND ARTICLES

Aers, D., *Community, Gender, and Individual Identity: English Writing, 1360-1430* (London and New York, 1988).

Allan, D. G. C., 'The Rising in the West, 1628-1631', *The Economic History Review*, New Series, 5, 1 (1952).

Anderson, B., *Imagined Communities: Reflections on the Origin and Spread of Nationalism* (London and New York, 2006).

Anstis, R., *Four Personalities from the Forest of Dean; Sir John Wyntour, Catharina Bovey, Timothy Mountjoy, Sir Charles Dilke* (Coleford, 1996).

Anstis, R., *Warren James and the Dean Forest Riots: The disturbances of 1831* (Coalway, 1986).

Arnold, J. H., *Inquisition and Power: Catharism and the Confessing Subject in Medieval Languedoc* (Philadelphia, 2001).

Bachelard, G., *The Poetics of Space* (Boston, 1964).

Bakewell, P. J., *Silver Mining and Society in Colonial Mexico, Zacatecas 1546-1700* (Cambridge, 1971).

Bakhtin, M., *The Bakhtin Reader: selected writings of Bakhtin, Medvedev and Voloshinov / edited by Pam Morris* (London, 1984).

Barthes, R., *Mythologies: Selected and translated from the French by Annette Lavers* (London, 2000).

Bateson, M., 'The English and Latin Versions of a Peterborough Court Leet, 1461', *The English Historical Review*, 19, 75 (1904), 526-528.

Beattie, J. M., *Policing and Punishment in London, 1660-1750: Urban Crime and the Limits of Terror* (Oxford, 2001).

Beckwith, S., 'Ritual, Church and Theatre: Medieval Dramas of the Sacramental Body', in D. Aers (ed.), *Culture and History, 1350-1600* (Detroit, 1992), 65-89.

Beckwith, S., *Signifying God: Social Relation and Symbolic Act in the York Corpus Christi Plays* (Chicago and London, 2001).

Bertaux, D., (ed.), *Biography and Society: The Life History Approach in the Social Sciences* (Beverly Hills, 1981).

Beynon, H., Cox, A., and Hudson, R., *Digging up trouble: the environment, protest and open cast mining* (London, 2000).

Beresford, M., *History on the Ground: Six Studies in Maps and Landscapes* (London, 1971).

Bohna, M., 'Armed Force and Civic Legitimacy in Jack Cade's Revolt, 1450', *English Historical Review*, 118 (2003), 563-82.

Boivin, N., 'Life Rhythms and Floor Sequences: Excavating Time in Rural Rajasthan and Neolithic Catalhoyuk', *World Archaeology*, 31, 3, Human Lifecycles (2000), 367-388.

Bourdieu, P., *The Logic of Practice* (Cambridge, 1990).

Braddick, M. J., *The nerves of state: taxation and the financing of the English state, 1558-1714* (Manchester, 1996).

Braddick, M.J., *State formation in early modern England, c.1550-1700* (Cambridge, 2000).

Braddick, M.J. and Walter, J. (eds.), *Negotiating power in early modern society: order, hierarchy and subordination in Britain and Ireland* (Cambridge, 2001).

Braudel, F., *A History of Civilisations / translated by Richard Mayne* (London, 1993).

Broad, J., 'Parish Economies of Welfare, 1650-1834', *The Historic Journal*, 42, 4 (1999), 985-1006.

Brooks, A. and Verey, D., *The Buildings of England. Gloucestershire 2: The Vale and the Forest of Dean* (New Haven and London, 2002).

Bristol, M., *Carnival and theater: plebeian culture and the structure of authority in Renaissance England* (New York and London, 1989).

Bryson, W. H., *The Equity Side of the Exchequer: Its Jurisdiction, Administration, Procedures and Records* (Cambridge, 1975).

Bryson, W. H., *Cases concerning equity and the Courts of Equity, 1550-1660, Vol. 1* (London, 2001).

Bryson, W. H., *Cases concerning equity and the Courts of Equity, 1550-1660, Vol. 2* (London, 2001).

Bryson, W. H., 'Exchequer equity litigation', *The American Journal of Legal History*, 14, 4 (1970), 333-348.

Bulmer, M., (ed.), *Mining and Social Change; Durham County in the Twentieth Century* (Croom Helm, London, 1978).

Bulmer, M. I. A., 'Sociological models of the mining community', *The Sociological Review*, 23 (1975).

Burgess, G., *The Politics of the Ancient Constitution: An Introduction to English Political Thought, 1603-1642* (Basingstoke, 1992).

Burke, P., *Popular culture in early modern Europe* (Aldershot, 1994).

Burke, P., *Languages and community in early modern Europe* (Cambridge, 2004).

Burke, P., *What is cultural history?* (Oxford, 2005).

Bushaway, B., *By Rite: Custom, Ceremony and Community in England 1700-1880* (London, 1982).

Campbell, A., *The Scottish Miners, 1874-1939* (Aldershot, 2000).

Canary, R. H. and Kozicki, H. (eds.), *The Writing of History: Literary Form and Historical Understanding* (Madison, 1978).

Carroll, S. (ed.), *Cultures of Violence: interpersonal violence in historical perspective* (Basingstoke, New York, 2007).

Cassell, P. (ed.), *The Giddens Reader* (Basingstoke, 1993).

Cattell, M. G. and Climo, J. J., *Social Memory and History: Anthropological Perspectives* (London and New York, 2002).

Cawley, A. C., *Everyman and Medieval Miracle Plays* (London, 1956; reprint, London, 1990).

Clanchy, M. T., *From Memory to Written Record: England 1066-1307* (Oxford, 1993).

Clark, S., 'The 'gendering' of witchcraft in French demonology: misogyny or polarity', *French History*, 5 (1991).

Cobley, P., *Narrative* (London and New York, 2001).

Cohen, M. and Hitchcock, T. (eds.), *English Masculinities, 1660-1800* (Harlow, 1999).

Cohn, S., *Popular Protest in Late Medieval English Towns* (Cambridge, 2012).

Collard, A., 'Investigating 'social memory' in a Greek context', in E. Tonkin, M. McDonald and M. Chapman (eds.), *History and Ethnicity* (London, 1989), 89-103.

Cook, A. B. 'The European Sky-God. VI. The Celts (Continued)', *Folklore,* 17, 3 (1906), 308-348.

Connerton, P., *How Societies Remember* (Cambridge, 1989).

Corbin, A., *Village Bells: Sound and Meaning in the Nineteenth Century French Countryside* (Basingstoke and Oxford, 1999).

Cox, J. C., *The Royal Forests of England* (1905).

Crehan, K., *Gramsci, Culture and Anthropology* (London, Sterling and Virginia, 2002). Cutting, G. (ed.), *The Cambridge Companion to Foucault*, 2nd Edition (Cambridge, 2005).

Davies, O., *Witchcraft, Magic and Culture 1736-1951* (Manchester and New York, 1999).

Davis, N. Z., *Fiction in the Archives: Pardon Tales and their Tellers in Sixteenth Century France* (Stanford, 1987).

De Coppet, D., *Understanding Rituals* (London, 1992).

De Vries, J., *The economy of Europe in an age of crisis* (Cambridge, 1976).

Decker, J.M., *Transitions: Ideology* (Basingstoke, New York, 2004).

Dennis, N., Slaughter, C., and Henriques, F., *Coal is Our Life* (London, 1956).

DiMaggio, P., 'Culture and Cognition', *Annual Review of Sociology*, 23, (1997).

Evans-Pritchard, E. E., *The Nuer* (Oxford, 1940).

Fabian, J., *Time and the Other: How Anthropology Makes its Object* (New York, 1983).

Fentress, J. and Wickham, C., *Social Memory* (Oxford, 1992).

Fisher, C., *Custom, Work and Market Capitalism: The Forest of Dean Colliers, 1788-1888* (London, 1981).

Foot, S., 'Remembering, forgetting and inventing: attitudes to the past in England after the First Viking Age', *Transactions of the Royal Historical Society*, 6th series, 9 (1999), 185-200.

Fortier, M., 'Equity and Ideas: Coke, Ellesmore, and James I', *Renaissance Quarterly*, 51, 4 (1998), 1255-1281.

Fox, A., *Oral and Literate Culture in England 1500- 1700* (Oxford, 2000).

Fox, A. and Woolf, D. (eds.), *The spoken word: Oral culture in Britain, 1500-1850* (Manchester and New York, 2002).

Foot, S., 'Remembering, forgetting and inventing: attitudes to the past in England after the First Viking Age', *Transactions of the Royal Historical Society*, 6th series, 9 (1999), 185-200.

Frazer, B., 'Common Recollections: Resisting Enclosure 'by Agreement' in Seventeenth-Century England', *International Journal of Historical Archaeology*, 3, 2 (1999), 75-99.

French, H. R., *The Middle Sort of People in Provincial England, 1600-1750* (Oxford, 2007). French, H. R., 'Social Status, Localism and the "Middle Sort of People" in England, 1620-1750', *Past and Present*, 166 (2000), 66-99.

Friel, B., *Translations* (London and Boston, 1981).

Friel, B., *Brian Friel: essays, diaries, interviews, 1964-1999 / edited, introduced and with a bibliography by Christopher Murray* (London, 1999).

Gaskill, M., *Crime and mentalities in early modern England* (Cambridge, 2000).

Godelier, M., 'Infrastructures, societies and history', *Current Anthropology*, 19, 4 (1978), 763-771.

Godoy, R., 'Mining: Anthropological Perspectives', *Annual Review of Anthropology*, 14, (1985).

Goody, J., *The Domestication of the Savage Mind* (Cambridge, 1977).

Goody, J., *The Interface between the Written and the Oral* (Cambridge, 1987).

Goody, J., *The Logic of Writing and the Organisation of Society* (Cambridge, 1989).

Godelier, M., 'Infrastructures, societies and history', *Current Anthropology*, 19, 4 (1978), 763-771.

Goldscheider, C., 'Migration and Social Structure: Analytic Issues and Comparative Perspectives in Developing Nations', *Sociological Forum,* 2, 4 (1987), 674-696.

Gough, J. W., *The Mines of Mendip* (New York, 1967).

Gingrich, A., Ochs, E. and Swedlund, A., 'Repertoires of Timekeeping in Anthropology', *Current Anthropology*, 43, (2002), S3-S4.

Griffiths, P., 'Meanings of nightwalking in early modern England', *Seventeenth Century*, 13, 2 (1998).

Griffiths, P., Fox, A and Hindle, S. (eds.), *The Experience of Authority in Early Modern England* (Basingstoke, 1996).

Greenblatt, S., *Renaissance Self-fashioning: From More to Shakespeare* (Chicago & London, 1984).

Halbwachs, M., *On Collective Memory* (Eng. Trans., Chicago, 1992).

Harris, M., *Carnival and other Christian festivals: folk theology and folk performance* (Austin, 2003).

Hallpike, C. R., *Foundations of primitive thought* (Oxford, 1979).

Harris, T. (ed.), *The Politics of the Excluded, c. 1500-1850* (Basingstoke, 2001).

Hart, C., *The Free Miners of the Royal Forest of Dean and Hundred of St. Briavels* (Newton Abbot, 1971).

Hart, C., *The Forest of Dean: New History, 1550-1818* (Stroud, 1995).

Hart, C., *The Industrial History of Dean* (Newton Abbot, 1971).

Hart, C., *The Verderers and Forest Laws of Dean: with notes on the Speech House and the deer* (Newton Abbot, 1971).

Hart, C., *Royal forest: a history of Dean's woods as producers of timber* (Oxford, 1966).

Harvey, D., *Spaces of Hope* (Edinburgh, 2000).

Hatcher, J., *The History of the British Coal Industry. Volume 1: Before 1700: Towards the Age of Coal* (Oxford, 1993).

Hay, D. and Snyder, F. (eds.), *Policing and Prosecution in Britain 1750-1850* (Oxford, 1989), 301-42.

Hayman, R., *Trees: Woodlands and Western Civilisation* (London and New York, 2003).

Herbert, N. M. (ed.), *A History of the County of Gloucester: Volume V. Bledisloe Hundred, St Briavels Hundred, The Forest of Dean* (Oxford, 1996).

Hill, C., *Change and Continuity in Seventeenth-Century England* (New Haven; London, 1991).

Hill, C., "Reason' and 'Reasonableness' in Seventeenth-Century England', *The British Journal of Sociology*, 20, 3 (1969), 235-252.

Hindle, S., 'Custom, Festival and Protest in Early Modern England: The Little Budworth Wakes, St Peter's Day, 1596', *Rural History*, 6, 2 (1995), 155-78.

Hindle, S., 'Hierarchy and Community in the Elizabethan Parish: the Swallowfield Articles of 1596', *The Historical Journal*, 42, 3 (1999), 835-851.

Hindle, S., *On the parish?: the micropolitics of poor relief in rural England, c. 1550-1750* (Oxford, 2004).

Hindle, S., 'Power, Poor Relief, and Social Relations in Holland Fen, c. 1600-1800', *The Historical Journal*, 41, 1 (1998), 67-96.

Hindle, S., *The birthpangs of welfare: poor relief and parish governance in seventeenth-century Warwickshire* (Stratford upon Avon, 2000).

Hindle, S., *The State and Social Change in Early Modern England, 1550-1640* (Basingstoke, 2002).

Hinks, J., 'Networks of Print in 'Radical Leicester'', *The Leicestershire Historian*, 46 (2010), 21-26.

Hinks, J., 'Richard Phillips: Pioneer of Radical Print', *The Leicestershire Historian,* 47 (2011), 22-26.

Hirsch, E. and O'Hanlon, M. (eds.), *The Anthropology of Landscape: Perspectives on Space and Place* (Oxford, 1995).

Horwitz, H., *Chancery equity records and proceedings 1600-1800: a guide to documents in the Public Record Office* (London, 1995).

Horwitz, H., *Exchequer equity records and proceedings, 1649-1841* (Trowbridge, 2001).

Hoskins, W. G., *The Making of the English Landscape* (London, 1985).

Howkins, A., *Reshaping Rural England: A Social History 1850-1925* (London, 1991).

Howson, G., *Thief-Taker General: The Rise and Fall of Jonathan Wild* (London, 1970).

Hoyle, R. (ed.), *The Estates of the English Crown, 1558-1640* (Cambridge, 1992).

Humphrey, C., *The politics of carnival: festive misrule in medieval England* (Manchester, 2001).

Ingold, T., 'The Temporality of the Landscape', *World Archaeology*, 25, 2 (1993), 152-174.

Ingram, M., 'Ridings, Rough Music and the 'Reform of Popular Culture' in Early

Modern England', *Past and Present*, 105, 1 (1984), 79-113.

Ivinskaya, O., *A Captive of Time: My Years with Pasternak* (London, 1978).

Jaffe, J. A., *The struggle for market power: industrial relations in the British coal industry, 1800-1840* (Cambridge, 1991).

Joll, J., *Gramsci* (Glasgow, 1983).

Joyce, P. (ed.), *The historical meanings of work* (Cambridge, 1989).

Kates, G., 'From Liberation to Radicalism: Tom Paine's Rights of Man', *Journal of the History of Ideas*, 50, 4 (1989).

Kerr, C. and Spiegel, A., 'The Industrial propensity to strike: An International Comparison', in A. Kornhauser, R. Dubin and A. Ross (eds.), *Industrial Conflict* (New York, 1954).

King, P. M., 'Morality Plays', in R. Beadle (ed.), *The Cambridge Companion to Medieval English Theatre* (Cambridge, 1994), 240-64.

Knights, M., *Representation and Misrepresentation in Later Stuart Britain: Partisanship and Political Culture* (Oxford, 2005).

Kriedte, P., *Peasants, Landlords and Merchant Capitalists, Europe and the world economy, 1500-1800* (Providence, 1983).

Landes, D. S., 'The Ordering of the Urban Environment: Time, Work and the Occurrence of Crowds 1790-1835', *Past and Present*, 116 (1987), 192-199.

Langton, J., *Geographical change and industrial revolution: coalmining in south west Lancashire, 1590-1799* (Cambridge, 1979).

Lefebvre, H., *The Production of Space* (Eng. Trans., Malden, Oxford and Victoria, 1991).

Lee, R., *Unquiet Country: Voices of the Rural Poor 1820-1880* (Macclesfield. 2005).

Levine, D. and Wrightson, K., *The Making of an Industrial Society: Whickham 1560-1765* (Oxford, 1991).

Lipset, S., *Political Man: The Social Bases of Politics* (New York, 1963).

Litzenberger, C., *The English Reformation and the Laity: Gloucestershire, 1540-1580* (Cambridge, 1997).

Lowenthal, D., *The Past is Another Country* (Cambridge, 1985).

Manning, R. B., *Village Revolts: Social Protest and Popular Disturbances in England, 1509-1640* (Oxford, 1988).

Marx, K., *A Contribution to the Critique of Political Economy*, M. Dobb (ed.), (Moscow, 1970).

Mason, P., *A glance back at Drybrook* (Lydney, 2001).

Mason, P., *A glance back at Mitcheldean* (Lydney, 2001).

Maurice, W., *A pitman's anthology* (London, 2004).

Massey, D. S., 'Social structure, Household Strategies, and the Cumulative Causation of Migration', *Population Index*, 56, 1 (1990), 3-26.

Martin, J. (ed.), *Antonio Gramsci: Critical Assessments of Leading Political Philosophers. Volume III: Intellectuals, Culture and the Party* (London and New York. 2002).

McLuhan, M., *The Gutenberg Galaxy: The Making of Typographic Man* (Toronto, 1962).

Meirion-Jones, G.I., 'The Use of Hearth Tax Returns and Vernacular Architecture in Settlement Studies: With Examples from North-East Hampshire', *Transactions of the Institute of British Geographers*, 53 (1971), 133-160.

Middleton, D. and Edwards, D., 'Conversational remembering: a social psychological approach' in D. Middleton, and D. Edwards (eds.), *Collective Remembering* (London, 1990).

Miller, J. C., *The African Past Speaks: Essays on Oral Tradition as History* (Folkestone and Hamden, 1980).

Misztal, B. A., *Theories of Social Remembering* (Maidenhead and Philadelphia, 2003). Moore, A. K., 'Mixed tradition in the Carols of Holly and Ivy', *Modern Language Notes*, 62, 8 (1947).

Moore, H. L., *Space, Text and Gender: An Anthropological Study of the Marakwet of Kenya* (New York and London, 1996).

Moore, L., *The Thieves' Opera: The Remarkable Lives and Deaths of Jonathan Wild, Thief-Taker, and Jack Sheppard, House-Breaker* (London, 1997).

Montgomery, M., *An Introduction to Language and Society* (London and New York, 1995).

Muir, E. *Ritual in Early Modern Europe 2nd edition*, (Cambridge, 2005).

Munn, N.D., 'The Cultural Anthropology of Time: A Critical Essay', *Annual Review of Anthropology*, 21, (1992).

Muriel Poggi, E., 'The Forest of Dean in Gloucestershire', *Economic Geography*, 6, 3 (1930).

Musson, A. (ed.), *Boundaries of the Law: Geography, Gender and Jurisdiction in Medieval and Early Modern Europe* (Aldershot, 2005).

Nash, J., *We Eat the Mines and the Mines Eat Us: Dependency and Exploitation in Bolivian Tin Mines* (New York, 1979).

Neeson, J., *Commoners: Common Right, Enclosure and Social Change in England, 1720-1820* (Cambridge, 1993).

Nicholls, Rev. H. G., *Nicholl's Forest of Dean: an historical and descriptive account and Iron Making in the Olden Times* (Dawlish, 1966).

Niditch, S., *Oral World and Written Word: Ancient Israelite Literature* (Louisville, Kentucky, 1996).

355

Ong, W.J., *Orality and Literacy: The Technologizing of the Word* (London and New York, 2000).

Orlikowski, W. J., and Yates, J., 'It's about Time: Temporal Structuring in Organizations', *Organization Science*, 13, 6 (2002), 684-700.

Ortner, S., *Anthropology and Social Theory; Culture, Power, and the Acting Subject* (Durham, New Jersey and London, 2006).

Outhwaite, R. B. 'A Note on the Practice of the Exchequer Court, with its Several Offices and Officers; by Sir T.F.', *English Historical Review*, 81, (1966).

Owen, C. C., *The Leicestershire and South Derbyshire Coalfield 1200-1900* (Ashbourne, 1984).

Parkhouse, N., *A glance back at Lydney* (Lydney, 2001).

Parkhouse, N., *A glance back at Lydney Docks* (Lydney, 2001).

Parolin, C., *Radical Spaces: Venues of Popular Politics in London, 1790-1845* (Canberra, 2010).

Paulin, T., Powell, D. and Robinson, E. (eds.), *John Clare: Major Works; including selections from the Shepherd's Calendar* (Oxford, 2004).

Perks, R. and Thomson, A. (eds.), *The Oral History Reader* (Abingdon, 2005).

Peterson, L. H., 'From French Revolution to English Reform: Hannah More, Harriet Martineau, and the 'Little Book'', *Nineteenth-Century Literature*, 60, 4, (2006), 409-450.

Pettit, P. A. J., *The Royal Forests of Northamptonshire; a Study in their Economy, 1558-1714* (Gateshead, 1968).

Pfau, T., "Elementary Feelings' and 'Distorted Language': The Pragmatics of Culture in Wordsworth's Preface to Lyrical Ballads', *New Literary History*, 24, 1 (1993).

Phelps, H., *A glance back at Newnham-on-Severn* (Lydney, 2001).

Philp, M. (ed.), *The French Revolution and British Popular Politics* (Cambridge, 1991). Pickering, K., 'Decolonizing Time Regime's: Lakota Conceptions of Work, Economy and Society', *American Anthropologist*, New Series, 106, 1 (2004), 85-97.

Poggi, E. M., 'The Forest of Dean in Gloucestershire', *Economic Geography*, 6, 3 (1930). Pollard, A. J., *Imagining Robin Hood: the late-medieval stories in historical context* (Abingdon, 2004).

Potter, D., *The changing forest: life in the Forest of Dean today* (London, 1962).

Powell, W. W. and DiMaggio, P. (ed.), *The New Institutionalism in Organizational Analysis* (Chicago, 1991).

Prince, A. E., 'The Army and Navy' in J. F. Willard and W. A. Morris (ed.) *The English Government at Work 1327-1336 Vol. I: Central and Prerogative Administration* (Cambridge, Massachusetts, 1947).

Proctor Hirst, R., *A glance back at Bream* (Lydney, 2001).

Raymond, J., *Pamphlets and Pamphleteering in Early Modern Britain* (Cambridge, 2003).

Reay, B. (ed.), *Popular Culture in Seventeenth-Century England* (London, 1985).

Ricoeur, P., *Time and Narrative*, 3 Vols. (Eng. Trans., Chicago and London, 1984).

Rivers, I. (ed.), *Books and their Readers in Eighteenth-Century England: New Essays* (London and New York, 2001, reprinted 2003).

Rollison, D., *A Commonwealth of the People: Popular Politics and England's Long Social Revolution, 1066-1649* (Cambridge, 2010).

Rollison, D., 'Exploding England: The Dialectics of Mobility and Settlement in Early Modern England', *Social History,* 24 (1999), 17-38.

Rollison, D., *The Local Origins of Modern Society: Gloucestershire 1500-1800* (London and New York, 1992).

Rutherford, J. (ed.), *Identity: Community, Culture, Difference* (London, 1998).

Ryan, M., 'Self-Evidence', *Diacritics*, 10, 2 (1980).

Said, E., *Orientalism* (London, 1995).

Scott, J. C., *Seeing Like a State: How Certain Schemes to Improve the Human Condition Have Failed* (New Haven and London, 1998).

Sewell, W. F. 'A Theory of Structure: Duality, Agency, and Transformation', *The American Journal of Sociology*, 98, 1 (1992).

Sewell, W. H. Jr., 'Geertz, Cultural Systems, and History: From Synchrony to Transformation', *Representations,* 59, (1997), 35-55.

Sharp, B., *In Contempt of All Authority: Rural Artisans and Riot in the West of England, 1586-1660* (University of California Press, 1980).

Sharpe France, R. (ed.), *The Thievely Lead Miners 1629-1635* Lancashire and Cheshire Record Society, 52, (Preston, 1947).

Shaw-Taylor, L., 'Parliamentary Enclosure and the Emergence of an English Agricultural Proletariat', *The Journal of Economic History*, 61, 3 (2001), 640-662.

Shaw-Taylor, L., 'Proletarianisation, Parliamentary Enclosure and the Household Economy of the Labouring Poor: 1750-1850', *The Journal of Economic History*, 60, 2 (2000), 508-511.

Simon, R., *Gramsci's Political Thought: An Introduction* (London, 1985).

Skipp, V., *Crisis and Development: an ecological case study of the Forest of Arden, 1570-1674* (Cambridge, London, New York and Melbourne, 1978).

Sokol, B. J. and Sokol, M., 'Shakespeare and the English Equity Jurisdiction: The Merchant of Venice and the Two Texts of King Lear', *The Review of English Studies,* New Series, 50, 200 (1999), 417-439.

Smith, A. H., *The Place-names of Gloucestershire Part III: The Lower Severn Valley, The Forest of Dean* (Cambridge, 1964).

Smith, B. R., *The Acoustic World of Early Modern England: Attending to the O-Factor* (Chicago, 1999).

Spufford, M., *Contrasting Communities: English Villagers in the Sixteenth and Seventeenth Centuries* (Cambridge, 1974).

Spufford, M., *Small Books and Pleasant Histories: Popular Fiction and its Readership in Seventeenth-Century England* (Cambridge, 1981).

Stallybrass, P. and White, A., *The politics and poetics of transgression* (Ithica and New York, 1986).

Steinberg, M. W., 'A Way of Struggle: Reformations and Affirmations of E. P. Thompson's Class Analysis in the Light of Postmodern Theories of Language', *The British Journal of Sociology*, 48, 3 (1997).

Tannen, D., (ed.), *Spoken and Written Language: Exploring Orality and Literacy* (Norwood, 1982).

Stewart, P. J. and Strathern, A. (eds.), *Landscape, Memory and History: Anthropological Perspectives* (London, 2003).

Tawney, R. H. *The Agrarian Problem in the Sixteenth Century* (Harrington, 1912).

Tonkin, E., *Narrating Our Pasts: the social construction of oral history* (Cambridge, 1992).

Tonkin, E., McDonald, M. and Chapman M. (eds.), *History and Ethnicity* (London, 1989), 89-103.

Thirsk, J., *Economic Policy and Projects: The Development of a Consumer Society in Early Modern England* (Oxford, 1978).

Thompson, E. P., *Customs in Common: Studies in Traditional Popular Culture* (New York, 1993).

Thompson, E. P., 'Time, work-discipline and industrial capitalism', *Past and Present*, 38 (1967), 56-97.

Thompson, E. P. *The Making of the English Working Class* (London, 2005).

Thompson, E. P., *Whigs and Hunters: the origin of the Black Act* (Harmondsworth, 1977).

Thirsk, J., 'Seventeenth century agriculture and social change', *Agricultural History Review*, 18 (1970).

Townley, E. L., 'The medieval landscape and economy of the Forest of Dean' (Unpublished PhD, Bristol University, 2005).

Turner, R. V., 'The Origins of the Medieval English Jury: Frankish, English or Scandinavian?', *The Journal of British Studies*, 7, 2 (May, 1968).

Turner, V., *Dramas, Fields and Metaphors: Symbolic Action in Human Society* (New York, 1974).

Tyler, I., *Thirlmere Mines and the Drowning of the Valley* (Keswick, 2005).

Underdown, D., *Revel, Riot and Rebellion: Popular Politics and Culture in England, 1603-1660* (New York, 1987).

Vernon, J. (ed.), *Re-reading the constitution: New narratives in the political history of England's long nineteenth century* (Cambridge, 1996).

Voloshinov, V. N., *Marxism and the Philosophy of Language* (Harvard, 1973).

Wales, T., 'Thief-takers and their clients in later Stuart London', in P. Griffiths and M. S. R. Jenner (eds.), *Londonopolis: essays in the cultural and social history of early modern London* (Manchester, 2000), 67-84.

Walter, J., 'A 'Rising of the People?' The Oxfordshire Rising of 1596', *Past and Present*, 107 (May, 1995).

Warwick, D. and Littlejohn, G., *Coal, capital and culture: a sociological analysis of mining communities in West Yorkshire* (London and New York, 1992).

Wasson, E.A., 'The Spirit of Reform, 1832 and 1867', *Albion: A Quarterly Journal Concerned with British Studies*, 12, 2 (Summer, 1980).

Webb, K. and Webb, J., *A glance back at Coleford* (Lydney, 2001).

Whittle, J., *The Development of Agrarian Capitalism: Land and Labour in Norfolk, 1440-1580* (Oxford, 2000).

Whyte, N., 'The deviant dead in the Norfolk landscape', *Landscapes*, 4, 1, 2003, 24-39.

Whyte, N., 'The afterlife of barrows: prehistoric monuments in the Norfolk landscape', *Landscape History*, 25, 2003, 5-16.

Williams, R., *Keywords* (London, 1983).

Williamson, B., *Class, culture and community: a biographical study of social change in mining* (London, 1982).

Williamson, T., *Shaping Medieval Landscapes: Settlement, Society, Environment* (Bollington, 2003).

Wood, A., 'Custom and the social organisation of writing in early modern England', *Transactions of the Royal Historical Society*, 6th series, 9 (1999), 257-69.

Wood, A., *Riot, Rebellion and Popular Politics in Early Modern England* (Palgrave, 2002).

Wood, A., *The Politics of Social Conflict: The Peak Country, 1520-1770* (Cambridge, 1999).

Wood, A., *The 1549 Rebellions and the Making of Early Modern England* (Cambridge, 2008).

Woolf, D. R., 'The "Common Voice": History, Folklore and Oral Tradition in Early Modern England', *Past and Present*, 120 (1988).

Wrightson, K., *English Society, 1580-1680* (London, 2002).

Wrightson, K. and Levine, D., *Poverty and Piety in an English Village. Terling, 1525-1700* (Oxford, 2001).

Wrightson, K., 'The Social Order of Early Modern England: Three Approaches', in L. Bonfield, R. M. Smith & K. Wrightson (eds.), *The World We Have Gained: Histories of Population and Social Structure* (Oxford, 1986), 177-202.

Wrightson, K., 'Estates, Degrees and Sorts: Changing Perceptions of Society in Tudor and Stuart England', in P. J. Corfield (ed.), *Language, History and Class* (Oxford, 1991), 30-52.

Yates, F. A., *The Art of Memory* (London, 2005).

Index

Abenhall, 26, 27, 31, 97
Anstis, Ralph, 226, 319, 320-322, 324, 331
Ann, Captain, 169
Assizes, 5, 119, 294, 296, 322
allegory, 41, 171, 173, 328
Arlingham Wharf, 88, 214, 215

bailiwicks, 54
Bankes, Sir John, 77, 133, 134, 135, 222, 225, 227, 241
Barthes, Roland, 62, 64, 167
Black Act (1723), 46, 290
Bond,
 Christopher junior, 265, 266
 George, 266
 family, 71, 90, 117, 118, 205
 family papers, 265-280
bounds, of the Forest, 8, 36, 50, 53, 58, 61, 63, 65, 66, 78, 84, 129, 182, 194, 197, 202, 213, 218, 269, 270, 275
Bourdieu, Pierre, 37, 38, 94, 95, 243,
Bream, 26, 92, 134, 320, 321
Brooke, Sir Basil, 75, 129, 133, 220, 222, 223
Burke, Edmund, 306
butty system, 262, 283, 285, 337

cadastral state, 181, 183, 198, 206, 211, 224, 225, 243, 250, 267, 269, 274, 275, 276, 286
Callowe, Anthony, 57, 254
Cannop, 11, 132, 183, 269
Catchmay,
 Sir Richard, 119, 120, 162, 205
 Edmund, 71
cattle, 35, 51, 78, 79, 86, 139, 160, 196, 207, 215, 230, 274, 282
charcoal burning, 12, 13, 221
Charles I, 168, 211, 212, 214, 217, 223
Charles II, 246, 254, 324
charters, 1, 3, 44, 45, 49, 73, 78, 203, 213, 272, 286, 330
Charter of the Forest (1217), 49, 60
Chepstow castle, 13, 30, 84, 232

civil wars,
    popular allegiance, 231-241
    and the Mine Law Court, 254-264
Clearwell (Clowerwall), 26, 57, 93, 193, 254, 265, 266
Coleford, 11, 26, 57, 88, 92, 93, 131, 137, 138, 158, 201, 226, 254, 289
Connerton, Paul, 192, 191, 192
coal,
    mining, 1-6, 11, 13, 14-32, 56, 119-123, 131, 141, 142, 144, 147, 148,
149, 157, 160, 165, 228, 234, 235, 237, 258-269, 277, 296, 336-339
    demand for, 26-32, 57, 95, 195, 214, 215, 235
colliers, 16, 30, 139, 157, 159, 183, 184, 190, 259, 295, 296, 337
commoners, 6, 53, 63, 78, 99, 101, 129, 135, 136, 140, 141, 153, 154, 161,
188, 189, 196, 199, 215, 229, 230, 249, 253, 267
common rights,
    estovers, 17, 49, 54, 65, 68, 77, 78, 103, 124, 128, 140, 141, 148, 215,
221, 230, 253, 291
    grazing, 17, 40, 50, 52, 54, 74, 90, 132, 134, 139, 140, 141, 144, 221,
230
    pannage, 17, 40, 50, 54, 128, 135, 198, 200, 201, 203, 214, 221, 230
    and free miners, 8, 17, 40, 141, 144, 230
commonalty, 6, 17, 41, 78, 81, 98, 101, 140, 144, 154, 155, 158, 188, 241,
248, 253, 278, 285, 301, 322
commonweal/th, 51, 63, 118, 126, 162, 169, 170, 171, 225, 226, 227
cottagers, 130, 132, 136, 140, 188, 325
Crehan, Kate, 112, 114, 115, 121, 248
cultural hegemony, 73, 109, 110, 111, 112, 114, 120, 209, 264, 287, 298,
308, 335, 339
custom,
    and popular memory, 1-7, 14, 32-39, 43, 56, 86-97, 197-204, 320-340
    and ritual, 18, 40, 144-180
    as *lex loci*, 5, 8, 19, 32, 112, 113
    as *jus non scriptum*, 32, 44-52, 69-72, 86
    function of, 6, 14, 21, 31, 32-39, 41, 42-52, 54, 56, 62, 63, 64, 69-74,
197-204, 298
criminal justice reform, 42, 287-300

Dean Forest Mining Act, 336, 337, 338
Dean Forest (Reafforestation) Act 1668, 8, 254, 262, 330
deer, 51, 122, 130, 196, 294
Denis, Book of, 42, 288

DiMaggio, Paul, 186, 187, 189, 242, 253
Dorothy, Captain, 169
dramaturgy, 145, 167, 175, 180, 326, 327

education, 3, 56, 166, 190
enclosure, 4, 5, 7, 35, 42, 47, 86, 107, 120, 131, 135, 138, 145, 160, 161, 173, 174, 175, 237, 250, 251, 252, 262, 265, 269, 282, 298, 315, 322, 324, 325, 326, 329
encoppicement, 76, 215, 219, 225, 226, 246, 267, 273, 297
English Bicknor, 26, 27, 30, 131, 132, 158, 159, 174, 263
equity courts, 61, 72, 81, 103, 113, 183, 183, 185, 189, 200, 201, 202, 204, 206, 208, 210, 211, 234, 236, 240, 243, 249, 252, 253, 257, 265, 276, 279, 287, 300, 308, 342
Exchequer, Court of the, 76, 78, 81, 85, 90, 119, 126, 128, 133, 134, 140, 141, 148, 160, 183, 184, 185, 199, 200, 207, 210, 211, 213, 215, 221, 228, 229, 233, 234-238, 241, 242, 248, 249, 251
Eyre,
   Justice Seat (1634), 122, 129, 130, 132-149, 183, 189, 183, 216-230
   Justice Seat (1656), 246, 266

fencing, 76, 79, 86, 165, 198, 275, 322, 326, 327, 328, 339
Fentress, James, 2, 4, 37, 283-285
Flaxley, 26, 31, 65, 113, 202, 304
folklore, 143, 145, 146, 154, 166, 169, 171, 178, 179, 180, 182, 303, 319

gavellor, 57, 58, 183, 193, 195, 216, 233, 268, 270, 271, 279, 299, 325, 336
Goffman, Erving, 167, 168, 172, 173, 279, 326
Gramsci, Antonio, 110, 112, 114
Gloucester, 10, 12, 29, 53, 84, 119, 130, 214, 218, 231, 235, 236, 309, 321, 325
Grant of Gales, 336, 337, 338, 339
groves, 11, 88, 273
Gyes,
   John, 71, 72, 73, 205
   William, 73, 76
   Robert, 72

habitus, 6, 37, 38, 39, 48, 61, 94-96, 192, 194, 243
Hart, Cyril, 14, 24, 58, 78, 84, 148, 193, 203, 217, 230, 231, 287, 288, 299, 213